# GLOBALIZATION, SECURITY,
# AND THE NATION-STATE

SUNY SERIES IN GLOBAL POLITICS
James N. Rosenau, editor

# Globalization, Security, and the Nation-State

*Paradigms in Transition*

Edited by
Ersel Aydinli
and
James N. Rosenau

STATE UNIVERSITY OF NEW YORK PRESS

Published by
State University of New York Press, Albany

For information, address State University of New York Press,          ·
90 State Street, Suite 700, Albany, NY 12207

Production by Michael Haggett
Marketing by Susan M. Petrie

**Library of Congress Cataloging in Publication Data**

Globalization, security, and the nation-state : paradigms in transition / edited by
Ersel Aydinli & James N. Rosenau
     pp. cm. — (SUNY series in global politics)
   Revised papers originally delivered at an international Conference on Globalization
and National Security in Ankara, Turkey, June 2002 and sponsored by the Center for
Eurasian Strategic Studies (ASAM).
   Includes bibliographical references and index.
   ISBN 0-7914-6401-6 (hardcover : alk. paper) — ISBN 0-7914-6402-4 (pbk. : alk.
paper)
   1. Security, International. 2. National security. 3. Globalization. 4. World politics—
1989– I. Aydinli, Ersel, 1967– II. Rosenau, James N. III. Conference on Globalization and National Security (2002 : Ankara, Turkey) IV. Series.
JZ5588.G594 2005
355'.033—dc22

                                                                    2004014331

10 9 8 7 6 5 4 3 2 1

# Contents

# Part III
## Regional Reflections

# Part IV
## Emerging International Patterns

# *Acknowledgments*

This edited book arose from an international conference on Globalization, Security, and the Nation State, held in Ankara in June 2002. The conference and subsequent volume would not have been possible without financial and administrative support from the Center for Eurasian Strategic Studies in Ankara, and in particular its director, Dr. Ümit Özdağ.

Thanks to the chapter contributors, whose tremendous skills and professionalism made the organizing of the conference and compiling of the resulting volume a smooth process. Thanks as well to Özgür Çiçek and Çağrı Konur, graduate research assistants at Bilkent University.

Special thanks to Dr. Julie Matthews of Bilkent University, for her extensive assistance with the editing of the volume.

Ersel Aydinli
James N. Rosenau

# Introduction

James N. Rosenau and Ersel Aydinli

We live in a time of enormous contradictions, of dualities that are moving people and societies in opposite directions. Some paradigms are coming undone and yet others are as fixed as ever. Changes and transformations are pervasive and yet constancies persist. Globalizing processes are accelerating and yet localizing processes remain powerful. Many nations and states are weakening and yet others are undiminished in their competence. Wealth is expanding and yet poverty is omnipresent. New technologies are adding to the pleasures and comforts of daily life and yet insecurities are ubiquitous. Regions are unifying and yet others are mired in conflict and war. People are becoming ever more skillful and yet they are marked by a sense of losing control over their lives. The world's prime superpower is flexing its muscles and yet it is forced to seek assistance from the United Nations.

Tensions and ambiguities are prime consequences of these contradictions, and some of the main ones constitute the focus of the following chapters. We collectively seek to comprehend the changing paradigms that are altering the structures of world politics and adding new issues to the global agenda. More specifically, we are concerned with the impact of globalization on the conduct of international affairs, on the capacities of states, and on the security of both peoples and their collectivities. The various authors do not share similar perspectives on such matters, but the differences among them make for lively writing and provocative ideas that are bound to be clarifying for the reader.

More specifically, differences can be discerned over whether the course of events are overtaking nations and their states and leading to some of their competencies being superseded by activist nongovernmental organizations and local authorities. Some of the contributors argue that world affairs continue to be a state-dominated system, but others highlight ways in which the system has been undermined by the dynamics that have unfolded since the end of the Cold War and that, in effect, have led to a bifurcation of global structures into state-centric and multicentric worlds. One focus in this regard is the impact of global terrorism on the so-called security dilemma of states. None of the authors denies that the advent of terrorism on a global scale constitutes a major alteration of international structures that calls into question the nature of individual and collective security. But they differ over whether this and the military responses it has evoked are the only major sources of pervasive insecurity, with some contending that widespread poverty and discrepancies between the developed and developing worlds are no less significant as dynamics that underlie the insecurities now intruding on individual, national, and global well-being. And throughout this book there is a preoccupation with the extent to which globalization has served as a source of terrorism and insecurity.

Inasmuch as the dynamics of globalization continue to unfold at a rapid rate, estimating the ways in which it has fomented positive and negative transformations is not a simple matter. Much depends on how globalization is conceptualized. For some it is seen as primarily a set of economic processes, a paradigmatic transformation that, in turn, has fostered social, political, and cultural changes. Others perceive a more complex paradigmatic shift in which no single dynamic is perceived as the prime source of change. Rather, causal dynamics are conceived as overlapping and mutually reinforcing, with the social, political, and cultural dynamics interacting with and shaping economic processes as much as they are shaped by these processes.

A brief review of the thrusts of the various chapters serves to highlight these various themes and the different approaches to them. The book is divided into four sections that focus, respectively, on reconceptualizing security, state transformations, regional reflections, and emerging international patterns. The chapters were papers first delivered at an international Conference on Globalization and National Security convened in Ankara, Turkey, late in June 2002 and sponsored by the Center for Eurasian Strategic Studies (ASAM) and its director, Dr. Ümit Özdağ. All the papers were subsequently revised in response to suggestions made during the conference deliberations and subsequently by the editors.

## RECONCEPTUALIZING SECURITY?

The three chapters in Part I offer different perspectives on modern-day security. The chapter by Mohammed Ayoob, "Security in the Age of Globalization: Separating Appearance from Reality," argues that globalization is overestimated. He views globalization rhetoric as a deliberate attempt by the realist northern world to disguise a still realist world and at the same time further its dominance over the South. Ayoob's analysis springs from a state-centric perspective in the sense that he believes in the resilience of the state and that it remains as the primary starting point for International Relations (IR) paradigms. New security concepts such as human, societal, and environmental security are seen as secondary to state security.

Assuming a very different perspective, Ken Booth's chapter, "Two Terrors, One Problem," presents globalization as a real, transformative phenomenon with concrete consequences. He sees the interaction between the state-centric and multicentric worlds as producing largely negative consequences. In so doing, he disavows state-centrism and embraces the new era of globalization. Booth believes that the state has to share its space with increasingly powerful and numerous other types of actors. Thus, the state is likely to be challenged in its relations with society, which is being empowered by globalization. Even though his analysis reveals a conflicting relationship between the security outcomes of the state-centric world (state security) and those of globalization (human security), Booth warns us to avoid either/or thinking (e.g., security vs. ethics, us vs. them, politics vs. economics).

T.V. Paul's chapter, "The National Security State and Global Terrorism: Why the State Is Not Prepared for the New Kind of War," treats global terrorism as a key manifestation of a transformed, globalized, and insecure environment. While he asserts that the traditional threats and responses within the state-centric system remain intact, he also sees these same mechanisms as being challenged by an outside threat. He portrays 9/11 as part of an asymmetric strategy; a new level of threat is seen as emerging from the multicentric world and striking at the state-centric world, which is unprepared to respond to such a "nonfrontal" hit. Accordingly, Paul proposes revisions of four foundations of military strategy: offense, defense, deterrence, and compellence. Globalization in this chapter is seen as having given new impetus to certain old security threats. By affecting their formats and magnitudes, globalization turns the old threats into new ones capable of threatening the old, state-centric system. He perceives the multicentric world as having produced a threat capable of shaking the state-centric, "Clausewitzian" understanding of world affairs.

## STATE TRANSFORMATIONS

Part II focuses particularly on the state itself and its responses to globalization. Mark Brawley's chapter, "*The Rise of the Trading State* Revisited," examines a question posed by Richard Rosecrance in the mid-1980s. In considering state choices between trading strategies and strategies of conquest, Brawley proposes that dramatic changes in military technology, the so-called Revolution in Military Affairs, should cause us to reconsider the findings of Rosecrance's earlier work. Interestingly, he argues that the state's traditional security orientations and aggressiveness, rather than being called into question by and whittled down by globalization's effects, may in some ways be increased.

Georg Sørensen's chapter, "State Transformation and New Security Dilemmas," begins with the basic argument that the classical security dilemma argument that Herz described as a "vicious circle of security and power accumulation" is no longer appropriate or adequate to explain every state's security dilemmas because of subsequent changes in the nature of states. With the transformation of states, new security dilemmas emerge. Sørensen proceeds to identify three different state types and the corresponding shifts in economic, political, and "nationhood" security dilemmas that states encounter as they undergo transformations from "modern" states to "postmodern" ones. He focuses his analysis particularly on two of the three state types outlined, the postmodern state and the weak postcolonial state.

Ersel Aydinli's chapter, "Anarchy Meets Globalization: A New Security Dilemma for the Modernizing State," follows up on Sorensen's discussion by looking in depth at the dynamics of the modern state's transformation in response to the pressures posed by political globalization and the security dilemma. His particular focus is the modern state of the developing world, which he identifies as the "second" or "modernizing" world. His model postulates that these modern state structures, pressured simultaneously by the power-diffusing effects of globalization and power-centralizing demands of security agendas, frame a dual agenda of securitization and desecuritization that develops into an institutionalization of hard and soft state structures—a state-level adaptation to the tensions between state and multicentric worlds. States seek to centralize their power to better manage the transformation, but this tendency conflicts with the power diffusion agenda of societal actors. Thus, the model also suggests that the new security dilemma for transforming modern states is about the management and safety of power diffusion.

## REGIONAL REFLECTIONS

Part III consists of three regional case studies. The first is Alexander Sergounin's chapter entitled "Global Challenges to Russia's National Security: Any Chance for Resisting/Bandwagoning/Adapting/Contributing to an Emerging World Order?" What comes through in this chapter is a clear reflection of the distinction between the state-centric and multicentric perspectives or, as Sergounin calls them, "hard" and "soft" agendas. These two perspectives are viewed as being competitive, if not conflictual. They highlight tensions between the old and new worlds that mark Russia's security concepts—at least at the level of discourse. By analyzing and comparing security documents from the Yeltsin and Putin eras, Sergounin traces the swing between a more multicentric security conceptualization in 1997 (human, environmental security) and a sharp reversal toward state security in 2000.

The second of the regional cases is Bahgat Korany's chapter on the Arab Middle East and North Africa (AMENA), "Globalization and (In)security in AMENA: A Contextual Double-Pronged Analysis." Korany analyzes regional security questions in a balanced manner, giving due consideration to traditional security issues and new security agendas such as societal security and desertification. He offers the interesting observation that the new security challenges, although highly acute and threatening, have been overshadowed by traditional ones such as the Arab–Israeli conflict. The two are presented as being in a dichotomous relationship, though when traditional security issues cool off for brief periods, the new issues spring to the fore. He also touches on the uneven distribution of globalization benefits as a source of a number of new insecurities at the domestic level.

The last of the regional studies is Ole Wæver's "The Constellation of Securities in Europe." In this chapter, Wæver explains the dynamics of the EU-centered European Security Complex by applying securitization and regional security theories. He argues that moving away from a state-centric security understanding does not necessarily mean that a state or community has abandoned security and become desecuritized. Europe may be desecuritized in terms of state security, but it is still highly securitized in terms of other forms of security—as he puts it, Europe is "in the grip of security, even if in unusual forms." One of those forms, interestingly, may be Europe's own past. Wæver is in this sense skeptical about the extent to which globalization has actually changed traditional security concepts in Europe, given the region's continued preoccupation with its past as a security challenge.

## Emerging International Patterns

Part IV draws on various aspects and perspectives of the themes of globalization, security, and the state, and explores various implications for emerging international patterns in world affairs. The section leads off with a chapter by Barry Buzan entitled "The Security Dynamics of a 1 + 4 World." Buzan sets out to understand the security dynamics of the post–Cold War world. He first presents various possible scenarios involving the distribution of superpower(s), great power(s), and regional powers, and asserts that the most likely outcome is one of continued "1 + 4," in which the United States remains as the sole superpower, with China, Russia, Japan, and the EU classified as great powers. Although he does not directly focus on globalization processes or other challenges to the state-centric system, his analysis nevertheless indirectly suggests several ways in which an emergent multicentric world is competing with its state-centric counterpart.

David Goldfischer's chapter, "Prospects for a New World Order," develops a very different perspective. In light of the post-9/11 war on terrorism, he reconsiders E. H. Carr's 1940s inquiry into the combining of power and morality to create a peaceful world order. In so doing, Goldfischer focuses on the "capitalist security community" (CSC), generally composed of businessmen, scholars, state leaders, and their supporters, whose interests and security lie in the continuing spread of a free market economic system and Western values. On the one hand, he reveals the tremendous power of these actors in the multi-centric world. On the other hand, the state-centric system and the processes of globalization are posited as inextricably linked, since for most of the world the ideological, economic, and security interests of both converge and are supported by the CSC.

The final chapter is James N. Rosenau's introspection on the relevance of the post-9/11 world for his turbulence model. Entitled "Turbulence and Terrorism: Reframing or Readusting the Model?," he starts by pointing out that the events and subsequent effects of 9/11 require us to question existing theories of world politics. In particular, the nature of those events highlights a need to reconsider how we should think about security. Rosenau's model is founded on an understanding of change at the macro, micro, and micro/macro levels of aggregation. Change at the macro level refers to what Rosenau calls a "bifurcation of global structures" that differentiates the state-centric and multicentric worlds. The micro level refers generally to the individual, and the micro/macro level to links and interactions between individuals and their collectivities. The model presumes constant change sustained through interaction among the levels. Rosenau concludes that the 9/11 terrorist attacks are consistent with the premises of the turbulence model, that they are expressive of a war between a hegemon and actors in the multicentric world, thus revealing the disaggregated and bifurcated global structures at the core of the turbulence model. Even the one point that seemed early on to run counter to the model, the united surge of post-9/11 support in the United States for the state, has faded in the years since the attacks. An increasing questioning of authority, consistent with the model, has become ever more prominent today.

In sum, the reader is embarking on an exciting journey through the concepts, ideas, and processes that lie at the heart of world politics in the present era. It is an intellectual journey with twists and turns that mirror the course of events and lead one to pondering the best way to assess how they unfold.

# Part I

---

## Reconceptualizing Security

# 1

# Security in the Age of Globalization

## Separating Appearance from Reality

Mohammed Ayoob

## I

This chapter makes several arguments. First, it contends that the proponents of globalization (those who insist that the free market is now firmly in the driver's seat and will determine the future trajectory of the international system) and the exponents of a global society (those who advocate solidarist norms for global governance) overestimate the nature of economic, technological, and normative changes that impact the security arena. Second, it maintains that these same groups underestimate the resilience of the state and, even more, its role as the primary provider of security and the preeminent locus of security decision making. Third, it claims that there has been an attempt, deliberate in substantial part, by policymakers and analysts in the global North to portray a basically realist world as a liberal one by conflating rhetoric with reality. Fourth, it suggests that security relations among the countries of the global North have become subject to a different logic from the security relationship between the North and the South as well relations within the South itself. Fifth, it argues that neither of the major paradigms in the field of International Relations—neoliberalism or neorealism—is able satisfactorily to identify and explain the major security problems of the world we live in today. This is because both paradigms draw their data from a geographically circumscribed universe and are not adequately informed by the history of the evolution both of the modern state and the system of states. Sixth, it asserts that since the large majority of the members of the international system as well the overwhelming majority of conflicts in the international system are located in the global South, no adequate explanation of international security issues is possible without focusing on the Third World. Furthermore, that such attention to the Third World must be two-dimensional, focusing both on

9

intra-South relations and the relationship of the Third World with the global North (for details on this argument, see Ayoob & Acharya in Neumann, 1998).

Finally, at the most fundamental conceptual level, this chapter argues that the concept of security should not be unduly broadened and made so elastic as to lose all analytical utility. Security is a concept that addresses issues of order and authority and is, therefore, preeminently political in its connotation. The state, as the primary political institution, must, therefore, form the primary point of reference for any security paradigm. Variables from the ecological to the economic may impinge on the security arena, but their influence must be filtered through the political arena in order to become a part of the security calculus. Delinking security from the political realm and from the state does no service either to the concept of security or to other values that particular analysts would like to preserve and promote.

The various propositions that this chapter attempts to put forward are so closely interwoven that often it is difficult clearly to separate one argument from another. As a result, the reader may find that more than one argument is made in the same paragraph if not in the same sentence. The reader will have to bear with me on this score because, given the interrelatedness of the arguments, one cannot completely disentangle them.

## II

When discussing the notion of "security," proponents of globalization and those who subscribe to the notion of a global (rather than international) society make two arguments to which they are wedded in different degrees.[1] However, they rarely, if ever, test these arguments against international realities. When they do, they choose their data from a restricted universe and even then distort the data considerably to fit their conclusions.[2]

The first argument made by the proponents of globalization is that "security" concerns as traditionally conceived by scholars and practitioners of international relations have become marginal, if not totally irrelevant, to the functioning of international society. Therefore, the study of security should be relegated to a secondary position in International Relations curricula. This argument is based on the assumption that the privileged position occupied by states in the arena of international relations has declined dramatically as a result of globalization. It is also based on the premise that issues of economic exchange and interdependence, resulting from advances in the technology of production, communication, and information, now occupy positions of primacy in the international agenda. Therefore, the argument runs that security issues that had dominated a state-centric world should no longer occupy the pride of place in discussions about the international system.

Second, even those enthusiasts of globalization and the proponents of a global society who concede the relevance of security concerns assume that "security" needs to be redefined in the current context to focus on "human security" rather than the security of states and regimes. Thus, they challenge the integral connection between state and society that has formed a part of the conventional wisdom in the field of International Relations. They do so in two ways. On the one hand, they argue that states are no longer able to protect their citizens from external threats because the nature of these threats has undergone fundamental transformation. States are not equipped to meet these new challenges and, in many cases, new technologies of communication, information, and warfare have made state boundaries redundant. Security of individuals, therefore, has to be ensured through different mechanisms and institutions. However, they refuse to elaborate what these mechanisms and institutions are likely to be and how they are expected to carry out the functions currently performed by the state. Above all, they decline to evaluate the capacity and the efficacy of either IGOs or NGOs, in whom they put a great deal of trust, to provide order to territorially defined political communities.

Many critics of the integral relationship between state and society also argue that often the state is the primary threat to the security of its citizens. Drawing on examples of selected predatory regimes in the Third World, they argue that the notion of human security should, therefore, be delinked from that of state security because in these cases the two appear to be polar opposites.[3] They argue that, for individuals to be secure, the state, especially in the Third World, must of necessity be weak or ineffective so that it is unable to harm individuals and groups in arbitrary fashion. They argue further that given recent changes in international norms, especially with regard to human rights, issues of human security must take precedence over those of state security. Where the two come into conflict the former must prevail over the latter, if necessary with the help of agents of international society such as the United Nations and other multinational organizations.

All these arguments against privileging both the institution of the state and the concept of security carry certain ingredients of truth. However, they disproportionately magnify the diminution in the role of the state and radically underestimate the operation of the traditional state-centric security paradigm in the current context. Thus, they fail to portray the existing realities in the international system and are unable to provide satisfactory explanations for the current workings of the international system. Their inability to explain hampers their capacity to adequately predict the future of the international system and prescribe strategies that may help mitigate conflict and produce greater order in the system.

The devotees of globalization and human security fail to provide intellectually satisfactory explanations of the way international politics operates for a number of reasons. Above all, they fail to do so because they conflate rhetoric with reality. As Graham Allison has pointed out, "As currently used, globalization is too often an ill-defined pointer to a disparate array of phenomena—frequently accompanied by heavy breathing that implies that behind these phenomena, or at their root, is some yet-to-be-discovered substance" (Allison, 2000: 72). The proponents of globalization, both as fact and as a positive phenomenon, especially in academia, often fail to recognize that much of the rhetoric on which they base their conclusions is not merely out of sync with reality but is deliberately self-serving.

This is especially the case with the rhetoric emanating from the policy-making community in the West, particularly the United States, and their hangers-on among the journalist and academic communities. The neoliberal rhetoric about an interdependent world in which absolute gains are not only far more important than relative gains but are also distributed relatively fairly is the example par excellence of deliberate obfuscation that flies in the face of the reality experienced by most societies. It makes a great deal of sense for the powerful to portray their own relative gains as absolute gains for the entire international society. It also makes great sense for them to make a strong case that the status quo that protects, in fact enhances, the advantages they enjoy is best for all humankind. Similarly, denigrating the normative barriers to their domination constructed by notions of sovereignty and nonintervention works enormously to their advantage.[4] However, it is the duty of serious academics to scrutinize such claims very carefully before they accept them.

The self-serving nature of such claims is very obvious in the economic arena. Bringing down barriers imposed by state boundaries allows the economically powerful states to penetrate weak and vulnerable societies and perfect the system of an international division of labor in which all societies know their place. Even the rigidity of the Indian caste system pales by comparison to the caste system embedded in the international economy under the guise of economic liberalization and globalization. Benefits of economic liberalization go disproportionately to the industrialized countries of the global North.[5] The overwhelming majority of economic interactions that make for interdependence in a "globalizing" world take place among the triad of North America, Europe, and Japan. As Hirst and Thompson have pointed out, "Capital mobility is not producing a massive shift of investment and employment from the advanced to the developing countries. Rather foreign direct investment (FDI) is highly concentrated among the advanced industrial economies and the Third World remains marginal in both investment and trade, a small minority of newly industrializing countries apart"(Hirst & Thompson, 1999: 2).

That the disproportionate benefits of globalization go to the developed states is not limited to FDI flows alone. In different forms this argument also applies to the protection of intellectual copyrights and patents as well as access to markets and cheap labor in the Third World by MNCs headquartered in the global North. It also applies to the imposition of tariff and nontariff barriers on the import of selected commodities, both agricultural and nonagricultural, on grounds either of dumping or of much needed subsidies required to satisfy important domestic constituencies.

The recent American decision to impose steep tariffs on the import of steel and the EU's policy of subsidizing agriculture under the Common Agricultural Policy (CAP) form prime examples of this phenomenon. The attempt to use stringent social and environmental criteria to curb cheaper imports from the global South further stacks the cards in favor of the industrialized countries of Europe and North America while denying Third World states the one competitive advantage they possess, namely, low production costs of low-tech manufactured goods.

The skewed nature of globalization is especially demonstrated by the fact that while there is much made of the need to provide for the unfettered mobility of capital globally, no voices are raised in the global North in favor of the unfettered mobility of labor, and therefore of human beings, across the globe. The logic of economic globalization is obviously supposed to apply selectively to cases that enhance the interests of the powerful against the weak, of the rich against the poor, but not vice versa.

In the political arena, tearing down the sovereignty barrier in the name of humanitarian intervention serves much the same purpose of preserving the dominance of the global North. Such interventions undertaken selectively to punish "rogue" states, such as Iraq and Yugoslavia, unwilling to fall in line with the wishes of the great powers, send the clear message that opposing the international establishment is likely to incur heavy costs. These could include the severe derogation of sovereignty and immense damage to state capacity. The use of the U.N. Security Council to endorse such actions provides the veneer of international legitimacy under which decisions based on realpolitik are disguised. The refusal of the P-5 to seriously countenance the issue of expanding the permanent membership of the Council as well as their refusal to consider the suggestion that they should abjure the use of veto in cases of humanitarian intervention demonstrate the unrepresentative character of that body.[6]

When the façade of U.N. endorsement is not available, as in the case of the Kosovo intervention in 1999, the services of the Security Council are dispensed with altogether. This is done on the basis of the argument, to quote then NATO Secretary General Javier Solana, that NATO "is a serious organization that takes a decision by consensus among serious countries with democratic governments" (cited in Daalder, 1999: 10). Reactions to the NATO bombing of Yugoslavia made it very clear that many important countries, China and India foremost among them, vehemently rejected the argument that NATO can claim the right to speak and act on behalf of the international community.

The selectivity with which the ground rules of globalization and of the emerging global society are applied makes this charade very clear. Interventions take place when it suits the strategic and economic interests of the "coalition of the willing and the able" (read the North Atlantic Concert). Where it does not suit the global hegemon or the dominant concert, norms of the evolving global society are disdainfully disregarded. Interventions in Iraq and Yugoslavia are undertaken enthusiastically without regard for the normative barrier provided by the concept of state sovereignty. Northern Iraq is declared a safe haven where the exercise of Iraqi state authority is barred. Kosovo, for all practical purposes, is treated as an independent entity from which Yugoslav state authority is expelled.

At the same time, however, all attempts at international intervention in occupied Palestinian lands face the threat of U.S. veto despite the fact that Israel has defied a plethora of U.N. Security Council resolutions, supposedly mandatory in character, on a number of issues ranging from settlements to Jerusalem. Many more draft resolutions favored by the overwhelming majority of the members of the Security Council have been either vetoed by the United States or died because of the threat of such a veto. This even though Israel has not merely thumbed its nose at the Security Council, it has also regularly violated major provisions of the Fourth Geneva Convention prohibiting demographic changes in the occupied territories. Such defiance and violation if committed by any other state would have immediately drawn the threat of international economic and military sanctions. The recent Israeli rejection of the U.N. fact-finding mission to Jenin and the subsequent decision by the U.N. secretary general to disband the mission drives home the point that some states are more equal than others, not only in terms of power but also in their "right" to defy international opinion and international law. There is no better refutation of the argument for a solidarist conception of international society than Israeli behavior over the past 35 years and American support for its defiance of international law and opinion.

The unilateral American decision to invade Iraq in order to effect regime change makes clear that the neoliberal paradigm does not apply even in the sphere of intra-NATO relations when the interests of the global hegemon diverge from those of other members of the coalition. This was symbolized by American Secretary of Defense Donald Rumsfeld's statement in the run-up to the war against Iraq that declared unequivocally that for the United States "the mission determines the coalition and the coalition ought not determine the mission"(U.S. Secretary of Defense, 2002). The expectation that the United States, unlike earlier hegemons, was a "liberal" (as opposed to a presumably "realist") hegemon was given a decent burial with the launching of the military campaign against Iraq. This "hyperrealist" example set by the most powerful state in the international system is bound to have a major effect on the behavior of other states. It can also be expected to seriously erode the international norms that the global North was attempting to propagate in the post–Cold War era.

The selectivity demonstrated in the application of the norms of global society leads one to draw two important conclusions. One, sovereignty continues to be a cherished value as far as powerful states and their clients are concerned. Advising the weak to dispense with sovereignty and with their preoccupation with state security is one thing—applying it to powerful states and their coalitions is quite another. As Lyons and Mastanduno have pointed out, the argument that sovereignty has been superseded as the organizing principle of international political life cannot be successfully sustained unless it is demonstrated "by reference to 'critical' cases. . . . The clearest set of critical cases would involve instances in which the exertion of some form of international authority significantly constrained major powers in their pursuit of their interests. . . . If we look at the present processes of international decision making [the veto power of the P-5 in the U.N. Security Council and the G-7's domination of international financial institutions], however, the prospect of finding such critical cases appears to be unlikely" (Lyons & Mastanduno, 1995: 17).

Two, the rhetoric of globalization and of the global society is employed to provide a veneer for the operation of a very realist paradigm by the powerful states of the global North in their relationship with the states of the global South, many of whom continue to be weak and vulnerable and, therefore, incapable of ensuring their own security. Australian scholar James Richardson has captured this reality very lucidly. According to him, "The realist dictum 'the strong do what they can, the weak do what they must' draws attention to the dark shadows in North-South relations. . . . Realism survives not only in the North-South economic relations but also in the military preparedness of the major powers. . . . Self interest now appears to dictate that the leading powers remain associates rather than rivals, as balance of power logic would have required, but the anarchic system structure points to their retaining a military capability to protect their favored position against the less favored" (Richardson, 1993: 45–46).

## III

I would like to explore these points further. That sovereignty is considered a cherished value by the powerful states is demonstrated by recent decisions taken by Washington not to ratify the CTBT, to build BMD systems in violation of the ABM treaty, to refuse to adhere to the Kyoto Protocol on the protection of the environment, and, most recently, to withdraw its signature from the treaty setting up the International Criminal Court (ICC). The importance of sovereign decision making on issues of war and peace has been demonstrated most dramatically in the U.S. decision to invade Iraq in March 2003 despite the opposition of the large majority of states, including several NATO members.

Paradoxically, it is also demonstrated by the decision on the part of West European states to surrender part of their sovereign functions to the EU but at the same time strengthen border and immigration controls vis-à-vis non-EU countries and their populations, thus forming a laager in order to protect their privileged lifestyle. What the European project seems to be achieving is the creation of a European quasistate that may evolve into a European sovereign state one day. Whether this project culminates in a single European state or not, the European vision does not include the sacrifice of sovereignty at the altar of global society, something Third World states are constantly advised to do. Such sacrifice is aimed at bolstering the capacity of an exclusive club of rich states to ward off economic and political challenges and unwanted intruders from outside their borders.

The doublespeak on the part of the industrialized and powerful states of the global North points to another phenomenon—namely, the difference in state capacity among different categories of states. States that are administratively effective, socially coherent, and economically affluent are able to regulate transborder transactions in such a way that they do not harm the political, social, and economic interests of the populations they preside over. They are also confident enough to sacrifice portions of their sovereignty in order to enhance their collective capacity and affluence while protecting their economic and political core interests against the barbarians knocking at their gates. The EU is a product of such calculations on the part of effective, affluent, and cohesive states. These states do not fear partial loss of sovereignty as long as such loss translates into strengthening the patrician institutions of the global North and protecting them from challenges from the hordes inhabiting the plebeian South. They also do not fear such partial loss of sovereignty in favor of a multinational institution composed of states with similar socioeconomic characteristics because they are at a stage of development in which no external party can dare intervene forcefully into their societies' affairs.

Adequate regulatory capacity is essential for states to benefit from the processes of economic liberalization. As Peter Evans has demonstrated in a well-argued and well-documented article, the logic of the current international economy does not point toward the "eclipse of the state." According to Evans, those societies that have effective states as regulators of internal and external economic transactions have fared, and will fare, far better in a globalized economy than those that do not. He bases this conclusion on the data on OECD countries that demonstrate that "countries that are more exposed to trade have bigger governments." He also bases it on the argument that "those who sit astride the international financial system need capable regulators." And, finally, Evans reinforces his conclusion on the grounds that "powerful transnational economic actors may have an interest in limiting the state's ability to constrain their own economic activities but they also depend on a capable state to protect their returns, especially those from intangible assets." He concludes, therefore, "In this optic, the persistence of the state's institutional centrality looks more likely than eclipse" (Evans, 1997: 62–87). In plain English, this means that those states with the institutional capability to regulate economic transactions within and across their borders will have an enormous advantage in the age of globalization compared to those who do not have such capacity or possess it in inadequate measure.

Societal cohesiveness is equally essential for states to remain largely immune from external intervention. Such cohesiveness is a function of the longevity of the state and its ability to bring to bear superior force against recalcitrant elements among its population. It is also based on its ability over time to weld a diverse population into a "nation" by the standardization of laws, language, and often religion, and the construction of historical memories that provide the foundational myths both for the nation and the state. Longevity, effectiveness, and successful mythmaking are essential ingredients of the state legitimacy formula. The developed states of Europe and North America have had the time and coercive capacity to attain such societal cohesiveness and to create shared myths and memories (for one of the best accounts of state formation in Europe, see Tilly, 1985). However, most Third World states are very far from reaching this goal. It is no wonder, therefore, that developed, industrialized states are the greatest exponents of economic liberalization and humanitarian intervention. They are the primary beneficiaries of the former and unlikely targets for the latter.

This happy situation does not apply to the large majority of states that collectively form the Third World. Their regulatory capacity is weak and their societal cohesiveness is low. Additionally, their economies are vulnerable, in many cases dependent on the export of a couple of primary products (oil-producing countries are essentially one-product economies), and their per capita income (even in the case of countries with relatively diversified economies and large GDPs, such as India) is low. In other words, the political, social, and economic dices are all loaded against them. They are quintessentially the losers in the process of economic liberalization and the potential targets for humanitarian intervention.

Historical experience shows that late industrializers need substantial state intervention in their economies for the latter to reach the takeoff stage. Similarly, the history of state formation demonstrates that states in the early stages of state making need to insulate themselves from external intervention so as not to jeopardize their task of imposing and maintaining political order, which often entails the use of force. The processes of economic liberalization and humanitarian intervention are not conducive to providing them the environment in which they can industrialize and mature as autonomous political actors.

Therefore, to demand that such states emulate the attitudes of the developed, powerful states on liberalization and humanitarian intervention is akin to making many of them sign their own death warrant. One should not be surprised that their sense of insecurity escalates as their economies are forced open and international norms begin to favor coercive intervention and the consequent derogation of state sovereignty. They suffer from what I call the "Opium War syndrome," the perception that what was done to China in the nineteenth century by the overt exercise of force is being done to them today by a far more subtle form of coercion.

## IV

As a result, the security predicament of most states in the global South appears both to these states and to informed observers of the Third World scene to be very different from the challenges faced by the states of the global North. It is no wonder that this division between the North and the South has been referred to as "the tale of two worlds" (Goldgeier & McFaul, 1992). The neoliberal paradigm that seems to prevail in the relationship of the northern countries among themselves cannot explain either the security predicament or the economic quandary faced by states in the Third World. One can reasonably argue that the realist paradigm continues to determine outcomes both in intra-South relations and in many of the interactions between the countries of the North and the South. The West's neoliberal rhetoric ignores this chasm between the security situation prevailing in the South and in North–South relations as compared to that operating among the countries of the global North.

Globalization makes the North more secure and dominant while making the South more insecure and increasing its subordination to the centers of economic and military power. Add the Revolution in Military Affairs (RMA), also called the Military Technological Revolution (MTR), to this equation and you get a very bleak picture from the perspective of the Third World. The RMA capacity has been summed up succinctly by Eliot Cohen in the following words: "What can be seen by high-tech sensors can be hit, what can be hit will be destroyed" (Cohen, 1996: 45; see also Freedman, 2000). The concentration of such capacity in the hands of a very few states makes one thing very clear—the hierarchy of military power has never been as rigidly stratified as it has become today as a result of RMA. The United States, the leading RMA power, sits in lonely glory at the top of the technological-military pyramid.[7] A group of major industrialized countries is clustered probably two-thirds of the way up. Then there are the rest who form the base of the pyramid, except for a few, such as China and maybe India, who have been able to claw their way up to about a quarter of the pyramid's height. For those located at the base of the structure or close to it, this would appear to be a prospect that could range from the very uncomfortable to the extremely scary.

The RMA's lessons regarding the extreme disparity in military power and its political consequences have been driven home over and over since 1990. It was made explicit during the Gulf War and with even greater clarity during the bombing of Yugoslavia in 1999 and the U.S.-led military campaign in Afghanistan in 2001–2002. What impressed much of the Third World with regard to these military ventures was not the righteousness or otherwise of the causes espoused by the dominant Concert, but the enormous destructive power the coalition, and especially the United States, brought to bear on its enemies from long distances, thereby making itself immune to retaliation. The precision and impunity with which the U.S.-led Concert could destroy the vital military nerve centers of Iraq and Yugoslavia and render them incapable of defending themselves were perceived as a technological miracle that dwarfed even the nuclear weapons revolution in terms of its actual impact on military affairs.

The use of RMA weaponry by the United States and its allies has left an indelible mark on the psyche of the Third World political elite. One the one hand, it has increased their feeling of insecurity manifold. On the other, those among Third World elites who continue to harbor a defiant streak have been spurred to find "equalizers" that may deter RMA powers from initiating military action against them. These equalizers are obtainable only in two forms. They can be procured either as weapons of mass destruction accompanied by delivery systems that can reach RMA troop and weapons concentrations at relatively long distances or as "terror" tactics that render RMA weapons militarily irrelevant, thereby reducing their political utility.

The attempt to attain weapons of mass destruction and missile capability by "states of concern" as well as the terrorist attacks on New York and Washington on September 11, 2001, should be seen at least in part as the response of certain states and groups in the Third World to the acquisition and use of RMA weapons by the United States and its allies. For those in the Third World bent on defying the dominant Concert, weapons of mass destruction and terrorist attacks seem to be the only instruments that can act as "equalizers" of sorts against the precision-guided conventional weaponry that can be unleashed by the United States and the coalition it leads. This adds to their attraction for those who are unwilling to embrace the New World Order that the dominant coalition is intent on imposing on the rest of the members of the international system.

## V

A response needs to be made to the argument mentioned earlier that in today's world the requirements of human security run counter to the imperatives of state security. Such a response should also be able to address the issue of state failure that poses a major threat to the security of the citizens of the failed or failing states. This response must begin by stating baldly that human security and state security are not the same thing and that on occasion their logics may diverge quite considerably. Nevertheless, the security of individuals, who by necessity form part of a political community, cannot be guaranteed unless the security of the entire political community is first ensured. This is clearly demonstrated by the fact that where the state has failed, as has been the case recently in Somalia, Liberia, Sierra Leone, the Congo, and Afghanistan, life has become truly "poor, nasty, brutish and short." In the final analysis, state security and the security of the society over which the state presides cannot be disassociated from each other.

Anyone with a passing knowledge of Thomas Hobbes would immediately realize the veracity of this assertion. The state acts as the primary provider of order and, therefore, of security to its citizens. It is, as Charles Tilly (1985) has pointed out, the ultimate "protection racket." When the state fails to do this job, the entire political and societal structure collapses and individuals and groups are left to their own devices to ensure their security as best as they can, usually at the expense of each other. Societal competition, indeed most societal interaction, becomes a zero-sum game and countries descend into the bleakest form of social Darwinism. Conflict entrepreneurs with vested interest in the continuation of civil war and state infirmity adopt very "rational" strategies to prolong civil conflict in order to extract major economic and political gains from the uncertainties and insecurities accompanying state evaporation.[8]

Therefore, while it is indeed the case that in some instances states, or predatory regimes acting on behalf of states, act as the major source of threat to their citizens (or at least to some part of their citizenry), one should not generalize from this argument that state security and human security are antithetical. Such an argument is akin to throwing the baby out with the bathwater. In fact, it is worse, for it amounts to throwing out the baby but still retaining the filthy bathwater in the form of an aggravated situation of insecurity for citizens who experience state collapse. Where the state poses a threat to the security of its citizens, it needs to be tamed—that is, legitimized on the basis of a social contract that constrains the arbitrary exercise of power. It certainly cannot be dispensed with altogether or weakened to the extent that it can no longer provide for the security of its citizens.

This is the major reason why, I believe, the concept of security must be rescued from its newfound friends who insist on hyphenating it with the word "human" or prefixing other adjectives such as "economic" or "ecological" to what is essentially a concept that derives from one's understanding of the "political." It needs to be reiterated that the "political" is that sphere of human activity that deals with the exercise of authority and the provision of order. The business of "securitizing" all sorts of phenomena from the economic to the ecological detracts from the quintessentially political nature of security and delinks it from its primary referent, the state. It thereby renders the notion so elastic that the concept of security loses all analytical utility.

This does not mean that economic and other concerns do not have the potential to affect the level of security enjoyed by the state and its citizens. All it means is that for such phenomena to have an impact on the security arena, they must become potent enough to intrude in a major way into that arena. Economic and ecological problems, and for that matter the problem of human rights, do not become security issues until and unless they become so salient as to be perceived as posing a threat to the state's institutions or boundaries and/or the regime that is recognized as acting in the name of the state (for details, see Ayoob, 1991). In other words, for any phenomenon to become "securitized," it must first be "politicized." In the absence of politicization, securitization cannot take place.[9]

# VI

Such a political definition of security must at the same time be accompanied by the clarification that it is not exclusively driven by the perception of external threats, but that it is equally applicable to, and useful for, deciphering threats emerging from within the boundaries of the state. This will ensure that the security discourse in International Relations does not become the preserve of neorealists who live in a reified world of their own, refuse to look beyond the anarchical nature of the international system and the security dilemma that such anarchy generates, and theorize on the basis of the sameness of states.

To understand the problems of security that states face, it is essential that one looks inside the black box. Once one does that, it will become clear that despite the diversity that states demonstrate, they can be categorized roughly into two groups based on two interrelated variables—the time when they became full members of the international system and the stage of state building at which they find themselves. Based on these two variables, one can determine the types of threats they are likely to face and the primary source or sources from which such threats can be expected to emanate.

The large majority of states today are relatively young states that have entered the system late and are at early stages of state building and nation construction.[10] These include not only those states of Asia, Africa, and Latin America traditionally recognized as belonging to the Third World, but also states in Central Asia, the Caucasus, and the Balkans that emerged in the

1990s following the disintegration of the Soviet Union and the dismember-
ment of Yugoslavia. In addition to other factors complicating their security
problematic, their newness means that they have not been able to establish
either their effectiveness or their legitimacy in the eyes of their populations. As
a result, threats to their security originate to a substantial extent from within
these states and are by-products of the attempt to impose political order on
societies that have only recently emerged into independence within colonially
crafted boundaries.

The domestic origins of most conflicts in the international system today
also denote that in several cases attempts to consolidate state power and
monopolize the instruments of violence in the hands of the state have not succeeded.[11] This has led in some cases, as discussed earlier, to state evaporation
or collapse with the political and security vacuum being filled by conflict entrepreneurs purporting to speak on behalf of ethnic, regional, or religious constituencies. State collapse also has major implications for regional order.
Conflicts linked to state failure displace persons both internally and across
state boundaries.[12] Transborder human movements have important consequences for neighboring states as they complicate the latter's attempts to
impose and maintain order within their own territories. They also have the
potential to trigger inter-ethnic conflicts, which often take on cross-border
dimensions. Thus, state failure has grave implications for regional peace. This
has been demonstrated in Africa, the Balkans, and Afghanistan, to name the
most obvious examples.


# VII


In most cases, however, states in the Third World have not failed. They have
been challenged, sometimes severely, but have continued to function as the
primary providers of order, in however imperfect a fashion, to most of their citizens most of the time. Furthermore, the challenges they have faced have not
been exclusively domestic in character. State and nation building in the Third
World is carried out within a context in which contiguous and proximate states
are simultaneously engaged in these extremely important political endeavors
crucial to their survival as coherent polities. The proliferation of interstate conflict in Third World regions is intimately connected to the fact that the process
of state and nation building is usually under way concurrently among contiguous and proximate states.

The simultaneous nature of this endeavor among contiguous states has
often made the success of state making and nation building crucially dependent on the existence or creation of regional balances of power favorable to particular states. Those states that have been able to create a favorable regional
balance for themselves, either through their own endeavors or by borrowing

## FLORIDA INTERNATIONAL UNIVERSITY
*Miami's public research university*

# PROGRAM IN NATIONAL SECURITY STUDIES

**The Jack D. Gordon Institute for Public Policy & Citizenship Studies**
University Park, Miami, FL 33199 • Tel: 305-348-2977 • Fax: 305-348-2924 • www.fiu.edu/~ippcs
Florida International University is an Equal Opportunity / Access Employer and Institution • TDD via FRS 1-800-955-8771

### FLORIDA INTERNATIONAL UNIVERSITY
*Miami's public research university*

# PROGRAM IN NATIONAL SECURITY STUDIES

**The Jack D. Gordon Institute for Public Policy & Citizenship Studies**
University Park, Miami, FL 33199 • Tel: 305-348-2977 • Fax: 305-348-2924 • www.fiu.edu/~ippcs
Florida International University is an Equal Opportunity / Access Employer and Institution • TDD via FRS 1-800-955-8771

FLORIDA INTERNATIONAL UNIVERSITY
*Miami's public research university*

# PROGRAM IN NATIONAL SECURITY STUDIES

**The Jack D. Gordon Institute for Public Policy & Citizenship Studies**
University Park, Miami, FL 33199 • Tel: 305-348-2977 • Fax: 305-348-2924 • www.fiu.edu/~ippcs
Florida International University is an Equal Opportunity / Access Employer and Institution • TDD via FRS 1-800-955-8771

FLORIDA INTERNATIONAL UNIVERSITY
*Miami's public research university*

## PROGRAM IN NATIONAL SECURITY STUDIES

Book
———

Clash of Civilizations

George Will
The Negro President
——

Alex Hamilton
——

Washington & Barbados

power from external great power patrons, have succeeded to a greater extent in consolidating state power, imposing order among their populations, and controlling territories that are also claimed by their neighbors. Those states that have operated within an adverse regional balance have found their state- and nation-building enterprise made increasingly difficult as their more powerful neighbors have encroached on the demographic and territorial space claimed by them. Their inability to fend off such incursions has further delegitimized such states in the eyes of their own populations and eroded their capacity to construct effective domestic political orders.

Regional balances have, therefore, crucially influenced the consolidation of state power among postcolonial states and thus become an essential component of their security problematic. It is no wonder that, given this linkage between domestic and regional variables, intrastate and interstate conflicts have become so closely intertwined in most regions of the Third World that it is difficult to determine where one ends and the other begins. Issues of internal and external security, therefore, play off each other, making the security predicament of most states in the international system very complex and resistant to easy solutions.

# VIII

The process of globalization and attempts at changing international norms to make them conform to a solidarist rather than pluralist notion of international society have not changed the basic security predicament of most states. In fact, they have immensely complicated the security problems that these states inherited at the time of independence.[13] Imposing solidarist norms on states that have not completed the process of state consolidation and that continue to suffer from inadequate nation formation intensifies their security dilemmas. Demanding that Third World states transcend the Westphalian model when many of them have not even approximated that model to any significant extent flies in the face of common sense. One cannot transcend a stage that one has not reached. The necessity for such states today is to attain the Westphalian model of effective and legitimate statehood rather than attempt to transcend it.

In these circumstances, elevating human security above state security and applying this logic indiscriminately without reference to context does not serve to enhance the objective of ensuring the security of individual citizens. It may in most cases end up making individuals more insecure as the state begins to lose its capacity to enforce its will and to monopolize the instruments of violence in its hands. The loss of these capacities almost inevitably leads to the state relinquishing its role as the provider of protection to its citizens. Prizing open the borders of states that do not have adequate regulatory capacity in the name of globalization further exacerbates their problems of state effectiveness and political legitimacy, thus adding to their insecurity.

When one adds to these factors the unprecedented and unbridgeable stratification in the hierarchy of military power currently witnessed in the international system thanks to RMA, most states unsurprisingly suffer from an acute sense of vulnerability and helplessness vis-à-vis the dominant coalition. Unable to protect themselves from the combined onslaught of economic, military, and normative forces previously outlined, they either succumb and descend into state failure or attempt to consolidate their domestic base through a strategy based on unalloyed force and repression rather than the more painstaking process of building social compacts.[14] Sometimes they combine the worst of both worlds, first indulging in repression and then succumbing to state failure. Both these outcomes—state failure and domestic repression—contribute enormously to the insecurity of their populations as well as of their neighbors and dramatically increase the probability of both intrastate and interstate conflict.

# IX

This analysis makes clear that the forces of economic and normative globalization, whose beneficiaries are few but whose negative fallout affects many, contribute handsomely to making the insecure even more insecure. Pretending otherwise, and presuming that globalization somehow makes security concerns either redundant, contributes to their mitigation, or transforms the primary referent of security, is the grandest form of self-delusion from which a student of International Relations can suffer. Nevertheless, this self-delusion seems to have become a growth industry in this field. It is time that such academic pretensions are subjected to closer scrutiny because perpetuating self-delusion can turn out to be dangerous, not only for the discipline but for the future of the international system itself.

It is imperative, therefore, that "security" be defined as a political concept and its usage limited to issues dealing with authority, order, and protection. This need has become more acute as the process of economic liberalization, the revolution in military affairs, and attempted innovations in international norms make the majority of states feel highly insecure. These processes have not transformed the basic logic of the international system, which continues to be based on the classical foundations of realism (*not neorealism*). What they have done is to make unbridgeable the gap between the powerful minority and the weak and vulnerable majority in all arenas of interstate interaction—economic, military, and normative. They have thus increased the danger of economic exploitation and coercive intervention by the powerful in the affairs of the weak that is unrestrained by the operation of the traditional norms of international society and the "prudence" enjoined by classical realist thinkers (see Morgenthau, 1948).

This state of affairs appears to be extremely deleterious from the perspective of international society that emphasizes the importance of normative consensus and the existence of common institutions that mitigate the anarchical nature of the international system and make international political life tolerable and predictable. By wishing away security and denigrating sovereignty, the proponents of globalization and of a global society do great disservice to the fragile bonds of international society that alleviate the more extreme Hobbesian characteristics of the international system.

To save ourselves from greater international disorder, it is essential that the security discourse, which resides primarily in the political realm, be taken seriously and its links to the concept of sovereignty and of the state be reestablished firmly. Wishing away or obfuscating the concept of security, denigrating the state, and diminishing the importance of sovereignty as a normative barrier to coercive intervention, under the mistaken assumption that these phenomena are no longer relevant in a globalizing world, would be playing into the hands of the powerful beneficiaries of globalization. The result may be greater disorder than order and a system that is far more predatory than one based on the notion of an international society that proclaims sovereign statehood, and, therefore, the need for security, as its foundational principle.

## NOTES

1. For the difference between global, or world, society and international society, see Bull (1977), chapter 1.

2. For details of this argument, see Ayoob (2002b).

3. For a discussion of the genesis of the human security argument and its links to social constructivism, see Newman (2001).

4. For sovereignty, see James (1999). For the classical statement on non-intervention as a norm of international society, see Vincent (1974).

5. For trenchant criticism by a former chief economist of the World Bank of the policies adopted by international financial institutions and the major industrialized countries ostensibly to promote globalization and their deletrious effect on developing countries, see Stiglitz (2002).

6. For a discussion of the unrepresentative character of the U.N. Security Council and how this detracts from its legitimacy as the primary forum where issues of humanitarian intervention are decided, see Ayoob (2002a).

7. For a succinct and persuasive case that America's current global predominanace constitutes unipolarity, see Brooks and Wohlforth (2002).

8. For a perceptive discussion of conflict entrepreneurs, see Keen (1998).

9. This is the major difference I have with Barry Buzan's comprehensive analysis of "security" in Buzan et al. (1998).

10. Much of what follows is based on my book Ayoob (1995).

11. SIPRI yearbooks throughout the 1990s and into this decade provide data showing that the overwhelming number of conflicts since the end of the Cold War have been intrastate in character. Even many of those that exhibit interstate characteristics have their origins within one or both of the warring states. This is a pattern that was visible during the Cold War years as well. However, it gained greater salience after the end of the Cold War and the outbreak of post-Soviet and post-Yugoslav conflicts.

12. The UNHCR estimated that at the end of 1999 there were over 22 million refugees in the world. See UNHCR, *The State of the World's Refugees 2000*. New York: Oxford University Press, 2001.

13. For a solidarist conception of international society, see Wheeler (2000). For a pluralist conception of international society, see Jackson (2000).

14. Incidentally, the construction of social compacts includes coercive and persuasive strategies, both sticks and carrots. However, this is not the place to go into a discussion of how social compacts are constructed, maintained, and augmented.

# Two Terrors, One Problem

Ken Booth

The starting point of my argument is that when it comes to the theory and practice of security, we have seen the past and it did not work. To advance this proposition, I want to make three further claims: that human society is confronted by a world-historical crisis and not just a temporary period of international turmoil; that the interacting dynamics of the states system and globalization are producing generally negative consequences; and that a significant part of today's crisis in human society arises from dualistic thinking. The discussion will finally be crystallized around the continuing relevance of Mark Twain's idea of 'Two Terrors' reigning at the time of the French Revolution.

## WHERE ARE WE NOW?

To begin, I want to make five general claims about the grim state of human society in world-historical perspective (Booth, 2000a).

*Proposition one: human society is not as far along the path of progress as many would like to think.* It is sobering to realize that for the greater part of human history the most intelligent people of their era believed that the earth was flat. How will today's most intelligent people look to historians in 500 or 2000 year's time? Will contemporary society, like our distant ancestors, be seen as primitive?

I believe this is likely, and the key area will be the destructive relationship humans have developed with the rest of the natural world. We will surely appear as flat-earthers to distant generations—denying evident realities—as, in a blink of historical time, we destroy the environmental bounty it has taken millions of years to create. To those future generations for whom the tiger will be a mythical creature, for whom fish will be fewer and farmed, for whom the climate will be an unpredictable threat, and for whom agricultural land will be ever-more scarce, the primitive behavior of twentieth-century humankind will attract particular scorn.

*Proposition two: the self-image of Western elites as decent people is seriously flawed.* It is commonplace to hear people sneer at ancient Greek philosophers, pointing out that their distinguished culture was built on a slave economy. How can we take the ethical systems of such 'hypocrites' seriously?

But are we any better today? If history does sneer, nobody can complain. In truth, we are worse than the ancient Greeks; their ethical systems did not include slaves as equals. We have the Universal Declaration of Human Rights as one of the many measures of our hypocrisy. Despite the supposedly more egalitarian global culture of this era, there is a global "dictatorship of the rich" ruled over by the West. At the bottom of the pile live one billion people in absolute poverty, while the richest 225 individuals have a combined wealth equivalent to the annual income of 47% of the whole population (UNDP, 1998: 30). Those living in what J. K. Galbraith calls the culture of contentment (1992) are far removed from the real lives of most humans on earth. The wiring of the world is celebrated—with huge annual increments in the hundreds of millions of telephone sets already in existence—but the minority owning multiple sets seems unaware that most people on earth have never dialed a friend. According to U.N. figures, the additional annual cost of education for everybody on earth would be 6 billion dollars; 8 billion dollars is spent annually on cosmetics in the United States alone (UNDP, 1998: 37). In global society, the spirit of Marie Antoinette is alive and well.

*Proposition three: human society is presently at the start of the first truly global age.* The context for living, globally, is being reinvented in radical ways. We are in the first stages of one of the most decisive periods of human history, comparable with the invention of tools or the Industrial Revolution. This is the first truly global age—one of those step-changes in the human graph, leading to the reinvention of space, time, boundaries, economics, identities, and politics (Booth, 1998: 338–355).

Globalization refers to a set of dynamics that became manifest in the final decades of the last century: the transnational organization of production, the liberalization of markets, the growth of world cities, the spread of advanced information technology, the 24-hour global financial system, changing consumption patterns and expectations, pressures on family and emotional life, the penetration of cultural norms and political authority, the disruption of local communities, and on and on. Globalization is a contested term, but as Anthony Giddens, one of its leading theorists, has put it: "Something very new is happening in the world" (Hutton & Giddens, 2001: 1). What is more, there is a sense that it is not all it is cracked up to be and that nobody controls it; instead the global transformations control us. It is a "runaway world," a world of "turbulence," a world "on the edge" (Giddens, 1998: 309; Hutton & Giddens, 2001; Rosenau, 1990).

*Proposition four: this period of history is characterized by a multiplication of morbid symptoms.* "The old is dying and the new cannot be born; in this interregnum there arises a great diversity of morbid symptoms." Even before the end of the Cold War, these words of Antonio Gramsci seemed to offer a helpful way into thinking about the global predicament (Booth, 1991: 1–28). The years since have more than borne them out (Cox et al., 1999: 3–19).

The morbid symptoms of our time include: nuclear proliferation, the AIDS pandemic in Africa, the real threat of nuclear war in Kashmir, the millions of people seeking refuge in countries other than their original home, the increasing death toll year by year from terror tactics, the "new barbarism" in western Europe (Jacques, 2002), accelerating desertification in Africa, suicide bombers (female as well as male) in the Middle East, a preventive war strategy by the United States, the breaking away of massive chunks of the ice cap, diseased foods, the threat of nuclear, chemical, and biological attack by terrorists, and on and on. On the opening day of the 2002 World Cup, a major British newspaper published an editorial that described it as "not merely the biggest sporting event ever, but possibly the largest globally shared experience in history" (*Guardian*, 2002). In the same issue, with nuclear war looming in South Asia, was an article describing how Pakistan was shifting thousands of troops from its western border (weakening the "fading hunt for fugitive members of al Qaeda") to the front line in the possible war with India (Harding, 2002). The bread and circuses of ancient Rome have been swapped for pizza and soccer.

*Proposition five: human society prefers to "escape from the real."* Ignoring human wrongs and not facing up to some of the more cruel aspects of life is common, and even extends, paradoxically, to mainstream academic International Relations—a discipline frequently criticized for worst-case forecasting escapes the worst (Booth, 1995). The ideology directing the way the International Relations "camera" is pointed excludes as well as includes. It shows a picture of the facts that allows the telling of whatever stories the teller favors. According to Clement Rosset, the discipline of philosophy in the early 1990s represented an "escape from the real." It produced an endless interpretation of texts "totally oblivious to what exists," and created "the illusion of a truth which would remove us from the suffering necessarily entailed by an encounter with the real" (Rosset, 1993: viii, xiv). This warning was equally pertinent to International Relations.

A few years later, the playwright Jean-Claude Carriere (1999) compared human society to those wealthy and more than normally egocentric American businessmen (they are always men, I think) who over recent decades have had the idea of being deep frozen in old age, or when sick, and sealed in cryogenic cylinders. They believe that their fatal disease (or even old age) may one day be curable. Consequently, they are preserving their bodies in the expectation of eventual salvation. Globally speaking, human society has been behaving in a similar fashion. We carry on regardless—voraciously consuming, for example—in the hope that there will be solutions in a few generations time to the problems we have brought upon ourselves, and the world as a whole.

## HOW DID WE GET HERE?

If this grim picture is valid, how did it come about? I reject simple arguments deriving from biology or destiny—human nature or the will of god. Instead, I prefer to remember the words of the peace researcher Kenneth Boulding: "We are as we are because we got that way" (Booth, 2003).

If history was open, how is it that human society came to create for itself this age of anxiety? The broad answer lies, paradoxically, in the power of the very ideas that once seemed solutions to the biggest questions in human society. The ideas that came through history to set the broad parameters of societies have been—in rough chronological order of invention—patriarchy, proselytizing religions, capitalism, sovereign statism (together with nationalism), and consumerist democracy. Each of these ideologies promised answers to the great questions of life: patriarchy seemed to respond to biological realities, religions gave insight into the meaning of life, capitalism delivered the most effective means of production, sovereign states gave hope of security from internal and external threats, and democracy institutionalized a yearning for fairer governance. But each of these historical solutions had a dark side. Look around. Patriarchy produces systematic violence against women; religious fundamentalisms feed bigotry and intolerance and sometimes terrorism; multinational corporations deny AIDS victims cheap drugs; sovereignty allows governments to behave badly to their own citizens; and democracy has developed into a "culture of contentment." A distinctive global sociology was created by the interaction of 4000+ years of patriarchy, 2000+ years of organized religion, 500 years of capitalism, 350 years of statism, and about 100 years of consumerist democracy. By their excesses and successes, its elements have conspired to create a world-historical crisis.

The security dimensions of this crisis will be significantly shaped by two particular sets of dynamics: globalization and the states system.

## Globalization

Globalization is a defining feature of the contemporary world. This is incontrovertible, even for those who question how to define it and how to describe its 'real' character. The momentum behind it is twofold:

*1. Globalization as a politico-economic project.* Globalization here is synonymous with the growth of an integrated world economy. In this sense, it refers to the acceleration and triumph of capitalism, the domination of neoliberalism and U.S. hegemony/imperialism. Globalization is "always *for* someone and *for* some purpose," to use Robert Cox's characterization of all theories (1981: 128). In its politico-economic form, it is *for* the U.S. state and *for* its enhanced power and prosperity. Globalization is a U.S. project.

*2. Globalization as a techno-cultural process.* Globalization in this sense is synonymous with multiple and complex interpenetrations of the local and the global. It refers to the shrinking of space and time, the communications revolution, the 24/7 world, and the confrontation of "Western" and other identities. Globalization is the set of processes constructing a smaller world.

Globalization—as world economy/small world—is without doubt here to stay, though it need not take the forms that have dominated recent decades. It is difficult to imagine that the world economy would again become a patchwork of localisms. The character of politico-economic globalization might—should—change, but autarky is not on the horizon. Equally, failing some global catastrophe (comprehensive nuclear war, a worldwide plague, etc.) techno-cultural globalization cannot be turned back. Any reversal of the secular trend toward a smaller world would require a radical disruption of the growth of global communications, not to mention the collapse of those with an interest in their growth. Critics of globalization sometimes argue it is not a new phenomenon—they are right. They usually make the point to try to diminish its significance, here they are mistaken. Its long historical trajectory simply underlines that it is here to stay.

## The States System

The dynamics of the global economy have circumscribed the scope for autonomous action by the governments of juridically sovereign states. The power of the market was evident in the way the Soviet Union—a military superpower—had to bend before the global power of capitalism. Never before had such a powerful state surrendered without suffering military defeat in the traditional games of nations. The Westphalian states system is under transformation (Held et al., 1999), but (some) states continue to be key sites of power, and will remain so for the indefinite future. Whether it is taxes or welfare, conscription or human rights, state borders matter. If they did not, why are so many people on the move, seeking new homelands?

Sovereign states should be problematized as analytical categories, empirical power centers, and normative institutions/projects; nevertheless, they will remain significant organizational forms in global governance—that is, the relationships between forms of political authority, and the character of that authority, on a global scale. Future global governance will include states, but also other organizations such as international organizations and varieties of nonstate actors. What emerges from the mix will have a profound effect on theories and practices of security.

## GLOBALIZATION AND INSECURITY

Having made a start to describing where we are in history and how we got there, I want to suggest some characteristic insecurities that derive from the dynamics of globalization and the structure of the states system. Beginning with globalization, the most important overall feature is its uneven impact on different groups (classes, nations, genders, etc.), states, and regions. This is evident in the field of security, just as it is in economics.

The world economy produces a patchwork of differently affected local regions. In human terms, the most decisive aspect of the uneven impact of globalization has been to widen the disparities between the haves and the have-nots within and between countries. This trend, potentially, will play a decisive role in the security of individuals and groups, governments and political systems, and states and regions. The divisive potential of economic stratification raises the probability that definitions of class will again emerge as a categorical feature of human society.

A framework for thinking about the relationship between globalization and insecurity is provided by the "sectoral" schema of Barry Buzan and his colleagues. Five security-issue areas are identified (Buzan et al., 1998). The following arguments are neither original nor likely to be particularly controversial, and they lead to two generalizations: first, that globalization has both positive and negative impacts on security; and second, that generalization is difficult because the impacts of globalization on security are uneven. (The framework and some of the illustrations are from Scholte, 2000.) Space allows only a snapshot of each sector.

### Military

*Positive.* It might be argued that globalization has had two main positive impacts on military security at the state level. First, politico-economic globalization is strengthening historical trends against interstate war, alongside other trends, such as the increasing potential for destructiveness in war (Mueller, 1990). Major war between industrial powers has been in decline as an instrument of policy for decades (which is not the same as saying it has disappeared) and the interconnectedness of the global marketplace assists in this evolution.

Second, politico-economic globalization places extra incentives on conflict management, if not actual resolution. The difference in external (U.S. and EU) concern about instability in the Middle East as opposed to violence in the Great Lakes region of Africa is revealing in this respect.

*Negative.* What makes the global economy work so well in delivering fresh produce to supermarkets halfway round the world at a reasonable price (to consumers, if not the original laborers) also delivers less wholesome products. The international drug trade, for example, is one such globalized industry that contributes to the insecurities of streets, neighborhoods, and regions across the world. A similar globalized enterprise, but this time dealing in the currency of political violence, is terrorism. Several observers have pointed to the globalized character of al Qaeda. John Gray, for example, has written: "In organization, it seems to be a hybrid of the semi-virtual business corporations that were so fashionable in the Nineties and the loosely linked cellular structures that run the world's drug cartels. Like the most advanced businesses, al Qaeda is a worldwide network that is only vestigially territorial. Though some states may have sheltered it, it is not under the control of any of them. Thriving on weak government and the mercurial mobility of stateless wealth, it is a perfect embodiment of globalization" (Gray, 2002).

## Political

*Positive.* Whether globalization enhances security in "political" areas depends on the position particular states and societies occupy within the global capitalist system, together with their particular culture of capitalism. These considerations will affect issues such as the practice of human rights and the character of governance (Madeley, 1999). Winners in the global economy will have more resources than the losers, and this will give them relative independence and security, but it may be security at somebody's expense—never a totally comfortable situation. Some of the regulatory aspects of globalization, to help economies work more profitably, can empower workers who previously have been ignored.

*Negative.* Globalization has led some governments to make the lives of their people distressingly insecure by reducing public spending; this can affect health and other life chances, and also can have the effect of disempowering people. The Asian miracle obscured the vast difference in the actual daily lives of people; these differences in economic wherewithal translated into both political and economic insecurities for the have-nots (Jindy Pettman, 2003). Equally, while there may be improved regulatory aspects of globalization, the drive for profit by multinational companies can have negative human rights outcomes, as has been the case with some Western oil companies in South America and West Africa (Madeley, 1999: 121–127). Strong corporations and strong-arm governments ally against workers and their supporters seeking better life conditions.

## Societal

*Positive.* It is easy to exaggerate the significance of global civil society, but it would be even more of a mistake to ignore it (Ekins, 1992; Keck & Sikkink, 1998). On the positive side, there has been the growth of a global consciousness evident in the densification of networks of "global civil society." These "transworld solidarities" have helped indigenous peoples struggle against their governments and multinational corporations (Booth, 1999: 55–56). One example is the Survival International campaign organized on behalf of the Kalahari bushmen.

*Negative.* Identity politics and the politics of identity have become central concerns for some schools of thought about world politics. It has been argued, for example, that the security problem in Europe has become that of societies seeking to protect their identity rather than of states protecting their sovereignty (Waever et al., 1993). The insecurity of 'local' identities against the cultural power of Americanization is a widespread phenomenon. Counters to the threat of McWorld have taken several forms, including the fundamentalism of the Taliban in Afghanistan (Barber, 1996). Globalization puts pressures on local, traditional cultures, especially if they are small. Languages become threatened as the local is increasingly engulfed by outside influences, and global figures (world leaders, film stars, soccer players, etc.) become more recognizable than local politicians or even neighbors (Giddens, 1998: 311). But it is not only small societies that are suffering. Even before September 11, Americans seem to have become less happy, despite their steady rise in consumption (*New Internationalist*, 1999: 18; Putnam, 2001). The pressures of competing, even successfully, in the global economy can erode local community and personal fulfillment.

## Environment

*Positive.* Because of the need for companies to compete, environmental standards are not always high on their list of their priorities. But sometimes they are, and this promotes standards in places where previously there were none, especially if local governments attach importance to the environment; this is both a cause and consequence of the growing awareness within civil society, nationally and globally, of environmental issues. Such groups have learned to share knowledge and coordinate more effectively.

*Negative.* It is difficult to draw any other conclusion than that globalization has proved to be a net polluter, with resulting insecurities for local communities. Over a long time-scale, the overexploitation of fisheries and the disturbance of the global climate will provoke massive insecurity, affecting livelihoods, communities, and habitats. Many communities live in areas that are fragile in relation to the capacity of the natural world to keep delivering, and hence there is a growing fear of where it might end.

## Economic

*Positive.* There are many defenders of globalization (Leadbeater, 2002); they argue that it is having a benign effect on human society through global growth, increases in aggregate welfare overall, and rapid industrialization bringing jobs and wealth.

*Negative.* The key indicator affecting the security of people(s) at all levels is not the global aggregate, but how the figures play out in specific situations. Global growth figures hide particular insecurities. One potent symbol of the different perspectives one can adopt on these issues has been dam-building (Madeley, 1998: 115–120). Globalization pushes governments into attempting to compete internationally, create jobs, promote nationalism, and construct efficient infrastructure. Dam-building is often seen as a key element of economic progress and modernization. Others think differently, seeing their traditional land disappear as a result of such projects, and with it their livelihoods and identity. The Himba in Namibia faced greater insecurity from their own state's dam-building project than from the military attacks of the former apartheid regime in South Africa (Vale, 2003). Globalization also promotes stresses as the rich get richer, within and between countries, and the poor get poorer (Thomas, 1999). Internal violence may be provoked by the working of the global system. The end of the Cold War opened up space for the expression of old ethnic animosities in Europe—notably in the Balkans. But the disintegration of Yugoslavia was also shaped by the country's changing role in the global economy—from being a favored Cold-War recipient of credits to being a relatively unimportant region in the neoliberal world economy (Woodward, 1995). Economic change exacerbated ethnic insecurity.

These snapshots have attempted to suggest ways in which globalization produces insecurities at all levels of human society, even though there are some positive sides. But as long as today's highly competitive form of globalization persists—which looks like a very long time—it is bound to produce winners and losers. Although there has been movement away from the more fundamentalist Washington consensus that dominated globalization a decade ago—note the concerns of some of its former masters such as George Soros (2002)—there is a great distance to travel before a more humane globalization can emerge.

Without a radical transformation in the character of globalization, pressure on "human security" will increase. Business-as-usual will result in insecurities growing at the level of individuals, societies, and in important respects globally, too. The causes will vary: governments responding to globalization by reducing public spending and so exposing their populations to the insecurities that come from poverty and ill health; the incompetence, oppression, and corruption of elites dominating different global regions; crises of identity in the face of powerful economic, cultural, and political forces; the increase in environmental problems as long as growth and profit are valued above sustainability and conservation; and insecurities arising from hyperglobalization's creation of widening gaps between the rich and the poor. It is a sign of the deepening crisis that a higher profile is being given to human and not simply state security needs (UNDP, 1994). Human insecurities, magnified many times, can lead to serious international consequences. These range from the provision of the foot soldiers for terrorism to the collapse of economies. The former may result in Western interests being violently targeted, the latter in Western governments having to contemplate assistance or military intervention in failed states.

Traditional thinking about security assumes a states system characterized by domestic order and external anarchy; consequently, when a government is threatened (by the military power of a foreign adversary), the inhabitants are threatened as well. With globalization, the dynamics of insecurity are more complex. One's own government is a player in the world economy, and each state competes as local agents of the world capitalist good (to paraphrase Hedley Bull). Running hard to compete in the global marketplace, governments will often have different agendas and pressures to those of the mass of their people; certain classes will benefit, while others suffer. Attempts to adapt to the mechanisms of globalization—literally structural adjustment—have usually resulted in the victory of market advantage over human security. The first president of Tanzania, Julius Nyrere, put the choice with stark clarity between meeting the demands of structural adjustment programs or providing public spending on food subsidies. "Must we starve our children to pay our debts?," he asked (quoted in *New Internationalist*, 1997: 37).

The world is not working for most of its inhabitants; perhaps it never did. But today more of the world knows about it. Globalization spreads insecurities and also knowledge about the winners and losers. The insecurity felt by most people does not come from a neighboring army across the nearest border, but from the strengths and weaknesses of their own governments. Many feel additionally insecure because of low expectations about their governments. They perceive governments getting weaker in the context of a global economy run by corporations in the interests of their own profit, not by politics in the interests of the people (George, 1999; Klein, 2000; Korten, 1995; Madeley, 1998).

## DANGEROUS DYNAMICS IN A RUNAWAY WORLD

Two further dynamics, morbid symptoms both, could seriously exacerbate all the existing dangers.

### The Population Dynamic

On 12 October 1999 a baby was born in a hospital in Sarajevo and became, symbolically, the sixth-billionth human alive. There are lots of us already, but the number could double again before today's young adults reach late middle age.

The worst predictions may not come about—growth rates are slowing down—but nevertheless global public policy has not begun to appreciate the potential magnitude of the environmental, social, and political stresses that may lie ahead as a result of the population dynamic. Britain and other parts of Western Europe worry about a few thousand asylum seekers. Right-wing politicians are finding increasing favor in the liberal-democratic world, where the liberal spirit is declining alongside faith in politics. In Australia, the right-wing prime minister, John Howard, came from behind in the polls in the general election by manipulating the threat to Australian society supposedly posed by boatloads of refugees (Dunne & Booth, 2002). Meanwhile, in Denmark, another supposedly liberal and tolerant country, a law was passed in 2002 to prevent anyone under the age of 24 from living in the country with a non-EU spouse; it also prohibits asylum seekers from marrying while their applications are being processed (Smith, 2002). Xenophobia and racism are rising, and the major surge in the world's population growth has yet to come.

How will all the new mouths be fed? How will they get jobs when they reach adulthood? What will life be like in the 100-mile cities of the future? What will the vast armies of unemployed youth in Third World megacities do to pass their time, with their minds fueled by the global media and whatever else? Who will pay the pensions of the grey-haired world? Will race join class as a revived category in the ontology of world politics? What will be the consequences of mass migrations of desperate people? Population growth is a potential global time bomb.

## The Ideological Dynamic

As the Cold War wound down, there was a temptation among Western elites (and their counterparts elsewhere) to believe that the great political and economic questions of life had been settled. The "end of history" thesis of Francis Fukuyama, which was neither as brilliant nor as silly as it was greeted at the time, saw a world dominated by one way of life, based on democracy and capitalism (1993). Liberal triumphalists have been correct when they have argued that there is no immediate challenger to liberal capitalism, but I believe that the objective conditions over the next half-century will ensure that alternatives do arise, as the present system fails to work for most of humanity. Conflict creates convictions.

There are abundant warning signs. One is the growth of fanaticisms of all types. We are in an era when there seems to be a growing tendency for people(s) to reject reason in favor of fundamentalism, extremism, or hate. There was growing evidence of this worrying ideological dynamic in the 1990s: the brutal hypernationalism in the Balkan conflicts; the genocidal mentality in Rwanda; the medieval simplicities of the Taliban; the fundamentalisms of Islam; the "fascism" of Hindu nationalism; the back-to-basics Christianity of the religious Right in the United States; the anti-Semitism and anti-Roma attitudes in eastern Europe; the rise of the xenophobic Right in western Europe, and on and on.

Religion has been a traditional glue holding societies together, but it has been in decline in many parts of the world. G. K. Chesterton once said that the problem when people stop believing in God is not that they believe in nothing, but that they believe in anything. It is usual (in the West) to look for thought-extremism in "rogue states" or those outside their liberal homelands. But this is not always the case. I recently heard on the radio that there are more fortune tellers now in France than priests. According to polls, 40% of Americans believe that aliens have visited the planet, and a range of similar weird beliefs have been reported as having wide support (Linden, 1998: 122–133). Politically, some militia organizations in the United States consider the United Nation as a potential threat, and it is not long since a very popular president is supposed to have consulted astrologers. Under President Bush the country has moved to the political Right, in a fundamentalist manner that frightens much of the world.

No matter how persuasive Fukuyama's vision appeared in the short term, it seriously underestimated the interplay between material circumstances and convictions. In future circumstances of predictable social stress within countries (such as massive unemployment resulting from population growth) and unpredictable conflicts between them, it is likely that world politics will be witness to a new age of ideology. Human society feels primed for it, not least because massive inequality has the potential to make ideologues of us all. Desperation can lead people to believe in anything, and today the search for meaning and the will to dominate are both served by amazing technological wizardry. The circumstances are such that widespread crises will occur as disparities grow between and within countries, the global population will surge to 9–12 billion, environmental problems will increase, as key states will remain competitively militarized and suspicious, and a sense is growing of system overload and helplessness about the future. If all this is the case, it cannot be assumed that the ideologies to which the rich will be drawn (feeling insecure because they are rich) or the poor are drawn (feeling desperate because they are poor) will be characterized by benign and progressive social and political—and racial—views about the social order and its betterment.

In some ways it would be comforting to believe that poverty was the only or chief cause of fanatical ideologies, but their origins are more complex. This is evident in the growth of the Japanese 'cult' *Aum Shinrikyo* (Supreme Truth), which, according to one writer, was made up of the "highly educated, well-off children of an 'economic miracle'" (Buruma, 2002). This group, based on a complex mix of religions and nonreligions, was the product, according to one of its historians, of "the lack of a broad world vision" in Japanese life, which had narrowed into purely material, technocratic aims. The religious killers wanted "a meaningful Armageddon." Ian Buruma has argued that parallels exist between the situation in Japan and the rest of the industrialized world, though it is in an extreme form in Japan. His warning is worth quoting at length: "As politics become increasingly bureaucratic, as organized traditional religion fades away, as history is turned into a theme park and social life is usurped by television and the internet, we too become vulnerable to sudden eruptions of irrationality. In a society where masses of people cry louder over the death of a celebrity than for their own kin, strange cults are never far away. Here, too, we have searchers for absolutes. If they can no longer find them in churches, there is no telling where they will explode."

This is a snapshot of a world in which rage, hate and extremism are in season—a world in which fanatical leaders will readily gather fanatical followers. In the early 1990s, the manner in which ruthless leaders in disintegrating Yugoslavia were able to mobilize hatred for political purposes was instructive in its speed, depth, and violence. In many parts of the world in the years ahead there will be situations in which economic dislocation, prejudice, historical scores, and present tensions will match those that fueled the disintegration of Yugoslavia. The coming into season of fanaticism was evident before September 11, but that fateful morning, when mass murder came out of a clear blue sky, demands that we consider it a central dynamic when contemplating the future of global insecurity.

## Two Terrors

The meanings of that morning will be debated endlessly, and rightly so. A continuing controversy will be the motives of the perpetrators. My concern here is not with this important question, however, but how the events have been perceived, and what this tells us about Western thinking about globalization, security, and the nation-state.

The key insight comes from the great nineteenth-century American writer Mark Twain and his views about the French Revolution. This was highlighted in an editorial in the British weekly magazine the *New Statesman* shortly after the terror attacks on the United States (2001). Recalling the intense fear gripping Europe in the 1790s as a consequence of the French Revolution, Twain pointed out that there were two Reigns of Terror to consider, and not just the great terror that so dominated the history books. The first was the immediate and urgent one, which brought "the horror of swift death"; this was the terror caused by the French Revolution itself. The second was the daily terror affecting the poor, which resulted in "lifelong death from hunger, cold, insult, cruelty and heartbreak." The great terror "inflicted death upon a thousand persons, the other upon a hundred million." He went on to say that the one brief terror "we have all been . . . diligently taught to shiver at and mourn over," whereas the other we had never learned to see "in its vastness or pits as it deserves."

Twain could have been writing in the days after September 11, 2001, given the contrast between the fully reported horror of 9/11 in the United States and the generally unreported daily horror faced by the world's poor. The headline writers of the *New Statesman* noted that those killed in New York, Washington, and Pennsylvania on 9/11 added up to less than half the number of children who die somewhere in the world each day from diarrhea as a result of the lack of clean water.

I want to push this argument further. There are indeed two reigns of terror, today as in the 1790s. But they are not autonomous: we in the comfortable world are complicit in one of them, just as we are the targets of the other. Dirty water is not a geographical phenomenon: it is the result of dirty politics and economics. Children need not die from diarrhea, as is obvious from the fact that nowhere on earth do the children of comfortably off parents suffer from the lack of clean water. In this sense, the thousands of dying children across the world are not victims of diarrhea; they are victims of poverty. Their deaths are the result of governments—their own and others—behaving badly. And there will be no improvement until it is accepted that these children do not "die" from natural causes: they are killed by world politics.

In making this point I am not minimizing the horror of the mass murder and torture inflicted on their victims by the al Qaeda fanatics on 9/11. I am simply underlining the continuing relevance of Twain's insight that terror comes in different guises. Nobody should forget what happened in and to the United States on September 11, 2001. As it happens, there is no fear of that, because it will be kept alive by the world's most powerful media. Equally, nobody should ignore what happens in and to the world's oppressed people(s) between January 1 and December 31, every year. We may well, because this is the suffering of the largely silenced majority.

## ONE PROBLEM

September 11 was a wake-up call about the two terrors, though it remains to be seen whether it results in world order reform or a continuing snooze. The specific call to action in this chapter relates to the need to change orthodox (realist-inspired) thinking about security. In particular, I want to address the problem of dualism. (I am not using "dualism" here in the sense that philosophers employ it, to refer to the theory that mind and matter are two distinct things, or in the theological sense of humans having two basic natures, the physical and the spiritual). By dualism I mean the way in which orthodox conceptualizations of security operate in a series of twofold or discrete relationships: the separation of security/ethics, us/them, politics/economics, and ends/means. I believe such conceptualizations represent yesterday's tribal answers to tomorrow's global challenges. Each of these dualisms is based in turn on other features of traditional thinking about international politics: "problem-solving" approaches, ethnocentrism, statism, and instrumental reason.

### Dualism One: Security/Ethics

The problem here, paradoxically, is problem solving. Specifically, it is the way in which traditional thinking about security has been confined to Robert Cox's conception of problem solving theory (Cox & Sinclair, 1996: 87–88; Hoffman, 1987: 237–238). This type of theory works inside a particular framework of social or political (or security) ideas. It "takes the world as it finds it, with the prevailing social and power relationships and the institutions into which they are organized as the given framework of action. The general aim of problem solving is to make these relationships and institutions work smoothly by dealing effectively with particular sources of trouble." The alternative to this approach is what Cox calls "critical" theory.

Problem-solving theorists are concerned with technical questions: "how?," not "why?" Security policies are a technique, not an ethics. This leads some strategists to talk about "balancing" morality and power. But how can one balance what one cannot separate? Power is a currency from which morality cannot be extracted, and morality is the arena in which power always operates. The security/ethics bifurcation is evident in the history of nuclear deterrence strategy during the Cold War, not to mention its manifestations since. When the employment of military technology is seen simply as instrumental, it is strategic reductionism, not politics (Booth, 1987: 43–44). Such an attitude was brutally manifest in the plans of General Sherman in the American Civil War. "War is hell," he said, implying a context of unmitigated cruelty—the "Sherman simplifier" (Walzer, 1977).

But there are always choices, and all security practices have consequences; hence there are no ethics-free zones. Only the cruel and desperate and those in denial can persuade themselves otherwise. The negative results of so much done in the name of security might have been mitigated had the ethical dimension been explicit, as opposed to being theorized away, or otherwise rationalized. The traditional question about security would be something along the lines: How can we improve our security in the twenty-first century? In this problem-solving formulation, definitions of the problem, and possible answers, are predefined. A critical perspective—inclusive, open—would start by asking: Who should the twenty-first century be for? In the beginning of security is the who, not the how.

## Dualism Two: Us/Them

Ethnocentrism is a universal phenomenon, though its grip on thinking varies considerably between individuals (Booth, 1979: 14–15). In its broadest sense it is a synonym for being culture-bound; this refers to the inability of one individual or group being able to see the world through the eyes of others, and it is invariably associated with ideas of in-group superiority. It emphasizes "the right to be different" rather than "the right to be the same" (Malik, 1995: 277.

Dualistic thinking constructs a world of us/them. It turns possibilities into either/or instead of both/and. Such social reductionism seeks to impose an identity based on one characteristic (Muslim, black, gay, German) at a time when due recognition must be given to peoples' multiple identities, and the fact that people these days are more self-consciously members of different groups. Every society is becoming more porous as people live increasingly in each others' pockets under conditions of globalization. Identity politics have the effect of reifying a political, social, and cultural reality that is multifaceted and changing. One of the least helpful reifications is the postcolonial ritualization of "the West" and "the Rest." Not only were the lines never more blurred, but who, what, and where, these days, is the West? And when was the West? Analysts of security should never forget Adorno's view that "all reification is a forgetting" (quoted in Wyn Jones, 1999: 107).

To illustrate the importance of transcending us/them in favor of thinking about our community of fate (and collective responsibility), I offer what might not appear the most obvious case: AIDS, a pandemic that not only devastates the lives of individuals and families, but also threatens economies. It is a metaphor for security in the age of globalization.

When a disease spreads rapidly, its causes are "never merely biological" according to the French epidemiological pioneer Louis Pasteur (quoted by Ellwood, 2002: 10). This has been the case with AIDS. Before examining local causes, its etiology encompasses colonialism and the Western domination of the world economy; it also implicates everybody, however remotely, to the extent that any of our attitudes and behavior assists in the replication of poverty, gender, and class inequalities. AIDS is a global "us" issue. Looking at the social conditions for AIDS in sub-Saharan Africa, the South African photographer Gideon Mendel lists the following: commercial sex-work, urbanization, and poverty-driven job migration. These social forces he then relates to the political and economic conditions exacerbated by economic adjustment policies and debt. Further back, he argues, colonialism "set the template for African labour migration, tearing men away from their villages and families to work in mines and plantations." Mendel reports from one of the pandemic's battlefronts: "You go to some of the mines and there are between 20,000 and 30,000 men working there. They go home for two weeks a year. The mines are surrounded by squatter camps full of sex workers, many of whom are infected with HIV. If an evil genius were asked to design an ideal scenario for the spread of AIDS, he couldn't come up with anything better" (quoted by Ellwood, 2002: 10).

The AIDS pandemic is not simply a biological phenomenon of the 1980s and afterwards; it has been incubating in our history. It also challenges our futures, for it not only wrecks individuals and families, it also threatens economies (the following examples are from WHO/FAO reports quoted by Ellwood, 2002: 10). It is estimated that one-quarter of all families in Botswana might lose a wage earner to AIDS in the next 10 years, with obvious impact on household income. Zambia has already lost one in three teachers to AIDS. Across sub-Saharan Africa it is predicted that farm workers will die in the millions. Earning, education, agriculture are at risk; public health will not be able to cope. In these conditions, states can fail. When they do, others are called on to rescue them. AIDS is a potential security issue at all levels.

In its causes and consequences, AIDS underlines the importance of recognizing human relatedness under conditions of globalization. If ethical universalism has not so far been a persuasive argument for communitarians, self-interest should be. Humans increasingly share a community of fate. The old us/them dualism of the realist/communitarian outlook is illustrated in its most brutal political simplicity in the Bolshevik formula, *kto-kovo*—"literally, 'who-whom,' but in its most radical sense, 'who kills whom'" (Bell, 1971: 301).

In contrast to learning "Who/whom?" as the fundamental issue of politics—the world of us/them, nation/alien, self/other—we need to recognize the commonness of humans, based on the I-that-is-another in all of us (Booth, 1999: 31, 64–66). This is part of the need to privilege human equality over intra-human difference. Otherwise, as Kenan Malik has argued, "difference becomes resolved into *indifference*" (this is the theme of Malik, 1995: 217–259).

## Dualism Three: Politics/Economics

The problem here begins with statism. Among its top-down manifestations is the idea of 'high' and 'low' politics, with security issues belonging to the former, and economics to the latter. But politics and economics are not only separated hierarchically; they have too often become regarded as autonomous realms. Neoliberalism in the 1990s, for example, became management; only the victims and their supporters recognized the iron political fist hidden in the corporation's glove. Such a separation of politics and economics includes the privileging of the victims of politics over the victims of economics, as mentioned earlier. This dualism may serve national interests in terms of state security, but it is always unfriendly to security in the human interest.

An illustration of the politics/economics dualism was evident through the 1990s in the militant humanitarianism of some of the major liberal-democratic states, and in particular the United States and Britain (Booth, 2000b). In their rhetoric, no doubt those who speak for these states would spin in sympathy for the victims of all life's hardships. In the aftermath of 9/11, Prime Minister Blair spoke of reordering the world (Blair, 2001): but where is the follow-up? Actions always speak louder. Professors of security, for the most part, only have words, and for the most part those who have written about humanitarian intervention, focusing on the means of rescuing the political victims of tyrants, have not engaged with the economic system that has sometimes played a role in creating the conflict necessitating intervention.

When state leaders start using the term "international community" it usually serves as a warning that an interventionist initiative is on the way. During the Kosovo crisis of 1998–1999, the great power club who form the nucleus of the so-called international community behaved in ways that drew attention to some of the questions raised by the distinction between the victims of politics/economics. The basic issue can be stated baldly. Why did the great powers in 1999 give so much attention to the victims of politics in Europe—the targets of Milosovic's ethnic policies—as opposed to the far greater number being victimized (and dying) by global economics? The answer is self-interest. Those who would question this—convinced that NATO's motives were purely humanitarian—might ask themselves what would have happened had Milosevic been more subtle in his policies, and had history been kinder to him in the matter of timing. Would NATO have gone to war against Serbia at the end of 2001, had circumstances conspired to allow Milosovic to wait until after 9/11 before expanding his human rights abuses against the Kosovar Albanians? Or would the Serbian leader's "counterterror" against the Islamic extremists of the KLA have made him an ally, albeit an uncomfortable one, in the global struggle against international terrorism? It is inconceivable that NATO's humanitarian impulses on behalf of the Kosovar Albanians would have outlived 9/11 and a canny Milosevic. On the contrary, a diplomatic Milosevic could have made it virtually impossible, by prosecuting his counterterror at acceptable levels of violence while standing shoulder to shoulder with the U.S. president on all important world issues, such as their joint rejection of the idea of establishing an International Criminal Court.

The academic development of the discipline of International Relations has mirrored the politics/economics dualism of state policy. Dead soldiers have always been thought so much more interesting and important a source of study than the 14,000-a-day dead babies from preventable disease in the global South (Booth, 2000b). Dualistic thinking about politics/economics often serves to rationalize racial, patriarchal, and nationalistic prejudices. The victims of economics, like the victims of politics, are equally victims of world politics; they are presumably equally worthy of consideration by students of security.

## Dualism Four: Ends/Means

The separation of ends and means is deeply embedded in Western political theory, including the tradition of Machiavelli and Clausewitz. What Theodor Adorno and Max Horkheimer called instrumental reason, in which decision-making systems operate free from moral constraints in accordance with the ends and means logic of strategic action, is one way of representing this duality (Wyn Jones, 1999: 31–32, 35). It has been seen throughout history in political practice in the old question: Do the ends justify the means?

President Bush's war against terrorism illustrates some of the problems of dualistic thinking about ends and means. All his reactions to date have been calculated (whether consciously thought out and articulated or not) to return the challenge to comfortable categories. Declaring it a war was one move, which permitted a range of well-established means to secure the desired end. Military assets were deployed, bombs dropped, alliances formed, domestic critics silenced, troops inserted, and loyalty tests made. It was, ostensibly, a return to realpolitik (though falling short of the realpolitik originally conceived by Bismark, concerned with limited objectives and modest moves). A non-dualistic ends–means approach to the challenge of September 11 would lead to a different posture to that so far adopted by the White House. While accepting the obligation of the United States to protect its citizens and use violent means when unavoidable, the conception of victory would be different: dealing with terrorism would become a political process more than a military "end."

A nondualist strategy against terror would make conceivable the immediate declaration of victory, though not the immediate elimination of all terrorists. Albert Camus hints at the general idea by suggesting that the means one uses today shapes the ends one might perhaps reach tomorrow (Hoffmann, 1981: 197). Better still is the Ghandian idea, believing that "ends and means amount to the same thing" (Richards, 1995: 31–32). Such an approach is not about the ends justifying the means—the idea that has caused countless harm through history—but instead sees the means as equivalent to the ends. This involves employing means that embody everything implied in the end sought. In other words, some "end" might not be achievable, but means that are its equivalent are. So, for example, it might not be possible to lessen the gap between haves and have-nots quickly, but it is possible to implement policies equivalent to bringing about the humanization of globalization; it might not be possible to reverse the worrying trends in global climatic change, but treaties can be signed that change the daily behavior of consumers and corporations; it might not be possible to eradicate terrorists quickly, but victory over terrorism can be achieved if prisoners are treated properly, dissidents respected, and antiterrorism not used as an excuse to suspend the lawful values of society (Booth & Dunne, 2002: 21).

One way of expressing this nondualistic idea is Joseph Nye's distinction between process as opposed to end-point utopias (Nye, 1987). The dualistic response to terrorism prioritizes the military means to bring about the end of al Qaeda. The nondualistic response accepts that there are no end-points, when all will be well, only ethical and law-governed processes that are consonant with constructing the ethical and law-governed world one seeks.


## AFTER SEPTEMBER 11: BEYOND DUALISM?

Nondualism is vulnerable to the familiar mainstream put-down of idealism. But what about the projection into the future of the implications of old thinking, the grim world that realism has wrought? In comparison with the latter, nondualistic thinking about security in world politics appears tactically astute as well as a strategic necessity.

As long as the traditional games of nations and unstoppable globalization interact so dynamically, it is difficult to imagine that it will be possible to keep the two terrors of world politics apart. What is more, global and local winners and losers will be in more instantaneous and cognitive contact. The winners will feel threatened because they are winners, the losers because they are losers.

It would not be a surprise if ambitious, aggressive, or desperate leaders did not seek to take advantage of those with a sense of grievance—those who feel themselves victims, or can be made to feel so. The stoking of historic and not so historic wrongs can turn insecure people into violent thugs. This is the case at all levels, from ethnically threatened minorities to superpowers.

The world is getting smaller, but small will not necessarily be beautiful. At the moment, the image to keep in mind is less of a global village than a global inner city; that is, less of a real community than a tense and dangerous place, a world of volatility, not stability, of rage, not self-realization, and of ghetto wars, not friendly interaction (Booth, 1979: 178; Heilbronner, 1995). Human society faces the prospect of a "long hot century" (Booth, 2003).

In sum, human society has not progressed as much as we think; our ethics are flawed; we are living at the beginning of a radically new era; world politics are characterized by morbid symptoms; the dynamics of globalization and the states system combine to produce manifold insecurities; there is a sense of a runaway world with worrying trends and irrationalities; the events of September 11 underline a well-established tendency to conceive global insecurities in terms of two terrors, with one being prioritized; orthodox thinking about security is part of the problem; human society, in the long hot century ahead, needs a global cultural change if it is not to be rent by unprecedented levels and types of insecurity. The traditional global culture of the powerful in human society is running out of time; the ideologies and structures that have made us what we are today—the dominating ideas about patriarchy, capitalism, religion, sovereign states, and democracy—are calculated only to increase global insecurities to the breaking point.

The aim of this chapter has been to underline the case for one element in that global culture to change: from dualistic to nondualistic praxis. This involves thinking beyond the orthodox categories. In the vernacular of governmental officials, the holistic approach being proposed is sometimes called joined-up thinking. It has been badly lacking.

The resources for such thinking are all around; they are not the preserve of one country or period of history. I will illustrate it by an anecdote, a story that is more telling, memorable, and inspirational than most of what passes for political analysis these days. It concerns an episode during a recent book tour by the inspiring figure of Maya Angelou (Younge, 2002: 18). In the short paragraph that follows can be learned more about how to construct a more secure world politics than in 10 realist-informed books on strategic studies. Here can be detected the elements of joined-up thinking in the global human interest: ethics through action, captured in Aristotle's view that by acting virtuously we become virtuous (1985: 1104a 30–35); learning across borders, as celebrated in Leopold Senghor's emphasis on the way we all benefit from being cultural "half-castes" (Gordimer, 1999); equality as a key value, as expressed by Thomas Jefferson and enshrined in the U.S. Declaration of Independence (Callinicos,

2000: 20; Ishay 1997: 127–130); and practicing the nonduality of ends–means, as attempted in Ghandhi's political action (Richards, 1995: 31–32). The reporter who had interviewed Angelou wrote: "'When she began this current tour in North Carolina, the county commissioner was part of the official welcoming committee. When Angelou noticed he had tried to get her to sign his books ahead of others in line, she told the crowd: 'In West Africa, in times of famine, in times of drought, the chief tightens his belt first. I ask those of you who are leaders to wait.'"

It is a simple story. What it shows is that humans have choices. We have choices about where to stand in a book-signing line, just as we have choices about the way to deal with terrorism or the plague of childhood diarrhea. The choices can be made selfishly, ethnocentrically, hierarchically, and assertively, or by trying to act virtuously, being willing to learn from others, valuing equality, and being as concerned with the morality of the means as of the ends. We are all faced by choices, though some of our answers will obviously be more influential than others. Leaders, from the president of the United States downward, please take note.

# 3

# The National Security State and Global Terrorism

## Why the State Is Not Prepared for the New Kind of War

T. V. Paul

The effects of globalization on the national security state are multifaceted, as exemplified by the chapters in this volume. This chapter specifically addresses the question of global terrorism, a key manifestation of the transformed globalized threat environment, and its impact on the national security state. The rise of global terrorism as a major challenge to the nation-state has occurred in the context of the post–Cold War international order, characterized by the absence of a major power rivalry and near unipolarity, with the United States as the dominant power. While no nation-state is currently capable of directly challenging the U.S. dominance on a global scale, the subnational global terrorist networks with asymmetric strategies have adopted this mantle. This challenge is not an easy one to detect or defeat. In the following analysis, I present the constraints that traditional national security establishments face in fighting enemies with terrorist strategies. Asymmetric strategies rely on non-frontal hit-and-run approaches, and targets are often selected for their visibility and political message. The smaller asymmetric challenger is not capable of or expecting substantial victory in a positional, frontal collision that is the domain of regular armed forces. What he expects is the incremental weakening of the nation-state that he is challenging.

The terrorist attacks on the U.S. in September 2001 were based on asymmetrical strategy by a global network and they have suddenly raised several challenges in security policymaking for states around the world. Although terrorism is not a new phenomenon in world politics, and terrorists have been ravaging established states in many parts of the world for decades, the magnitude of the attacks, the suddenness of their impact, the massive casualties and the intensity of property destruction they caused, and the high-value nature of the targets (symbols of global and American capitalism, the World Trade Center, and the headquarters of the American military establishment, the Pentagon), all gave the attacks a much greater significance than any previous episodes of terrorism. Despite warnings by specialists and media analysts of the possibility of cataclysmic terrorist acts in the United States for well over a decade, policy planners in both the military and civilian realms were caught by surprise. The policymakers seemed to be under the misapprehension that the most likely route of massive attacks by terrorist groups would be the use of weapons of mass destruction against urban targets. The unusual instrument of the terrorist acts, commercial aircraft fully loaded with jet fuel, was not considered a serious possibility, since, barring individual instances on a much smaller scale in the Middle East and South Asia, terrorists until September 11 rarely used suicide as a means for causing massive destruction.

The apparent unpreparedness of the United States to prevent and confront terrorist attacks occurred in a context in which both policymakers and scholars have been generally focused on nation-states as the central makers or breakers of security. From a state-centric security point of view, substate actors could engage in nibbling activities on the periphery, often causing limited security challenges, but they were not perceived as a threat to the domestic security of states, especially in North America and Europe. Countries in protracted zones of conflict, such as Israel, India, and Russia, have long lived with terrorism, often initiated by terrorist groups sponsored by homegrown movements or adversarial states. But terrorism in the latter two countries has been confined largely to specific provinces such as Kashmir and Chechnya, without causing much of a global impact. Terrorist activities from the key breeding ground in the geographical arc stretching from the Middle East to Southeast Asia took a while to reach North America in their intense form.

In this chapter, I argue that most national military organizations, especially Western ones, are not fully equipped to meet the new security challenge posed by transnational terrorism. For more than a century, leading Western powers have structured their military forces and operational plans on Clausewitzian rational assumptions. Their defense policies have been very much state-centric because it is states that have traditionally posed the major security challenges to each other. War has been conducted by territorially organized states, often for rational purposes, and peace has been attained through postwar settlements (Holsti, 1996). In the Clausewitzian world, "war is politics by other means" in which opponents array forces to make political, economic, or territorial gains through the use or threat of organized violence.

For well over two hundred years, the main Western conception of security has been state-centric. At least since 1792, warfare has been national, fought by citizen armies against similar forces of nation-states. In most Western countries, "the army reflected the state. . . . The officers whose incentive was honor, class consciousness, glory or ambition and soldiers enlisted for long terms who fought as a business for a living, who were thought incapable of higher sentiments, and whose strongest attachment was usually a kind of naïve pride in their regiments" (Palmer, 1971: 50). Because war has been "organized violence carried on by political units against each other" (Bull, 1977: 184), the main purpose of military force has been to confront other similarly organized military forces of enemy states. As Bull characterizes it: "it is war and the threat of war that help to determine whether particular states survive or are eliminated, whether they rise or decline, whether their frontiers remain the same or are changed, whether their peoples are ruled by one government or another, whether disputes are settled or drag on, and which way they are set- tled, whether there is a balance of power in the international system or one state becomes preponderant" (1977: 187).

Since the Napoleanic era, leading Western strategic analysts, from Henri Jomini to Karl von Clausewitz to Basil Liddell Hart, have spoken in rational terms when discussing war and its conduct (Moran, 2002: 17–74). To them, war has been an instrument of state policy to maximize territorial, political, or economic gains. To Clausewitz, war was an "act of force to compel our enemy to do our will" (1976: 75). The political culture assumed in Clausewitz's *On War* was state-centric. For Clausewitz, the European states were the principal actors, with strong central governments, armies, commanders, and populations mobilized politically, under the direction of a powerful state (Gray, 1999: 102). Although the colonial European armies sometimes fought guerrilla forces in the colonies and were able to adopt flexible strategies, the principal nature of the organization of warfare remained largely intact (Porch, 2000). The United States also imbibed these notions of warfare. From the U.S. historical perspec- tive, war meant total war, and victory in war implied victory over nation-state enemies, often achieved through the use of massive air power (Brodie, 1946).

The Cold War conflict reinforced the state-centric approach to security. The arrival of the nuclear age made it all the more imperative that states remain the principal possessors and managers of security. The bipolar compe- tition under the leadership of the two superpowers also meant the broad con- trol of Moscow and Washington over the conduct of military forces of the allied states. The Cold War was waged between states, organized as two com- peting blocs that quarreled over political and strategic objectives. Both the superpowers knew that they could hurt each other if they crossed a certain line in their conflict. They could engage in crisis behavior, but, when the crisis was about to get out of hand, they could sit down and negotiate and manage the endgame, thereby precluding an all-out war. Large military and institutional structures were created to conduct the Cold War conflict, deter potential wars, and influence global politics involving secondary actors. No effective sub- national challenge emerged to their dominance, as the superpowers managed to maintain their aura of invincibility. In the Soviet case, effective control over its empire in Eastern Europe was often achieved through coercive means.

With the demise of the Cold War, this situation has changed. As the possibility of a major-power war declined dramatically, large military organizations with the primary mission of fighting interstate wars became somewhat redundant. The new security challenges that arose, be they transnational terrorism, drug trafficking, illegal migration, or ethnic conflicts, all required new or modified instruments to combat them. In the meantime, the number of interstate wars began to decline, although there is dispute over whether the waning of major wars is a reality or a temporary phenomenon (Vayrynen, forthcoming). Most of the new wars of the post–Cold War era have been characterized by a blurring of the distinction between interstate wars, organized crime, and large-scale violations of human rights. While the main issue of contention has been identity politics, the weapons have been a combination of the old and the new and the units of combat have not been vertically organized hierarchical entities (Kaldor, 1999).

Military planning in established states, however, remained almost on the same earlier lines so as to be ready to fight other states, as military organizations refused to change their ways in a big way. The Clausewitzian conception of war as a means to serve state interests continues to form the "intellectual and conceptual foundation for international organizations, national military institutions and practices of diplomacy and the academy" (Holsti, 1996: 6). States seem to be driven by the assumption that, although the Cold War has ended, the potential for new systemic and subsystemic rivalries exists. Major powers proceeded as if they should always be prepared for the eventual arrival of a challenger or challengers. In the U.S. case, the general expectation has been that China would emerge as the most powerful rising challenger to American dominance. The United States has also been focusing on a small group of regional challengers (e.g., Iraq, Iran, and North Korea) with ambitions to acquire weapons of mass destruction while preparing to fight in two different regional theaters simultaneously. In addition, security planners have been attempting to keep up with the revolutionary changes taking place in arms technology and information warfare. In the past, terrorism rarely struck security planners as a core security threat and the defensive measures against it were confined to intelligence and political solutions aimed at eliminating the root causes of the problem.[1] Moreover, state military organizations have not often been equipped with the operational skills to deal with highly motivated ideological or religious fanatics whose goals and strategies are often difficult to pin down.

## ASSUMPTIONS BEHIND NATIONAL MILITARY STRATEGIES AND DOCTRINES

Military strategies and doctrines of major states, especially the United States, have remained relatively constant, although the political environment has changed since the end of the Cold War. Armed forces often base their security planning on worst-case assumptions involving other states, as the main challengers to security have been territorially organized states with military organizations founded on rational organization and planning. The four foundations of military strategy—offense, defense, deterrence, and compellence—all assume that the opponent is a rational actor who would make cost/benefit calculations and would not engage in war if the costs of attacking are higher than the payoffs. National militaries often project one or a combination of these elements in their strategic approaches. These four aspects of military strategy need further elaboration.

## Offense

The key offensive function of a military force is to launch an attack if and when an opportunity or need arises. First-strike and surprise attacks are favored as these may achieve major payoffs since the attacker could gain initial advantage over the defender. If the attacker can sustain the offensive, the defender will lose the will to fight and concede the object in question. Taking the offensive is severely costly and risky unless the attacker holds advantages in term of numerical, technological, or terrain-based strengths. Offense can, however, achieve battlefield dominance, especially if the political environment is conducive to such a strategy and if the available weapons capability is in favor of the power engaging in offensive action (Van Evera, 1984). However, the political costs of offense have to be factored into the calculations for war, as these are often unpredictable.

## Defense

Unlike offense, a defense-based strategy assumes that the first strike would come from the opponent. In defensive mode, states deploy forces to ward off an attack and, if the attack takes place, try to minimize the damage that the attacker can inflict. Invariably, the defender will direct his military against the attacking forces and not the civilian populations (Art, 1980: 5). If defense is to succeed, the defender should be able to thwart the attack even after absorbing the costs of the first strike. Historically, a numerical advantage of 3:1, and in some cases 5:1, was required to decisively defeat a well-entrenched defensive force. However, most limited wars are not conducted for a long duration and the attacker's goal in such wars often has been to end the war as quickly as possible in order to gain tactical and political objectives (Paul, 1994: 24–25). Armed forces most of the time prepare for defensive operations. They go by the assumption that victory can be denied to an attacker and that offense can be made costly if the defense is superior.

## Deterrence

A military strategy based on deterrence assumes that opponents will not launch an attack, as the retaliatory punishment would be so high that the attacker has no rational reason to launch a strike. Rationality is thus the basic assumption behind the strategy of deterrence. Both *deterrence by denial* and *deterrence by punishment* are based on the expectation that a rational opponent will desist from attacking if he believes that victory will be denied or, as in the latter case, that the punishment will be higher and that the attacker will suffer more harm than the benefits he is likely to gain (Morgan, 1977: 30–32).

## Compellence

A compellent strategy assumes that, when threatened with massive use of force, an adversary would back down, fearing incalculable harm. The threat of retaliation is assumed to be especially credible if it involves destruction of the opponent's society. Although compellence is often a risky and uncertain strategy, as it involves the reputation of the power forced to back off, it is a tempting strategy, nevertheless, for a state with enormous advantages in air power. In modern times, compellence has been more nuanced and it has been combined with diplomacy in the aim of achieving the goals of the initiator without using force (George, 1991; Schelling, 1966: 72).

Being a status quo world power, the United States has made deterrence and compellence the most salient features of its defense policy. The United States has historically been secure from the major wars of Europe and Asia. Both deterrence and compellence served its security interests fairly well because the enemy forces could not reach the U.S. mainland easily. In the nuclear age, major-power challengers were deterred from undertaking military action against the U.S. homeland because of the threat of massive retaliation, while regional powers were often coerced not to undertake certain actions against U.S. vital interests. This strategy was pivotal in both world wars. In the period after World War II, even when the United States could not win against guerrilla-type armies such as the Korean and the Vietnamese, the effects of these wars reached the home front only indirectly. Those who seriously challenged U.S. interests (e.g., Iraq) faced massive air strikes and, as a result, gave up their territorial ambitions. Conventional deterrence also has been the bedrock of U.S. strategy in other regions such as East Asia. The September 11 terrorist strikes have, however, affected the long-standing assumptions behind US security strategy, although it is not apparent how deep the changes are because state-centric security strategies still dominate the policy process.

# THE ASYMMETRIC STRATEGY OF TERRORISM

War against terrorism poses fundamental problems for state actors. The terrorist adversary does not hold the same Clausewitzian rationality assumptions, although one can argue that a form of instrumental rationality is inherent in the calculations of terrorists. Military strategies that are relevant in the interstate context may not be very applicable in the war against terrorism. Let us look at each of the traditional foundations of military strategy and examine their application to combating terrorism.

*Offensive* action against terrorism is hampered by the fact that terrorists rarely possess fixed targets that are easily detectable for offensive action. Terrorists are elusive actors who often work amid their sympathizers in heavily populated cities or sparsely populated tribal areas. For regular forces, terrorists constitute more difficult targets to conduct offensive action against as compared to guerrilla forces that operate from hideouts and sometimes within possibly identifiable areas. States that sponsor terrorism can be made targets for offensive action, but such actions may not result in major victories against terrorists themselves. The targeted states may be deterred from future support for terrorism, but the terrorists can change their locations of operation. Offensive action against terrorists is further constrained because states often cannot use the same tactics that terrorists employ, such as indiscriminate killing of innocent people, due to moral, legal, and political (both internal and external) constraints. In the past, when states attempted offensive action against terrorists and their sponsors, the results have been mixed, as in the cases of Israel in Lebanon, India in Kashmir, and the United States in Afghanistan.

*Defense* against terrorist attacks is heavily constrained by the surprise element in terrorist acts. States can defend against terrorism only if they know where the terrorists are coming from and what their strengths and weaknesses are. For this reason, conventional defensive as well as preemptive strategies may be ineffective against terrorists; unconventional defensive and preemptive strategies could be more suitable, but national military organizations are not often equipped with such operational skills. Unconventional limited defensive strategies are often the domain of police and intelligence agencies but, in order for such unconventional strategies to succeed, high levels of intelligence on the whereabouts and plans of terrorists are needed. Targets such as high-rise buildings, major industrial and population centers, and transportation and communication networks are sitting ducks for terrorist attacks and poorly suited for defensive action. Defense against terrorists is further complicated when they engage in suicide attacks.

*Deterrence* may not work with substate actors of this nature, because the terrorists are prepared to die for the particular ideological cause that they expound while committing acts of terrorism. Massive retaliatory strikes on the state or the population that supports terrorism would simply make the terrorists' cause gain an even wider appeal among hitherto ideological fencesitters. Such retaliation may not even touch the center of gravity or focal point of terrorist operations, which may be a basement in a Western city. If the terrorist group holds millenarian objectives, the "ultimate disaster is a joyful prospect rather than something to be dreaded. Rational calculations, such as the likelihood of doing damage to themselves, do not apply" (Laqueur, 1998: 266).

Deterrence against terrorism is hampered by many factors. A successful deterrence strategy requires adequate capability, commitment to use force, credibility in the threat of retaliation, and the ability of the deterrer to communicate to the target tacitly or openly about its determination to retaliate. The adversary needs to know that it will get hurt in a major way if it undertakes military action. Societal destruction is the ultimate price that deterrence may call for, especially if it involves nuclear weapons. The deterrer needs credible information about the adversary's motives, intentions, and capabilities for immediate deterrence to succeed. For general deterrence, capabilities and military postures need to be kept ready for retaliation even though no immediate attack is expected (Morgan, 1977: 30–32). This is where terrorism generates difficulties for states, as military planners may not have sufficient information regarding the intentions and capabilities of terrorists. If the adversaries do not mind their own destruction or the destruction of the societies they come from, deterrent threats will not work. Terrorists who operate in small, ad hoc groups or cells have little to lose against their state enemies. Terrorists who are driven by religious zeal would like to see chaos, as martyrdom may be their ultimate goal. Deterrence has no meaning against groups that aim for Armageddon or total societal destruction (Stern, 1999: 131). State sponsors of terrorism are more deterrable, but even in their case deterrence may not work, if they believe that they can "camouflage their involvement, that they have nothing to lose, or that their adversaries lack the will (or the ability) to retaliate harshly" (Stern, 1999: 131). A case in point could arguably be Pakistan vis-à-vis India in Kashmir.

*Compellence* also has its limitations in overcoming the challenge of terrorism as the opponent, knowing the larger power's inability to execute a war that could bring victory, can ignore the compelling threats altogether. Further, the opponent can retaliate years later when, from the perspective of the status quo power, the military operations have ended. In this case, compellence might have succeeded in the short run but, in the long run, compellence has led to more strikes and counterstrikes.

Likewise, coercive diplomacy is unlikely to work because a negotiated settlement may be virtually impossible to achieve with terrorists who may be holding millenarian ideological objectives. Their strategy is war by indirect means, which implies avoiding direct contact by all means. Because of the extreme secrecy surrounding most terrorist groups and the surprise or lack of warning employed by them, the gathering and assessing of accurate intelligence warnings are at best difficult. Negotiations with terrorists also create great difficulty for states. When states negotiate with terrorists, they may lend them legitimacy. States generally wage war or conclude peace with other states that are legitimate entities in the international system. Terrorists often lack legitimacy, both in the societies they come from and in the eyes of the state they target. The problem gets especially complicated if the terrorists are fighting for religious causes, as there is no real solution to their grievance other than the final victory of the religious view that the terrorists uphold.

Thus, the key element of coercive diplomacy that states employ vis-à-vis one another—that is, coercion plus diplomacy—may not be appropriate at all in the case of terrorism. Part of the problem is that the threat posed by terrorism is so diffuse because terrorism is changing in terms of its nature, instruments, adherents, and objectives as years pass by. As Paul Kennedy states: "What was needed to defeat the Spanish Armada or Hitler's Panzer columns may not be all that useful against a new amoeba-like foe, which attacks from within and through civilian instruments and in a decentralized and shadowy form" (Kennedy, 2001: 60).

Terrorists wage a form of asymmetric conflict vis-a-vis militarily and politically superior states. Terrorism thus is a form of power struggle between inferior and superior entities in conventional military terms. Contemporary terrorists themselves are pursuing a form of compellence vis-à-vis nation-states. By definition, terrorism involves the "systematic murder, maiming and menacing of the innocent to inspire fear for political ends"(Harmon, 2000: 1). As terrorist mastermind Osama Bin Laden puts it, the aim of his activities is to create a "balance of terror" to equalize the "geopolitical score between Muslims and Americans" (Kurtz, 2002: A2).[2] By showing that even the most powerful states are vulnerable to terrorism, the terrorists do gain a symbolic sense of powerfulness, in their own perceptions and in the perceptions of others. Although the power they receive is temporary, successful terrorist acts can weaken, even if in a limited sense, the power of an established nation-state, especially if the terrorists succeed in attacking and destroying the symbols of the power of that state (Juergensmeyer, 2000: 132–133). It is the interaction of politics and indiscriminate violence that gives terrorism an unpredictable character. Unpredictability is also a source of power for terrorists, as regular military organizations tend to favor predictable military behavior.

A number of features that characterize asymmetric wars also exist in the terrorist form of violence. First, terrorists with intense religious or ideological positions are highly motivated. They are prepared to suffer the consequences of their action. The threshold of the willingness to take pain increases with the intensity in motivation of the terrorist group. Second, the terrorist strategy rarely involves a direct head-on collision, but war by indirect means. The terrorist combatants are irregular forces who rely on "unconventional methods of fighting to inflict disproportionate damage on more powerful conventional forces." In place of the traditional "heavy metal weapons—[such as] tanks, combat planes, warships, it employs cheap, low-tech weapons and commercially available technologies (including biotechnology)" (Klare, 2001: 433). Third, innocent victims are selected for the horror impact created for the targeted audience. Finally, conventionally superior armies tend to follow rigid organizational patterns, often making them inflexible to confront indirect strategies. Terrorists, on the other hand, use unconventional and flexible organizational patterns and strategies.

The use of unconventional methods by terrorists has become especially prominent in the age of information revolution. John Arquilla refers to this as "netwars," in which the "protagonists use network forms of organization and related doctrines, strategies and technologies attuned to the information age" (Arquilla & Ronfeldt, 2001: 6). Terrorists who rely on information technology adopt strategies such as "swarming," which involves a "deliberately structured, coordinated, strategic way to strike from all directions at a particular point or points, by means of a sustained pulsing of force and /or fire, close-in as well as from stand-off positions" (12). Individuals are linked by internal and external networks that may have only temporary lifecycles and are sustained by shared norms, beliefs, and trust (Zanini & Edwards, 2001: 31–32.). The new terrorism strategies thus generate immense difficulties for hierarchical organizations to combat and to prevent.

For states, the difficulties in confronting terrorism are magnified by the increased use of the terrorist weapon, *suicide bomber*, that is, an individual carrying high explosives and willing to die for the cause. The protective shield of the state cannot reach each and every possibility of suicide bombing by individuals who otherwise look normal and above suspicion. Even a police state with tremendous reach cannot protect citizens in all public places where they gather. Democracies are especially vulnerable to such attacks, as surveillance and preventive action can often infringe upon cherished individual rights. By adopting too many draconian laws against terrorism, a democratic state can become a police state. The dilemma the United States has been facing since September 11 is how to protect its citizens while at the same time not abandon cherished individual rights or create paranoia among the public.

## WHY HAS THE U.S. BECOME A KEY TARGET?

The United States has emerged as the single most powerful enemy for terrorists. More than one-third of international terrorist incidents in the 1980s and 1990s were directed against the United States (Pillar, 2001: 57). The United States is targeted because of its dominant power position, global involvement, support or opposition vis-à-vis allies and adversaries in the terrorism-breeding regions such as the Middle East and South Asia, and because attacks on U.S. targets tend to receive the maximum publicity for terrorist groups. The preponderant power position of the United States is the key reason for disgruntled groups and individuals to adopt terrorist strategies against it. In the contemporary world, no state or coalition of states is in a position to frontally challenge the United States in a military conflict. Terrorism is an asymmetric challenge that can, however, create difficulties for the lone superpower. Terrorists realize that no other instrument can have the same effect as terrorism can have on the U.S. sense of security. Terrorism is thus one weapon that a weaker challenger can employ against the United States that may have a decisive effect (Pillar, 2001: 57). Moreover, "the physical vulnerability of the US with a large and open society," the largest overseas presence of any state, and the "past examples of U.S. withdrawals from regions after being a target of terrorism" all give incentives to terrorists to engage in strikes on U.S. targets. The United States is the "prime terrorist target not only because of what it really is like or really is doing, but because of what the terrorists believe it is doing" (Pillar, 2001: 65–67).

Modern terrorism has become somewhat similar to the wars of attrition waged between guerrilla forces and regular forces, where "superior motivation is often the key to the successful compellence of an adversary, and terrorism is a way of demonstrating their determination and power. When civil war is expanded to the international system, vulnerability may be the inevitable accompaniment to the exercise of power" (Crenshaw, 2001: 432). The effort of the terrorists is to compel the United States to withdraw or modify its external commitments (425). Their aim is also to serve notice to the regional allies of the United States to modify their policies vis-a-vis the secessionist or freedom movements that these states attempt to contain. Terrorist motives may include regime change and withdrawal of U.S. support for the regimes that the terrorists would like to overthrow. Invariably, terrorists calculate that their strategy can work as an equalizer in their otherwise immensely asymmetric power equation vis-à-vis the United States.

Another problem is that some of the states that are formally allies of the United States in the struggle against terrorism are the breeding grounds of terrorism. These allies themselves may pursue policies that sometimes help defeat the American strategy against terrorism. Examples of such allies are Pakistan and Saudi Arabia. Over the years, the regimes in these states have used terrorism for state purposes or have allowed terrorists to flourish in their countries to further their domestic or regional political goals. After September 11, they have been forced to change their positions, but institutions (such as the Inter-services Intelligence (ISI) in Pakistan) and societal groups (such as the Wahabis in Saudi Arabia) that have invested so much in terrorism in the past have little incentive to alter their policies. Many members of these societal groups and organizations oppose the United States for religious or ideological grounds.

From the early 1990s, Afghanistan became the most significant source of terrorism for the United States, to some extent due to its own policy failures there. The U.S. policy in Afghanistan, although it succeeded in ejecting the Soviets out of the beleaguered country, led to failure in the post–Soviet phase. This failure occurred because of an "overestimation of Soviet power during the Cold War and an underestimation of the U.S. interests after the Soviets withdrew" (Khalilzad & Byman, 2000: 66). The bleeding of the Soviets was done through aid to radical fundamentalists with scant attention being paid to postwar implications. The United States hurriedly withdrew from the region, leaving power with the radical forces and their state sponsors such as Pakistan and Saudi Arabia (Khalilzad & Byman, 2000: 65–78). The Taliban regime that captured power in 1996 became the major sponsor of the terrorist organization al Qaeda and its wealthy mastermind, Bin Laden. The U.S. policy did very little to influence the Taliban or its neighboring ally, Pakistan, until the September 11, 2001, attacks.

## GLOBAL NETWORKS OF TERROR AND MILITARY PLANNING

The United States was caught unprepared for the terrorist strikes because of the low level of attention paid by it to subnational challenges in the immediate post–Cold War era. It seems that the national security establishments, including that of the United States, have not properly adapted to the changing global security environment since the early 1990s. The post–Cold War world system, characterized by the absence of major systemic conflicts, has given most policymakers, especially in the West, a false sense of security. The semi-unipolar order, in which the United States dominates the world's economic and military power structures, is assumed to provide collective goods fairly uniformly to all. Indeed, this order does provide a certain amount of stability and prosperity to those who are closely associated with it. However, the masses of people who are not beneficiaries of this order, even though the elites in their countries may be successful in gaining their own economic and political objectives, are generally ignored. It is precisely the small splinter groups in these societies that are outside the global order who intensely hate it for various political, religious, or ideological reasons. The easy flow of people, money, weapons, and ideas in the post–Cold War world has provided these groups an unprecedented global network for their particular form of power in asymmetrical warfare. While continued economic prosperity and technological innovation of the advanced states require the smooth flow of people, ideas, and money across borders, the smaller groups with messianic ideologies also squeeze through the cracks. Moreover, the revolution in information technologies has increased the global reach of the terrorist groups. The new technologies "have facilitated the conduct and control of operations over long distances while minimizing the need for a large, fixed physical presence" (Pillar, 2001: 48).

The technological changes that have brought about closer and faster communications and travel opportunities have also made the reach of the terrorists and the scope of their activity extend much farther beyond the geographical regions from where they operate. Homer-Dixon calls this phenomenon the rise of "complex terrorism." The dramatic technological and economic advancements in the past decades have made the rich nations targets of sudden terrorist attacks because in order to maintain economies of scale and thereby prosperity, these states tend to concentrate their vital assets and key workforces in small geographical areas. Terrorists who realize the value of such targets have now developed strategies to attack the "right nodes" in order to make their point and achieve their objectives (Homer-Dixon, 2002: 52–62).

Al Qaeda represents the new global terrorist group fighting the sole superpower using highly asymmetric strategies. The strength of al Qaeda is derived from stealth—the ability of its forces to disappear in societies where it conducts secret operations and then chooses the time and place for surprise terrorist attacks. While the United States possesses overwhelming technological capabilities, allowing it to strike at fixed targets if and when it chooses, it is less well endowed to fight a stealthy opponent. The politico-military aims of the two are also different to the extent that the United States wants to maintain its presence in the Middle East and other key regions, and preserve the liberal world's dominance, while "al Qaeda's goal is to see the creation of a Pan-Islamic movement to establish a transnational Islamic state based on its reading of Islamic law. The purpose of the state would be to insulate the Islamic world from the economic, political, and cultural power of the non-Islamic world, and by logical extension serve as the foundation for an expanded Islamic world" (Starfor.com, November 6, 2001). The U.S. strategy is to rely on traditional air war, but air power is often successful against fixed targets and heavy concentrations of armed forces. In the war that began in the fall of 2001, the United States and allied forces succeeded in toppling the Taliban and the fixed targets of terrorists, especially the caves where al Qaeda members were operating from. However, it also allowed al Qaeda and Taliban members to vanish amid their supporters in the tribal areas of Pakistan and Afghanistan, where they could prepare to strike for years to come. Partly because of U.S. reluctance to use ground troops due to its antipathy to taking casualties, the terrorist forces may prove to be much more difficult to eject from their hideouts.

The changing faces of terrorism also generate difficulties for states to come up with appropriate strategies. The most significant example of this change is the rise of the radical religious variety in the place of secular terrorists who fought for ideological or nationalist causes. The worldwide resurgence of radical religious movements has made a major impact on terrorism as it is practiced today (Laqueur, 1999: 127). The rise of religious terrorism has also been helped by the demise of Communism and other political ideologies with large numbers of followers. The spread of Western materialism and consumerism throughout the globe, with masses of people not having the wherewithal to acquire wealth, generates the political conditions for the rise of terrorism in some parts of the world (Harmon, 2000). No wonder that the largest number of terrorists are drawn from the unemployed or underemployed young adult males, "with weak social and familial support and with poor prospects for economic improvement or advancement through legitimate work" (Pillar, 2001: 31).

A major change that marks contemporary terrorism is that previous terrorism avoided "massive bloodletting." The strategies of the Palestine groups or the IRA since the 1960s "was the calibration of violence" to gain "potential sympathizers and winning for those groups a place at the bargaining table, where the status quo could be revised." Their strategy precluded too many barbaric attacks that would have made them ineligible for a seat at the bargaining table. The new terrorists, on the other hand, express their grievances in religious terms and deliberately attempt to "maximize carnage" (Campbell & Flournoy, 2001: 38).

Terrorism in the past was practiced by individuals and groups with ethnic, separatist, and ideological motives through "selective, discriminate acts of violence," with clear political or ideological goals and led by a "command and control apparatus," which often took credit for their actions. The new terrorism, on the other hand, is distinguished by its "amorphous religious and millenarian aims," high level of lethality due to the easy access to weapons, increasing number of amateurs as well as professionals because of open availability of information on terrorism, and the ability of terrorists to operate for longer duration without being captured or detected (Hoffman, 1999: 7–38).

There have thus been substantial changes in the goals of terrorists. Terrorists previously sought incremental changes in their opponent's policies, and their causes were mostly limited to specific issues that had little or no global significance. The new terrorists, as epitomized in Bin Laden's al Qaeda, seek to make radical changes with major geopolitical connotations. This group wants to expel the United States from the Arabian peninsula, end alleged repression of Muslims everywhere, establish an Islamic empire stretching from Spain to Afghanistan, achieve religious change in almost all Muslim countries, and inspire traditional Islamic law (Campbell & Flournoy, 2001). It also uses modern capabilities such as computer and telecommunication links, e-mail, along with cellular and radio networks. It has been successful in defeating airport security, engaging in a global network of economic exchange, using nongovernmental organizations to collect money, conducting narcotics trade, engaging in sophisticated public relations campaigns, and making inroads to obtain materials for weapons of mass destruction (Campbell & Flournoy, 2001: 44–49). This group has been especially adept at engaging in terrorism in front of the global television audience. Terrorism has thus become a "public performance of violence—as a social event with both real and symbolic aspects" (Juergensmeyer, 2000: 144). Thus, the combination of 'strategic' or 'utilitarian terrorists' with millenarian terrorists, fighting for the "Empire of God" but with some geopolitical goals, has changed the lethal nature of terrorism (Gill, 2001). Although the United States has succeeded in creating a temporary wedge between the promoters of strategic terrorism (e.g., Pakistan's Pervaiz Musharaff) and millenarian ones (Taliban and al Qaeda), the societal links between the two are so strong that the connections linger on. The religious terrorists do elicit substantial sympathy among disgruntled masses in their key theaters of operation, and they may find new sponsors as time passes.

## CONCLUSIONS

Global terrorism is somewhat akin to the war on drugs, organized crime, or communicable diseases. Even the most sophisticated states have not been able to confront these challenges fully. Counterterrorism by states "is a fight and a struggle, but it is not a campaign with a beginning and an end." A central lesson for counterterrorism is that terrorists "cannot be defeated . . . only reduced, attenuated, or some degree controlled. Individual terrorist or terrorist groups sometimes are defeated, terrorism as a whole never will be" (Pillar, 2001: 218).

Terrorism thus presents multifarious problems for the nation-state. These problems arise from the global reach of terrorist networks, the religious connection, the ability of terrorists to wreak havoc on key economic centers of the advanced world, and the asymmetrical strategies that they follow that are difficult to confront using traditional national security approaches. Any effort to solve the problem of terrorism purely through a traditional state-centric military approach is not likely to succeed. The consequences of war are generally unpredictable, this time in a more profound way, as the nation-state is fighting an invisible enemy who adapts his asymmetrical strategies continuously and has operational bases spread across the globe. Although elements of a military approach may be relevant in some situations, they will most likely give more political and ideological legitimacy to the "martyrs." On the other hand, not taking any military action also holds risks as groups may become emboldened by their "victory" and pursue even greater terrorism. Either way, the stability of the regions in question is at considerable risk. The challenge for national security planners is to find balanced short-term and long-term policies that effectively address the military, diplomatic, economic, and political dimensions of the problem. The battle against terrorism needs to be fought on different fronts—political, ideological, economic, and military. Any quick-fix solutions and scapegoating, however tempting, will breed further terrorism and insecurity and challenge to the global order.

## NOTES

1. Even after September 11, the U.S. defense priorities may not have changed drastically, if one goes by the defense spending and procurement patterns of the U.S. military. The U.S. annual defense spending of $396 billion in 2003 is expected to grow to $470 billion by 2007, but much of the money will be devoted to procurement of new weapons to replace old ones and other traditional expenses, such as pay for servicemen, rather than combating terrorism (O'Hanlon, 2000: 61).

2. In an interview with the Arab television network al-Jazeera, Bin Laden claimed that just as the United States and the United Kingdom are "killing us, we have to kill them so that there will be a balance of terror" (Kurtz, 2002: A12).

# Part II

State Transformations and Responses

# 4

# *The Rise of the Trading State* Revisited

Mark R. Brawley

In 1986, Richard Rosecrance's *The Rise of the Trading State* captured the sense and imagery of a new era, as international relations were evolving toward a greater emphasis on economics rather than security. Rosecrance powerfully and persuasively argued that shifts in technology had made conquest for economic gain foolhardy. In the current era, states were much more likely to improve their welfare by pursuing an economic or "trading" strategy. The most powerful and successful states of the late twentieth century were those that had eschewed territorial expansion through military dominance and were aiming to develop their economies through international trade and investment. The models to emulate were Japan and West Germany—states actively engaging in interdependent economic relations with their neighbors. The losers in international competition were those continuing to pursue economic self-sufficiency through the domination of vast swathes of territory, such as the Soviet Union.

If we focus on the economic changes that have swept the globe in the years between the book's publication and today, Rosecrance's views have been borne out in impressive fashion. The Soviet Empire has collapsed through economic exhaustion, the "Washington Consensus" (emphasizing market relations as the key motor for economic development) is widely held, and economic globalization has taken off. The United States and its closest allies are clearly the models for other states to imitate—so much so that Francis Fukuyama could argue that we have seen "the end of history." As journalist Thomas Friedman put it in his best-seller *The Lexus and the Olive Tree*, "When

I would like to thank Ersel Aydinli for inviting me to participate in the conference in Ankara, Turkey. I thank Ersel and Bill Weininger for helpful comments. I thank ASAM for holding such a stimulating meeting. Finally, I would like to thank the Security and Defense Forum, run by Canada's Department of National Defense, for support through the Research Group in International Security.

it comes to the question of which system today is the most effective at generating rising standards of living, the historical debate is over. The answer is free market capitalism" (2000: 104). Friedman goes on, "If you want higher standards of living in a world without walls, the free market is the only ideological alternative left."

The general proposition Rosecrance's book is remembered for centers on the impact of technology on trade. Advances in technology improve the ability to transport goods over borders and to communicate; these advances lower the costs of engaging in international economic relations and raise the potential benefits. Proponents of globalization would argue that the net mutual gains from economic intercourse have risen in a fashion quite consistent with the portrait Rosecrance painted. Economists and political scientists may argue over how the gains from economic globalization are distributed both between countries and within them, but there is a broad consensus that greater international economic integration delivers additional benefits overall. Yet the changes occurring in economic relations accounted for only half of Rosecrance's argument. Rosecrance pitched the trading strategy as one option for increasing a state's welfare. The alternative is conquest. He argued that the benefits from conquest were also shaped by changes in technology and communication. Technology had reduced the potential benefits from engaging in war significantly, by increasing the costs associated with military conflict.

The last fifteen years have seen dramatic changes in military technology, which should cause us to reconsider how states will choose between these two strategies in the future. The Revolution in Military Affairs (RMA) has affected how military forces are organized and employed. The U.S. military in particular has demonstrated in the Gulf War, operations in the Balkans, and in the war in Afghanistan, that technological change has altered the face of battle. Satellite imagery and communications, global positioning, precision-guided munitions (PGMs), drone aircraft, and a host of other innovations have reduced the costs to going to war in terms of lives, if not money, for those states that possess such weapons. How will these innovations affect the balance between the trading and conquest strategies, especially as the barriers to operating such weapons systems inevitably fall over time?

In effect, I am merely posing the same question as Rosecrance (1986: 31). As he put it, "What balance will future generations choose between trading and territorial worlds?" His own answer was not that trading would dominate conquest forever. As he answered his own query: "That depends upon the cost and benefits of waging war on the one hand and engaging in trade on the other. The greater the restraints on trade and the fewer its likely benefits, the more willing nations have been to seek to improve their position through military force. The higher the cost of war and the more uncertain its benefits, the more nations have sought trade as a livelihood."

## ELABORATING THE CHOICE ON STRATEGIES

Rosecrance was careful to set up his claims about the rise of the trading state by noting that each strategy had dominated at points in the past, and that at any given point in the past, different states had chosen different strategies. He was also clear in pointing out that greater economic contact between states did not necessarily lead to peace or greater understanding. Such contacts could also be the ingredients for conflicts of interest and strife. Rising interdependence could increase the costs of going to war, but this was only one piece in the overall calculation states would undertake.

What is also often forgotten about the logic of his argument is that the benefits of the trading strategy could remain high, or even increase over time, but be washed out by changes on the other side of the calculus. Perhaps the best way to illustrate my point would be to think explicitly of a simple formulaic calculation. One side of the equation comes from evaluating the costs and benefits of the trading strategy; this is contrasted with the costs and benefits of a territorial expansion/acquisition on the other side.

The benefits associated with the trading strategy = $B_t$
The costs associated with the trading strategy = $C_t$
The benefits associated with the strategy of conquest = $B_c$
The costs associated with the strategy of conquest = $C_c$

Rosecrance's argument can then be restated as the claim that the trading strategy is more beneficial when

$$(B_t - C_t) > (B_c - C_c)$$

My purpose for restating in this fashion is to underscore the point that there are four references (or variables) to consider in this argument. I do not set out to gather data to test when and where one strategy is dominant. Instead, I wish to use this formula to remind us what Rosecrance actually pointed to in his account of the rise of the trading state. He did not seek to measure these variables, but instead noted how particular trends influenced the values of each.[1] The development of containerization is a prime example. By placing cargo in standard sized containers that could be transported on flatbed trucks or railcars, easily and rapidly hoisted and stacked for short-term storage, or stacked on ships, the speed and cost of shipping a huge variety of goods were drastically reduced. (This is a case in which time equals money, since better management of transportation systems allows producers to lower costs by reducing inventories of both inputs and outputs.)

Most people focus on $B_t$ alone when they reflect on Rosecrance's propositions—undoubtedly due to the memorable title he penned. Debates over globalization tend to consider the left side of the equation only. These debates typically include questions evaluating tangible benefits from international economic ties combined with intangible costs. The benefits rise as increased trade and investment create wealth, but these gains are associated with losses in the form of greater social inequality, less government autonomy in economic policymaking, less strategic independence, and loss of cultural identity (to name but a few).[2] Attempts to think about economic globalization alongside changes in the military-security realm were few and far between before September 11, 2001.[3]

## EXPLAINING THE SUCCESS OF THE TRADING STATE: WHY THE ECONOMIC STRATEGY PAYS

Rosecrance identified a number of factors that have shaped the costs and benefits of pursuing the trading strategy. Having other states open their borders to trade and investment increases the possible gains from this strategy. This might best be seen in terms of open international regimes governing economic relations. When such sets of international rules and norms are well established and stable, they provide predictability and security to participants in international economic affairs. Established explicit rules guaranteeing compensation for international investments seized abroad, for instance, encourage many more investors to consider international opportunities. Having treaties or institutions that promise to keep borders open into the foreseeable future encourages producers to invest in specialized production to reap the benefits of trade.

The success of the GATT in promoting freer trade in manufactures is widely heralded. By providing predictability in terms of access to markets, GATT members have become more heavily involved in trade. In fact, this logic is usually employed to understand why GATT has been transformed into the WTO. Its membership has increased, its rules cover a wider range of goods than before, its status has been made more permanent, its mechanisms for settling disputes without disrupting economic relations improved, and its authority enhanced. Each of these changes should alter conditions to make the international political economy more conducive for international trade.

Economic conditions also affect the calculations of individuals, since trade is always more attractive when economies are growing rather than contracting. Trade leads to specialization; specialization involves adjusting the employment of people and assets, creating winners and losers. This adjustment is easier to bear politically and economically when economies are growing, since expanded economic activities generate new opportunities to employ labor or capital otherwise left in declining, less competitive sectors.

The example of containerization cited earlier illustrates how improvements in transportation can shift the balance between the costs and benefits associated with trade.[4] The number of containers shipped internationally last year hit approximately 72 million. Miniaturization of products also increases the benefits of trade by lowering shipping costs. Taken to the extreme, one can consider how digitization of products allows them to be shipped via the Internet. This reduces the costs of transportation quite drastically. Enhancement of technology in the future promises to reduce these costs—and therefore drive up the gains to the trading strategy—further.

Technological advances also improve communication. The greatest effect is in the falling costs of communicating long distances. This makes it easier to coordinate production abroad, allowing more international investment to succeed. Improved communication and better management techniques and equipment (i.e., computers) helped businesses manage their operations better. By one estimate, changes in infrastructure and managerial capabilities over the last decade have allowed American businesses to lower their inventory holdings significantly—from 25% of GDP to 15% (*The Economist*, 2002: 59). This is one reason why people fear that in the wake of September 11, increased inspections at border crossings will prove costly—businesses will be forced to sit on inventory for longer periods, adding to their overhead costs and reversing the impact of investments in infrastructure and technology.

We can therefore identify a number of trends contributing to an increased value generated by the trading strategy. Rosecrance highlighted several already present in the 1980s, and if these trends have changed since then, surely they have accelerated. This is the source of the discussion and debates centering on globalization (for details, see Brawley, 2002). Almost all economic analyses point to benefits arising from engaging in greater international economic interaction, though these gains are not distributed evenly (as previously mentioned). Antiglobalization protesters might point out a number of non-economic costs associated with these changes. Nonetheless, most states have shifted to the trading strategy in recent years.

Equally clear however was that interdependence had not prevented wars in the past. Norman Angell had argued before 1914 that a clash between the great powers would be self-defeating in economic terms. The great powers were so enmeshed economically that war would damage them all. Angell was largely right, but that didn't prevent the First World War from beginning. As Rosecrance put it (1986: 33), "The disincentives to engaging in war—it is likely to be expensive, destructive, and perhaps ultimately futile—do not prevent wars from taking place." There is little reason to think we have become much wiser.

## UNDERSTANDING THE OTHER HALF OF THE EQUATION: THE DECLINE OF THE CONQUERING STATE

Rosecrance identified two steps in judging whether territorial conquest was appealing. First, foreign territory would have to be seized; second, it would have to be exploited successfully. These costs and benefits would be calculated together and then compared with the potential costs and benefits associated with economic integration among independent states.[5] Given the success of European countries creating empires in the past and maintaining them for decades, the strategy of conquest must have paid off for them at some point.

The European states were able to dominate vast territories because of their superior military technology and organization. In the sixteenth and seventeenth centuries, European ships were able to transport men and material around the globe. Even though relatively small numbers of troops were sent, these soldiers were equipped with weapons that gave them a tremendous edge. This was clearest in the Western Hemisphere, where small Spanish armies led by Cortez and Pizarro conquered existing Native American empires. Clad in armor, wielding firearms, mounted on horses, and sailing in galleons, the Spaniards defeated armies of greater size.[6] They were also able to repel and then suppress revolts by the conquered peoples in subsequent years.

Rosecrance is clear that the military strategy includes not only being able to seize territory, but to command it effectively. If it is impossible to control the seized territory, it will be impossible to exploit it. If it is too costly to command occupied territory, then the territory may be seized and controlled, but not in a way that yields benefits for the occupying power. Studies by economic historians have questioned whether empires paid off economically for countries such as Britain or France, even when these countries' empires were at their height.[7] Such vast empires could yield political and strategic advantages rather than economic benefits, of course.

More surprising, perhaps, is that the European states could hold onto their empires with relatively little military effort. At the end of the nineteenth century, Britain ruled an immense empire with a small army (but large navy). It was able to raise soldiers from its seized territories—especially India—to employ in exercising authority over other parts of the empire. The same could be said of France; even such industrial laggards as Spain and Portugal could hold onto sizable empires up to the end of the nineteenth century.

One can point to several factors that eventually made the European empires too costly to maintain. Some of these factors were political and ideological—most important, the rise of nationalism. Yet poorly armed nationalists failed to rebel successfully. The advent of increasingly destructive small arms, combined with less and less need for these combatants to be highly trained to be effective, tilted the balance more in favor of the rebellious. In the early nineteenth century, European armies with soldiers who maneuvered and fired in units held the edge against less organized, less well-armed local forces. Advances in gunpowder, plus rifling of muskets, changed the accuracy and range of firearms by the middle of the century. Once we approach the end of the century, the Boers demonstrated how a small well-equipped force could tie down the armed forces of the greatest empire of its day.

Continued advances in the development of small arms in the twentieth century may have tipped the balance even further in favor of those resisting outside occupation. The weapons of choice for guerrillas defying great powers in the second half of the twentieth century were surely the AK-47 and the rocket-propelled grenade. Neither requires elaborate training, yet both can deal out death and destruction. Wherever the local population has supported them, guerrilla fighters seeking to disrupt local political order have been extremely successful, even though they have only been armed with these light weapons. Moreover, such light weapons have been produced in massive numbers and can be found around the globe.

We might conclude, therefore, that occupying territory no longer pays.[8] We cannot undo the development of small arms. We have not been able to regulate the production and trade of small arms either, though the international regime established to eliminate antipersonnel land mines points to possible ways to reduce the sheer volume of such weaponry. Still, many of these sorts of arms can be manufactured locally, and were, so that even embargoed countries in the midst of civil war (such as Bosnia) were quite capable of producing land mines, small arms, and large amounts of munitions.

Interestingly, many of the same changes that we would consider important for understanding the impact of technology on trade or international investment have also shaped the calculations regarding military strategies. Mass production shaped patterns of specialization in trade, but also led to the advances in the quality and quantity of small arms just described. Expansion of railroad networks and development of the steamship integrated markets in the late nineteenth century, but both also created new possibilities for projecting military forces.

As for the ability to seize territory, nuclear weapons have made this an extremely costly endeavor if it leads to conflict between the great powers. Both tactical and strategic nuclear weapons were important for deterring territorial conflicts between the two opposing sides in the Cold War. Whether the spread of this technology will continue to have this deterrent effect remains to be seen, and competing predictions have appeared. From the perspective of the Cold War era, when Rosecrance was writing, the balance seemed to have shifted solidly toward one result: the gains from the trading strategy were rising even as the gains from territorial expansion were falling.

On the other hand, Rosecrance stressed that military technology "is a volatile factor." Historically, war-fighting technologies have swung from advantages for the offense versus the defense, and back again.[9] These swings may even have been more pronounced than any changes in trade driven by technology. After all, the current period of globalization is based on a series of technological developments whose roots lie in the late nineteenth century. There was a period of economic globalization then. International investment took place on a large scale, trade as a percentage of GDP was extremely high for a number of the major military powers, and large-scale labor migrations were also occurring.[10] All that came to a crashing halt in 1914, and couldn't be reconstructed in the 1920s or 1930s. The advances in technology did not guarantee that the balance had tilted in one direction forever, as Angell proposed. There was not a permanent resolution in favor of one strategy over the other, as the Cold War also reminded us.

## THE REVOLUTION IN MILITARY AFFAIRS

Volatile changes in military technology have occurred in the last 20 years. We are still trying to decipher and interpret many of these changes. The striking success of the United States and its allies in employing combined arms in the Gulf War against Iraq illustrated that there was a qualitative difference between American military technology and those of regional powers. This point has been emphasized again by successes in Operation Allied Force and now again in the fighting subsequent to September 11, 2001. These military successes were founded on four elements: the use of precision-guided munitions (PGMs), the utilization of global positioning equipment (GPS), the enhancement of communications for command and control, and the increased development of information management.[11]

The use of PGMs rests quite clearly on computers. Computer chips, programming, and communications to link systems make it possible to guide missiles or bombs to their targets with stunning accuracy. Films of cruise missiles departing ships or turning left and right to follow specific routes to their intended targets have left indelible images, as do videos shot from warheads as they glide toward their targets. Analysis of the bombing campaigns in Afghanistan and Iraq show the technology delivers weapons on target with amazing consistency, but targeting can be quite faulty.[12]

In the Gulf War, only around 5% of the ordinance dropped from the air qualified as precision-guided.[13] The cost of PGMs used to be fairly prohibitive. Stocks of cruise missiles were easily depleted in the opening stages of the Gulf War, for instance. Only one or two states other than the United States had the means to deliver these weapons in 1991. When NATO air power was used in Bosnia in 1995 in Operation Deliberate Force, 708 of the 1026 bombs dropped were precision-guided. By the time of Operation Allied Force, several countries had acquired these means, including countries that do not have large military budgets, such as Canada and Spain. It seems that the main obstacle preventing American allies from adopting PGMs has been political will, not budget constraints. Still, only around 35% of the bombs dropped in the war for Kosovo were precision-guided. In both Operation Allied Force and Operation Deliberate Force, PGMs hit their targets some 60% of the time, and clearly reduced the impact on innocent civilians (Sloan, 2002).

The military technology continues to be improved, however. A new weapon used in Afghanistan shows how technological advances translate into reduced costs in this area. The JDAM, or "joint direct attack munition," is a tail kit for taking a "dumb bomb" and making it "smarter." The mechanism guides the bomb in its trajectory, using GPS and inertial guidance to steer the bomb as it falls. Whereas a Tomahawk cruise missile costs an average of $500,000 (and that price is as low as it is because the weapon has been in production for years), the JDAM costs only $18,000 apiece (U.S. Air Force, 2002; Federation of American Scientists, 2002). JDAMs can be fitted to bombs of different sizes, and with different warheads designed for different missions, giving them a greater range of capabilities than cruise missiles. The declining price of PGMs allowed the United States to drop many more of them in the war in Afghanistan—shifting the mix upwards so that 60% of the ordinance dropped was precise (Sloan, 2002: 149). This is also why the U.S. military was fairly confident about its confrontation against Iraq. Over the decade leading up to the war, Iraq's military capabilities deteriorated, while American capabilities rose. The combination of improved technology and cost-savings made it possible for an intensive, destructive and sustained air campaign ahead of the ground campaign.

This description of the JDAM underscores how much the RMA is linked to the use of global positioning system (GPS), which relies on a fleet of satellites in space—something that does not come cheaply. With it, military forces can locate themselves, their enemies, and their comrades with the requisite specificity to employ PGMs. GPS is also critical for exercising superior command and control over military forces. This is increasingly enhanced by the use of drones for aerial surveillance. Drones can remain aloft for hours on end, sending back real-time video images of what is happening on the ground. Canada's Coyote armored vehicle can do the same thing, along with heat-sensing imagery and ground radar.

To employ PGMs and the GPS successfully, military forces require the third and fourth elements: advanced information processing and communications. Military experts refer to these together as the ability to exercise "battle-space awareness and control" (Sloan, 2002: 6–9). American military doctrine currently emphasizes the need to be more effective with fewer troops, and the only way this can be achieved is through improved command and control, coupled with increased firepower. GPS provides information about locations, but these bits of information have to be gathered into a single picture and that picture relayed to all the respective players. When there is a breakdown along these lines, "friendly fire" incidents occur. The older AWACs aircraft serve as the nerve center for conducting air operations; the less well-known JSTARS system carried aboard aircraft serves a similar purpose for coordinating ground, sea, and air units. JSTARS stands for Joint Surveillance Target Attack Radar System. Its specific mission is to classify and track ground targets over a large swath of territory, but it also serves as a flying command post to coordinate combined ground and air forces. In the wake of the Gulf War, the United States accelerated development of this technology. AWACs are operated by a number of countries, but only the United States has the JSTARS capability.[14] Once again, the infrastructure does not come cheap.

Command and control issues highlight another way in which the U.S. military has tapped into technological changes. In the description of the economic benefits associated with improved infrastructure and communication, it was mentioned that businesses today operate with reduced inventories. The U.S. military has applied these same techniques to the management of its supplies, allowing for just-in-time delivery of military logistics on a global scale (Sloan, 2002: 12). Once again, the logic is to have smaller forces capable of doing more with less.

Such technologies may only be available to few states in the near future. On the surface, JSTARS aircraft do not appear expensive, at $225 million each. On the other hand, these are useless unless all other military forces have the requisite equipment to communicate and receive different forms of data when interacting with the JSTARS, and that includes tapping into the American GPS satellites. The European Union has decided to embark on the deployment of its own GPS system, Galileo, at a very high cost. So far this is only intended for commercial purposes. Other states may choose to follow Europe's lead for different ends—and thus the weaponization of space will likely follow. Currently, no state has both the economic ability and the political will to engage the United States in such a race.

In other words, the RMA has so far really only been exploited by the United States and, to a lesser extent, its allies. It also seems unlikely that the U.S.—the country that has so much "soft power" at its disposal in a globalized world—is likely to engage in wars of conquest. The costs associated with the second step in this strategy may deter any state: the balance of costs and benefits when controlling or exploiting seized territory. American experience in Afghanistan and Iraq shows that destroying an enemy's infrastructure and military assets is easier than exercising authority over occupied territory. Occupation against a hostile populace remains too costly to make economic sense—as the burgeoning expense of the American occupation of Iraq illustrates. Israel, a country with well-developed military technology and tactics (indeed the pioneer in several areas of electronic warfare and the use of drones) has not been able to effectively control the territories it has successfully seized. What the

RMA has meant so far for the United States is that they have the ability to exert punitive force on other states at declining costs. Rather than argue that the RMA will make the United States into a conquering imperial power, I argue instead that the RMA will reshape the mix of economic links and military conflicts we observe in the future.

## SMART SANCTIONS VERSUS SMART BOMBS

The RMA will have its most apparent impact in American decisions about coercing opponents. The trading strategy may remain the dominant choice for many states, if not most. The expense of the RMA makes it difficult for many other states to fully implement the set of changes necessary to construct and deploy such an array of forces. Yet, the United States can and has begun exploiting the RMA. It may therefore find it more useful to exert force in pursuit of its goals than it did in the past. The RMA is surely tilting the balance in calculating the net costs of using force in favor of additional benefits. I make this claim on the assumption that the United States prefers to limit its own casualties in military operations, as well as the "collateral damage" associated with conflicts. Both costs have been factors restraining the use of force in the past. They are unlikely to continue to cause self-restraint, though in the post–September 11 environment it is hard to separate out these effects from those creating greater public acceptance of casualties.

The RMA promises to allow U.S. forces the ability to deliver precise, punishing blows against opponents, while the majority of its own forces stay out of harm's way. By destroying opposing military forces with minimal civilian casualties, the political objectives for conducting military action are more likely to be achieved. Improvements in the ability to destroy opposing forces quickly also promise to create greater public confidence in support of the use of force by the United States. On the one hand, the U.S. public may have very high expectations concerning the performance of its own military in the wake of the largely successful operations of the last decade—meaning that minor failures (such as the loss of 18 soldiers in Somalia) caused policies to be reversed. On the other hand, the consensus among the public that present threats are high creates a willingness to bear higher costs in terms of American casualties.

A current example to consider is American attempts to alter the policies of Iraq. Economic sanctions have been applied for a decade—but to what effect? The United States is roundly criticized for creating "collateral damage" in the form of deaths and illness among Iraqi women and children. Convicted terrorist Ramzi Yousef stated this view clearly and concisely in his trial. On being charged with terrorism, he countered: "And now you [the U.S. government] have invented a new way to kill innocent people. You have so-called economic embargo, which kills nobody other than children and elderly people." He went on to equate the economic embargo with terrorism (Friedman, 2000: 404). (This thinking is skewed, since it absolves Saddam Hussein of any responsibility for how Iraq's allowed earnings are spent, but it does reflect commonly heard sentiments concerning the U.N. embargo.)

There has always been this problem with making economic sanctions more effective. Most sanctions are imposed in an effort to change the policy of a government. The target therefore tends to be the political leadership of the government or, even more precisely, of a political party or faction. Yet it has proven very difficult to tailor economic sanctions to hit only their intended victims. Sanctions against Iraq and Serbia in the past decade (or against Cuba for several decades) have largely served to heighten the popularity of the leaders the sanctions are meant to pressure. Sanctions allow these leaders to garner allegiance as defenders of the nation. These sanctions also tend to create economic shortages, which these leaders can exploit. Shortages enhance their ability to dole out privileges.

David Cortright, George Lopez, and Joseph Stephanides (2002) have argued that "smart sanctions" can be created. Their arguments rest on better logic in applying sanctions, though going from the logic to actual implementation remains frustratingly difficult (Tostensen & Bull, 2002). Technological solutions for making sanctions smarter do not exist, in the same way that we might anticipate technological advances to continue to make weaponry smarter. Moreover, improvements in technology will certainly bring the price of smart weapons down further, while economic advances are likely to bind states together more tightly, making the costs of implementing economic sanctions ever higher. When looking at the specific choice Americans face over which instrument to use for coercive diplomacy, the costs and benefits associated with using military force are increasingly positive, while the costs and benefits associated with economic sanctions are increasingly negative.

The characteristics of the target state clearly matter greatly in this calculation. The United States may find it particularly attractive to undertake quick, decisive military action against opponents that are industrializing and have well-developed infrastructures, yet are merely regional powers. An Iraq or a Serbia has clearly identifiable military, political, and economic assets that make these states vulnerable. Countries such as Somalia or Sudan have ineffective governments, lack infrastructure, and are therefore much harder to hit in a punishing fashion—precision-guided weapons are no good if targets cannot be identified. Of course, these same characteristics make them unsuitable for pressuring through economic sanctions as well. On the other hand, the Taliban in Afghanistan proved vulnerable, since its military forces in the field could be detected and defeated. I argue that the RMA has reduced the cost to the United States of going to war against several possible opponents. When we also include the greater chance of success employing military force, as opposed to the poor performance of economic sanctions, the likelihood of deciding to use force rises dramatically. When the stakes are high, expect the United States to turn to the military option more quickly than before.

## THE CONTINUED RISE OF THE TRADING STATE?

Rosecrance provided valuable insights into deciphering long-term trends. While his arguments have been remembered largely for predicting the turn toward economic strategies for the enhancement of national welfare, and the declining use of military force to pursue those same ends, he did not predict a permanent transformation of state strategies in one direction. He would certainly have anticipated that the majority of states would embrace economic globalization, especially since so many have adopted democratic forms of government in recent years. Yet the economic calculus was only half his logic.

Changes affecting the other side of the equation can tilt the balance as well. The effects Rosecrance identified and discussed pushed in the same direction. That conclusion no longer holds. The RMA could well refocus American thinking about the value of employing military forces for political ends. Seizing and controlling territory in the face of a hostile populace remain costly, so I am not arguing that there is evidence the United States will soon develop an empire. Instead, I claim the costs to deliver punitive blows in an effort to coerce other states has surely fallen. Moreover, the costs promise to fall further as technology advances, and as the American military implements further organizational reforms and acquires more advanced weapons. Its mastery over these weapons and tactics will also improve as it gains experience.

The trading state strategy will remain the one model widely adopted. As stated toward the beginning of this chapter, there really is no viable alternative at the moment. It would be wrong to think this means the end of the political-military strategy, however. In the short run, military operations may only be employed by those few states—led by the United States—capable of exploiting the RMA. We must remember, however, that it is possible that some other states with different interests and goals could eventually develop the economic base to allow them to exploit the RMA as well. Since the costs of various technologies will surely decline, this is a matter of "when" not "if." At some point in the future, the trading state strategy could well prove vulnerable. Despite the economic changes entailed in globalization, we need to continue to think about both security and globalization, and the way they interact to shape the evolution of international relations.

## NOTES

1. In that sense, I wish to parallel what Ellsberg (1961) did in his early piece on deterrence; by providing a formulaic depiction of the logic, he produced valuable insights on the impact developments in weapons technology or policy stances would have on the stability of deterrence.

2. Many of these themes are addressed very nicely in Kapstein (1999a).

3. One interesting exception is Hirst (2001).

4. Rogowski (1989) emphasizes precisely this point.

5. Note that Rosecrance remained within a largely realist framework by assuming states are rational unitary actors. For those approaching this issue from a liberal perspective, decision making concerning costs and benefits could vary depending on who it is in the society who makes the decisions. Thus, the spread of liberal democracies could also have a powerful effect on the spread of the trading strategy.

6. We shouldn't forget the impact of disease in aiding the invading Europeans, as Diamond (1997) reminds us.

7. One excellent example here would be Davis and Huttenback (1986).

8. Or at least it only pays in extreme cases, such as Iraq's seizure of Kuwait.

9. Quester (1977) remains a classic overview of this issue.

10. These comparisons have been well examined by economic historians (see Bordo, Eichengreen, & Ki, 1998; and Bordo, Eichengreen, & Irwin, 1999).

11. A number of other areas of technological prowess could also be factored in, such as the development of stealth capabilities, enhanced surveillance techniques, improved security of data transmission, and so forth.

12. Several journalists have investigated examples where civilians were hit by American air attacks in 2002 and discovered that Afghans had provided deliberately false information to call in strikes as a way to settle old scores against local rivals.

13. This figure is reported in the GAO's analysis of the air campaign. See the discussion in Appendix II in the report GAO/NSIAD 97–134.

14. The Europeans were offered participation in the system's development, but opted out.

# 5

# State Transformation and New Security Dilemmas

Georg Sørensen

The entire discipline of International Relations (IR) is predicated on the idea that sovereign states are valuable places. They are precious because they provide—or are at least expected to provide—basic social values for their citizens: security, freedom, order, justice and welfare. Historically, other types of social organizations have catered to these values, for example, bands, tribes, clans, or ethnic and religious organizations. After all, sovereign states have only been around for a comparatively short period of time (some hundreds or thousands of years, depending on definition), whereas people have been around for about half a million years, since *homo sapiens* evolved from *homo erectus*.

Yet, ever since sovereign states became the universally dominant form of political organization, the major responsibility for provision of basic social values has come to.rest with them. Political theory reflects the unique importance awarded to the state. Hobbes taught that security—and ultimately other essential social values—derives from the state. The state must be able to provide a sufficient level of protection of the population from external as well as from internal threats. Without the state, there can be no protection; people will live in the state of nature, where anarchy will reign because egoistic humans will get at each other's throats. Law and order, not to mention welfare, are absent: life is "solitary, nasty, brutish and short." Under the protection of the state, by contrast, people can enjoy relative safety and thus pursue happiness and well-being—"felicity" in Hobbes's term.

With the creation of states, the domestic anarchy of the state of nature is moved to the international level: "In all times, kings and persons of sovereign authority, because of their independency, are in continual jealousies, and in the state and posture of gladiators; having their weapons pointing, and their eyes fixed on one another" (Hobbes 1946: 101). Using that starting point, John Herz could, in 1950, formulate what we may call the classical security dilemma. Sovereign states taking measures to make themselves more secure may well increase their level of protection, but, given the existence of international anarchy—the absence of centralized authority—that very activity will lead to greater insecurity of other states. In a self-help system, the creation of more security for one state is inevitably the creation of more insecurity for other states. "Striving to attain security from attack, [states] are driven to acquire more and more power in order to escape the power of others. This, in turn, renders the others more insecure and compels them to prepare for the worst. Since none can ever feel entirely secure in such a world of competing units, power competition ensues, and the vicious circle of security and power accumulation is on" (Herz, 1950: 157).

This classical understanding of the security dilemma has been the guiding light of the profession for more than half a century. It's not entirely wrong of course; anarchy has led to security dilemmas in accordance with Herz's view many times. Still, the classical view is highly misleading because it is based on erroneous assumptions and because it leaves security problems of fundamental importance in the dark. It was misleading historically, but it is perhaps especially misleading today because states have been transformed in ways that have significant implications for their security dilemmas.

That is the argument this chapter aims to develop.[1] I review the problematic assumptions first. That leads to an emphasis on how the Herz–Hobbesian security dilemma is merely the most important one under certain, specific conditions (i.e., in a world of modern states). The next step in the argument is the claim that ours is no longer (and never was) a world of modern states. Today's world is inhabited by different main types of state. Postmodern states and postcolonial states are among the most important of these types. The distinctive security dilemmas pertaining to these states are then identified.

## PROBLEMS WITH THE CLASSICAL SECURITY DILEMMA

I focus on three problems: (1) the omission of not looking inside the state, but only at relations between states; (2) the assumption that the state provides a framework for 'felicity'; and (3) the assumption that violent conflict always lurks between states in anarchy.

The first point—not looking inside the state—is emphasized by Herz when he speaks of the hard shell of the modern state that protects it from foreign penetration. When this hard shell is in place, the state is "defensible and, at least to some extent, secure in its relation with other units" (Herz, 1959: 40). Security has to do with protection from outside threat, from the armed might of competing states. In this context, what goes on inside the state is not terribly interesting. Given protection from outside threat, the 'good life' is free to unfold in the domestic realm.

Hobbes reasoned along the same lines as we saw earlier. Protection by the state leads to security, order, and the good life. But why should there be protection with the state? Why would the state elite not be as self-interested and power-loving as anyone else? Herz actually hinted, in an earlier analysis, that domestic power relationships might be a serious security problem (Herz, 1951: 28), but he does not pursue the issue. As with Hobbes, he assumes away the problem of bad and self-seeking state elites through a strict specification of demands on the sovereign for protection of people and property. That is, a Leviathan in Hobbes's terms by definition honors the social contract in creating the basis for the good life of the citizens. The difficulty is, of course, that this is not a valid assumption; we cannot simply assume that security is taken care of when the hard shell is in order. We know that many of the most serious security problems for people have domestic rather than international roots. In most cases the security dilemma emerges from a peculiar interrelationship between domestic and international elements. The analysis of this whole relationship has been cut off by much of IR theory because it has omitted to look inside the individual state and, instead, focused exclusively on interstate relations.

Another argument in favor of purely systemic analysis comes from Kenneth Waltz. His neorealism builds its systemic analysis of the balance of power on the idea that domestic structures of states can be disregarded because they can be considered basically homogenous 'like units'. The argument is this: given that they want to survive, states are driven, under conditions of anarchy, to emulate the more successful states in the system, the theory says simply that as some do relatively well, others will emulate them or "fall by the wayside" (Waltz, 1979: 118). Socialization and competition are the two principal ways in which the anarchic structure affects states. They lead to the creation of like units. Therefore, we need not look inside the states; they are like units anyway.

Waltz's view is clearly wrong. Anarchy need not lead to like units through competition. Innovation can lead in entirely new directions. Moreover, the international society of states can suspend competition and accept the persistence of weak entities, as in the case of decolonization. In sum, the arguments for avoiding an analysis of domestic conditions when it comes to security dilemmas are not valid.

That leads to the second problematic point, the assumption that the state provides a framework for felicity. This assumption is only valid if the state in question has certain characteristic structures; in their absence there is no framework for felicity. It would appear that the modern state—the type of state that had emerged in the industrialized countries of Western Europe and North America by the mid-twentieth century and then spread to Japan and a few other places—provides the framework for felicity, that is, the good life. But in the early days of the Westphalian state—say, from the fifteenth through the nineteenth centuries—these modern domestic structures were not in place and, consequently, security and the good for citizens were not in place either.

Charles Tilly and others' description of state formation does not provide evidence to support that states in those days were places of security and the good life for the citizens (Tilly, 1990). Nor were citizens secure in such states as Stalin's Soviet Union; Stalin's obsession with domestic enemies sent 10 million people to the labor camps. Other millions died in his regime of terror and torture. The point bears repetition: the arguments for avoiding an analysis of domestic conditions when it comes to security dilemmas are not valid.

The final point concerns the assumption that violent conflict always lurks between states in anarchy. The critique that anarchy need not be as 'raw' as indicated by realists and neorealists has appeared in many different versions. The most important of these are probably the International Society, the liberal, and the constructivist views. All agree that cooperation and common rules are possible in the absence of a centralized authority above the states. Not all would go as far as the constructivist claim that "anarchy is what states make of it" (Wendt, 1992), but it is not necessary to go into these details here. The major general point is this: security dilemmas are connected not only to international relations between states but also to domestic structures inside states. Both in the domestic and the international realm, a variety of security dilemmas are possible. A much more nuanced analysis of security dilemmas than the discipline has been able to offer so far is called for. Especially, the domestic basis of the security dilemma has not been much addressed by IR theory, with a few notable exceptions (Berki, 1986; Buzan, 1991).

The interplay between domestic and international calls for much more concrete analysis that can be offered here. I propose to look at some major developments of sovereign statehood during the last half of the twentieth century. Recall that the classical Herz–Hobbesian security dilemma is relevant for the modern state. But, in ideal-typical terms, there are at least two other main types of state in the present international system: the postmodern and the postcolonial state. They are identified as follows and their peculiar security dilemmas are briefly discussed.

## MODERN, POSTMODERN AND POSTCOLONIAL STATES

States always change. There was no modern state in the seventeenth, eighteenth, and nineteenth centuries. There were developments—political, economic, social, and other changes—that would eventually lead to the modern state. Transformation is therefore the rule and not the exception. States have always undergone development and change; the present period of transformation merely adds a new chapter to that story.

It was demonstrated earlier that specific security dilemmas are tied in with particular structures of statehood. I have indicated that the classical Herz–Hobbesian security dilemma is relevant for the modern state. The basic structure of the modern state is set forth in Figure 5.1.

| Government | A centralized system of democratic rule, based on a set of administrative, policing, and military organizations, sanctioned by a legal order, claiming a monopoly of the legitimate use of force, all within a defined territory. |
|------------|----------------------------------------------------------------|
| Nationhood | A people within a territory making up a community of citizens (with political, social, and economic rights) and a community of sentiment based on linguistic, cultural, and historical bonds. Nationhood involves a high level of cohesion, binding nation and state together. |
| Economy | A segregated national economy, self-sustained in the sense that it comprises the main sectors needed for its reproduction. The major part of economic activity takes place at home. |

FIGURE 5.1. The Modern State

The modern state provides the context for the good life; the centralized system of democratic rule creates the basis for domestic peace and order as well as protection from external threat. Nationhood provides community that binds nation and state together; the national economy provides the basis for welfare as well as for resources to defend the realm. The existence of government, nationhood, and the national economy are the cohesion parameters that combine to forge the link between national security and the security of individual citizens. Modern states are characterized by a high level of social cohesion; in that sense they are strong states (Buzan, 1991: 97). But strong states in this sense emerged relatively late. The security dilemma in previous forms of state, as well as in contemporary postcolonial and postmodern states, is different because their domestic structures are different.

So Herz was right in connecting his security dilemma with the modern state (although he was wrong in implying that the security dilemma in the Soviet Union looked the same). But we know that the modern state has not stood still. The modern state of the mid-twentieth century has been transformed. We cannot be entirely sure about what has taken its place because the changes that are transpiring are still in process. Major developments are easier to identify in retrospect; the development of the modern state, for example, was under way for many decades, even hundreds of years. We now know, in retrospect, that the modern state came to full maturity by the mid-twentieth century. But we are much less sure where the current process of state change will take us, because that process has only lasted a few decades and is still unfolding.

That is why I suggest the label of "the postmodern state" as a way of summarizing those changes still under way. The post- prefix is an indicator that we are not quite clear about what shape and form the postmodern state will eventually take. But at the same time we are quite certain that it is different from the modern state. Our present situation can be compared with the observers of the modern state during the first part of the nineteenth century: they knew that big political, economic, and other changes were taking place, but they were not quite sure where they were going to lead in the end because the modern state came to full maturity only many years later. We also know that today big political, economic, and other changes are taking place, but we are not quite sure where they are going to lead. Still, we want to make sense of what is going on. The ideal type of the postmodern state is an attempt to do just that.

So what are the changes from modern to postmodern? The economy first. There has been a transformation of the economy, from a national economy toward a globalized economy. A globalized economy means deep integration, especially among the advanced economies. Transnational corporations organize production chains across borders, on a regional and global basis. Production by transnationals outside their home countries exceeds world trade. Trade, in turn, is typically intra-industry and intrafirm. Instead of purely national financial systems, a globally integrated financial market is emerging. So we must conclude that the economies of the advanced states are no longer aptly described as "segregated national economies." They have been transformed to globalized economies, where the major part of economic activity is embedded in cross-border networks. As a result, the "national" economy is much less self-sustained than it used to be.

What about politics? Governance is changing from an activity conducted by national administrations over well-defined territorial realms to an international, transgovernmental, and transnational activity that includes not only governments and traditional international organizations, but also nongovernmental organizations and other nonstate actors. There is great variation across countries and regions; clearly, regional cooperation has developed the most in Western Europe. But the general trend is away from governance in the context of national government, toward multilevel governance in several interlocked arenas overlapping each other. Some of that governance reflects a more intense conventional cooperation between independent states; some of it reflects a more profound transformation toward supranational governance in a context of highly interconnected societies.

The last item is nationhood. The nation is both a community of citizens (i.e., political, social, and economic rights and obligations) and a community of sentiment (people with a common linguistic, cultural, and historical identity). The community of citizens is being transformed by three factors: (1) the emergence of citizenship rights granted from other instances than the sovereign state and rights given to nonnationals; (2) the growth of regional movements; and (3) a reduced ability of states to deliver on social and welfare rights. The community of sentiment is challenged because the creation of identity is

| Government | Multilevel governance in several interlocked arenas overlapping each other. Governance in context of supranational, international, transgovernmental, and transnational relations. |
| --- | --- |
| Nationhood | Supranational elements in nationhood, both with respect to the community of citizens and the community of sentiment. Collective loyalties increasingly projected away from the state. |
| Economy | Deep integration: the major part of economic activity is embedded in cross-border networks. The national economy is much less self-sustained than it used to be. |

FIGURE 5.2. The Postmodern State

becoming individualized; that gives increased salience to collective identity 'above' the nation. In addition, various resistance identities (e.g., religious, ethnic, or narrow nationalistic identities) are of growing importance. In other words, nationhood is being transformed to incorporate new aspects. A major element of that transformation is that nationhood increasingly includes supranational elements, both with respect to the community of citizens and the community of sentiment. A further development is that collective loyalties are projected away from the state, toward other entities.

Taken together, as an ideal type, the postmodern state contains the features shown in Figure 5.2.

The transformation from modern to postmodern statehood discussed earlier is focused on the advanced states in the triad. This transformation does not accurately portray the states in the Third World, particularly the weakest states, primarily concentrated in sub-Saharan Africa. At the same time, it is clear that the weakest states are qualitatively different from the modern states. So how do we characterize these weak states?

Before answering that question, a few words about terminology. "Weak" is not an optimal term, because many will think of states that are weak with regard to military power and that is not the meaning here. Sometimes the term "weak" is used in another way, to designate states that have "strong" societies and "weak" states (such as the United States) in contrast to states that have "weak" societies and "strong" states (such as France), but that is not what is meant here either. As the term is used here, the weak state is weak in terms of all three core aspects of statehood: government, nationhood, and economy. The typical weak state in this sense has a colonial past: it is a postcolonial state (states can be weak without having a colonial past, but that is not the typical pattern).

So the state we are looking to characterize is the weak, postcolonial state (see Figure 5.3). It has not undergone a transformation from modern to

| Government | Inefficient and corrupt administrative and institutional structures. Rule based on coercion rather than the rule of law. Monopoly on the legitimate use of violence not established. |
|---|---|
| Nationhood | Predominance of local/ethnic community. Neither the community of citizens nor the community of sentiment have developed to become the primary bonds among people. Low level of state legitimacy. |
| Economy | Incoherent amalgamations of traditional agriculture, an informal petty urban sector, and some fragments of modern industry. Significant dependence on the world market and on external economic interests. |

Figure 5.3. The Weak, Postcolonial State

postcolonial because it was never modern in the first place. It is a state with a radically different type of background than the modern states of the triad. We need to know about it because there are several such states in the world today.

The next sections will discuss the peculiar security dilemmas pertaining to postmodern and weak postcolonial states, respectively. I am not claiming that an analysis of these ideal types will exhaust all empirical cases of sovereign statehood in the world today. There are some major states, including China, India, Russia, and Brazil, that are different mixtures of modern, postmodern, and postcolonial. They will not be treated in what follows. However, I hope to demonstrate how the security dilemma varies in conjunction with qualitatively different structures of statehood. The reader is also referred to the other contributions to this volume, several of which demonstrate variations in the security dilemma in different contexts.

## The Security Dilemma of Postmodern States

Relations between postmodern states do not correspond to a Hobbesian picture of anarchy in the sense of anarchy as "the state of nature." It does not even correspond to a more moderate realist picture of sovereign states in an anarchy with rules and institutions, where the balance of power is one significant institution. Among postmodern states there is legitimate authority. States continue to be formally independent, but they are increasingly tied to each other through networks of multilevel governance. Even if much of that cooperation falls short of the supranational governance especially developed in some areas of EU cooperation, the general trend is for more rather than less legitimate authority between postmodern states.

Peace between postmodern states is overdetermined because several different items each help produce a situation in which violent conflict is out of the question. These countries are liberal democracies, their level of cooperation through international institutions is very high, and they are highly interdependent, both in economic and other areas. In addition, they have developed a common Western civic identity at the core of which is "a consensus around a set of norms and principles, most importantly political democracy, constitutional government, individual rights, private property-based economic systems, and toleration of diversity in non-civic areas of ethnicity and religion" (Deudney & Ikenberry, 1999: 193).

So it is easy to understand why commentators believe that war between such states has become "subrationally unthinkable" (Mueller, 1989) and that the classical basis for violent conflict (i.e., aggrandizement through the conquest of territory) is historically obsolete (Rosecrance, 1995). The traditional security dilemma, based on anarchy as a state of nature, has been eliminated. Yet these countries still perceive possible traditional threats from modern or modernizing states, or even from weak postcolonial states, so the traditional security dilemma is not completely eradicated.

At the same time, postmodern states face new challenges. The first set of problems concerns the identification of the objects of security. Take the economy. For the modern state, it was easy to define economic security. It had to do with safeguarding the national economy and securing access to necessary resources, finance, and markets (cf. Buzan, 1991: 19). But when economies are deeply integrated across borders and different 'national' economies depend very significantly on each other for their reproduction, what then is the object of economic security: the larger economic space or merely the 'national' segment of it (to the extent that that segment can be singled out)? Insofar as national economic autonomy is no longer a viable option because the level of economic welfare and economic strength depends on continued successful economic integration across borders, there must be a corresponding shift in the object of economic security, away from the purely national economy, toward the regional/global economic framework in which this economy is now irrevocably embedded. Furthermore, political control over the economy becomes much more difficult because territorially limited regulations cannot effectively cover the relevant, larger economic space. So political measures to produce such core values as growth and welfare, as well as securing the economic basis for state power, must be increasingly challenged.

What about the political level? Again, there would appear to be a shift in the object of security. When the national political systems are parts of a complex of multilevel governance, the object of security is the entire structure of that governance including the supranational level, not merely the national and lower levels. This calls for a redefinition of political security. At the same time, the provision of other core values in addition to the economic ones previously mentioned faces new problems; this is the core message in Susan Strange's analysis of the Westfailure system, where she focuses on problems concerning environmental damage, financial infrastructure, and social inequality (Strange, 1999: 346).

There are also challenges to democracy in the postmodern context, and therefore challenges to the social value of freedom. So far, democracy has only developed within the context of independent states. Many theorists of democracy argue that the sovereign nation-state (i.e., the modern state) is a necessary precondition for democracy. There are obvious problems with democracy outside of that framework. First, there is no evident *demos*, that is, there is no well-defined political community external to that context. No *demos*, no democracy. Second, multilevel governance is not based on a well-defined constitutional framework; therefore, core decision makers are not subject to sufficient democratic accountability and control (Dahl, 1999: 31). In sum, the democratic link between rulers and ruled is challenged in the new context of postmodern statehood.

Nationhood is at the core of what Buzan calls "the idea of the state" (1991: 69). In the modern state, the identity of the nation was strong; a major aspect of national security was therefore the security of the nation. Strengthening collective identity with reference to the nation meant strengthening (the idea of) the state. Under postmodern conditions, by contrast, collective identities are projected away from the nation; they are much more differentiated and they develop in ways that may weaken rather than strengthen the idea of the state. The definition of national security in identity terms is much more difficult under postmodern conditions because the dynamics of change in identities turn them into a moving and more complex target. Collective identities are therefore no longer linked to the sociopolitical cohesion and thus to the strength of the state in any well-defined way. Postmodern statehood puts the component of the state that concerns the idea of the state on the agenda in ways that are not at all foreseen in most of the current analyses of national security. Some commentators find that the events of September 11 will reverse the new trend and create a return of the state; I comment on the consequences of September 11 later.

I have briefly discussed what the changes from modern to postmodern might mean in security terms for the economic, political, and nationhood level of the state. But there are other aspects of the new security agenda for postmodern states. One additional major aspect is the emergence of what sociologists call a risk society; another concerns the security agenda after September 11.

The idea of a risk society is linked to that fact that postmodern societies are densely interconnected, not merely with each other, but also with other countries. That is, postmodern countries are embedded in a globalized social context. Such a context is also a globalized risk environment in which risks are "largely without boundaries, not limited in space, and because they are also likely to affect future generations, not limitable in time either" (Lash, 1993). It is the influential analysis by Ulrich Beck (1992) that has termed this state of affairs "risk society," indicating that sovereign borders provide little in terms of effective protection in the postmodern context. A large number of different problems and risks emerging from single societies can therefore be quickly transmitted to other societies. Beck's focus is on environmental problems, but there are others, such as disease, crime, drugs, migration, and economic crises. The challenge to effective governance under these conditions is to continue to be able to provide the basic social values of security, order, justice, freedom, and welfare.

The most serious new challenge to security has emerged in full after September 11. The world was familiar with terrorism, of course. It was never confined to specific areas, such as the Middle East. There had been a number of serious attacks, also in the Western world. But we had not realized that terrorists were ready to commit mass murder of innocent civilians. Nor had we thought that it could be done so relatively easy; no need to be able to start or land an aircraft, merely to fly it straight. Bring a plastic knife on board—hardly a recipe for sophisticated, resource-demanding, technology-intensive operations. Moreover, there appear to be variants of chemical or biological terror that are not too hard to initiate either.

September 11 revealed how vulnerable open societies are to ruthless terrorism. There is a peculiar security dilemma here: how to create sufficient protection of the open societies without violating their major, defining quality—namely, their openness. Sufficient protection will require surveillance, undercover intelligence, and control of the behavior and movements of civilians, the citizens. Openness requires freedom of movement, speech, organization, and behavior in general, within constitutional limits. This dilemma is not entirely new, of course; it was present during the Cold War also. But it has become much more pertinent after September 11.

The dilemma has another dimension, related to the struggle against terrorism. How far are open, democratic societies allowed to go in the name of combating terrorism? Are they allowed to produce as many or more civilian casualties in the campaign against terrorism than the terrorists themselves murdered in the first place? Are they allowed to disregard international law in the name of fighting terrorism? The immediate answer to these questions would appear to be no, of course not. But the events in Afghanistan and Iraq have demonstrated the acute relevance of the dilemma.

The final major difficulty with mass-murder terrorism is that—unlike conventional war—one does not probably defeat it once and for all. It is, rather, an ongoing struggle in which one successful campaign risks producing new adversaries. At the same time, there is a complex set of causal layers behind this kind of terrorism. They include: (a) traditional Muslim elites in Saudi Arabia and elsewhere unable to accommodate processes of modernization and Westernization; (b) the Middle East conflict, especially the continuing clashes between Palestinians and Israelis; (c) the existence of weak states such as Afghanistan (more on this later); and (d) socioeconomic inequalities pushed by uneven economic globalization—more than one billion people exist on a dollar a day or less; another two billion on two dollars or less. That's half of the world's population. Yet there is no simple relationship between these underlying causes and the emergence of mass-murder terrorism; they are structural conditions, not the triggers, the concrete actors. In short, we don't really know how much more terrorism these underlying factors will actually help create.

September 11 has produced another result with at least potentially positive consequences for the security of consolidated states: it has presented us with a common enemy. Recall the comment of Colin Powell in 1991, when he was chairman of the Joint Chiefs of Staff: "I'm running out of demons. I'm running out of enemies. I'm down to Castro and Kim Il Sung" (Cover Story, 1991: 28). Mass-murder terrorism is a new common enemy. It will surely add another dimension to cooperation between postmodern states. But it will also increase the debate among friends about who is to pay for what and how each can best make the appropriate contributions; this is the issue on the table in current discussions in NATO between the United States and Europe. The expansion of NATO will not make the subject easier to handle. The prospect of a common enemy raises an additional set of problems: how far could or should that lead to tolerance of, for example, Russian abuses in Chechnya, or to cordial relationships with dictators in Pakistan and elsewhere?

In sum, the security dilemma of postmodern states is qualitatively different from the classical Herz–Hobbesian security dilemma. The latter is relevant for modern states, but it does not sufficiently incorporate the security consequences of the transition from modern to postmodern statehood. Postmodern states have developed legitimate authority between them, based on a set of common values and principles. War between them is out of the question.

At the same time, it has become much more difficult to define the substantial content of national security in economic, political, and nationhood terms. That is because under postmodern conditions the economies, the polities, and the collective identities of citizens are no longer neatly confined behind sovereign, territorial borders. Therefore, the standard way of protecting the state—by strengthening the hard shell behind which the good life can be pursued—is no longer a feasible security strategy. Because postmodern statehood does not simply involve the amalgamation of states to larger units, the hard shell cannot be established at any higher level either. The objects of security therefore remain suspended in a space that is not easily territorially demarcated and confined. That is a challenge to all conventional security strategies, because they are predicated on such demarcated and confined spaces as their objects of security.

Furthermore, there are new challenges to the postmodern state's provision of basic social values. This includes the emergence of a risk society and the new security challenge to open societies defined by September 11. Whatever the future trajectories of these challenges may be, there can be no doubt that postmodern societies face a security dilemma very different from the classical Herz–Hobbesian dilemma.

## The Security Dilemma of the Weak, Postcolonial State

The weak, postcolonial state also faces a distinct security dilemma, different from both the classical and the postmodern dilemma. Seen from the Herz–Hobbesian viewpoint, the mere existence of the weak states in the international system is a paradox: these entities are so unable to defend themselves against any serious external threat that they could most easily be swallowed by the much stronger states of the North. Yet this has not happened and there is no indication whatsoever that it will happen. The weak states are not involved in any kind of serious competition for survival in the international system. The Waltzian maxim of the weak needing to emulate the strong or "fall by the wayside" (1979: 118) is not valid for them.

They don't face any serious external threat because they are protected by the norms of the international system, norms that are backed by great powers and other substantial states. These norms were created in the context of decolonization. First, colonies were given the right to independence in a 1960 U.N. declaration that explicitly rejected demands for any kind of political or economic substance as a necessary precondition. Status as a colony became a fully sufficient ticket to sovereignty. What emerged from decolonization was a new type of very weak player in the international system.

Second, according to the new norms, borders are sacrosanct. As the main rule, they can only be changed with the consent of the affected parties. That new norm amounts to a kind of life insurance for weak states: no matter how weak, they will never be gulped up by stronger states. Yet this can also be a pass for predatory state elites to run 'their' states into the ground: no matter what the extent of misery and dissolution, a judicially sovereign state does not cease to exist; it continues to possess formal, juridical sovereignty. Even at the peak of violent disintegration, for example, the international society has continued to pretend that there was such a thing as a Somalian state. The weak are not taken over by the strong—they are merely allowed to disintegrate.

How did postcolonial state elites become predatory in the first place? Because of the overall domestic situation in the newly independent states. As already indicated, there was a lack of substantial statehood upon independence. The most important element appears to be the lack of cultural and political community. Independence meant independence for colonial territories, defined by colonial borders. The people inside those borders were communities only in the sense that they shared a border drawn by others. Their idea of nationalism was a negative one: get rid of the colonizers. When that project succeeded, there was no positive notion of community left over. The attempt by some elites to create community was quickly abandoned. What emerged instead were monopoly states: "Confronted by weak administrative structures, fragile economies, and in some cases dangerous sources of domestic opposition, political leaders sought to entrench themselves in power by using the machinery of the state to suppress or coopt any rival organization. . . . Rather than acknowledging the weakness of their position, and accepting the limitations on their power which this imposed, they chose to up the stakes and went for broke" (Clapham, 1996: 59).

Political community was thus not created; the communities that prevailed were the different ethnic subgroups that competed for access to state power and resources. State elites based themselves on patron–client relationships involving a select minority of such groups, shutting off the others from influence and resources. The predatory state was in place.

A predatory state is obviously no source of protection for the people: no hard shell and no basis for the good life. It is exactly the opposite: such states are sources of danger, including mortal danger for their populations. By no means do they provide security, order, or welfare. In weak, postcolonial states, the Herz–Hobbesian security dilemma has been turned on its head: because of the state, life for citizens can be solitary, nasty, brutish, and short. Meanwhile, the international community, staunchly supported by domestic state elites, agrees on one crucial point: let the weak state persist, no matter what.

The human cost of this peculiar kind of weak statehood has been extremely high. The three conflicts in Sudan, Ethiopia, and Mozambique each cost the lives of 500,000 to one million people (Copson, 1994: 29); casualties in Angola, Somalia, Uganda, and the Congo have also been very high.

How could it come to that? Who is responsible for the creation of weak states in the first place? One school puts most of the blame on external interests. The early colonizers were set on making a profit, not on creating good conditions for development of the colonies. After independence, dependency theorists claimed that postcolonial states were more or less doomed to underdevelopment as a consequence of their inferior status in the global capitalist system. It is certainly true that globalization is uneven and that there have been losers in the periphery of the system. But is it not true that postcolonial status or even a low initial position in the global capitalist hierarchy in itself means condemnation to underdevelopment. When it comes to the poorest countries in sub-Saharan Africa, for example, they have not been underdeveloped by global capital because global capital has not invested there; markets and production facilities have simply not been sufficiently attractive.

By contrast, the successes of Taiwan, South Korea, and others demonstrate how it was possible for newly independent countries to exploit the opportunities of the world market. At the same time, world market integration in itself is no guarantee for development success. Appropriate domestic conditions are critical, so both domestic and international circumstances are always in the picture.

Another tack on the question about the emergence of weak states is to focus directly on the worst cases in sub-Saharan Africa. For example, how could Mobutu's terrible rule in Zaire persist for so long? As a head of a desperately poor country, he was highly dependent on external interests. The book by Sean Kelly, *America's Tyrant* (1993), records how Mobutu relied on the CIA to save him from coup attempts by rival military factions on more than one occasion. One explanation for Mobutu then, is that he could conduct his dirty deals under CIA protection—he was a puppet on a string. This is not all wrong, but it is misleading in a basic sense because it stipulates that Mobutu was completely in the pocket of the CIA. He was not, for the simple reason that he was the leader of a sovereign state. Formal independence is not unimportant. At the moment of independence a new political, economic, social, and cultural sphere is created that has some substantial amount of autonomy. The new 'inside' can still be influenced by external forces, of course, but the conditions of operation are very different from before. On the one hand, there is a new need for the outsider to find domestic allies; that implies some sort of bargaining situation between insiders and outsiders. Mobutu was not merely in the pocket of the CIA; he bargained with them: you do this for me, I do this for you. At the same time, external intervention in weak states cannot be conducted in complete ignorance of the rules of international society. After all, the basic norm of judicial sovereignty is non-intervention, which means that acts of intervention have to be justified. So both in the domestic and the international sphere the rules of the game change in ways that provide increased autonomy to domestic actors. And, in the final analysis, the perpetrators are overwhelmingly local, that is, the violent conflicts are between domestic groups mostly fighting for the control of the state.

What can be done about the peculiar security dilemma of weak, postcolonial states? Overall economic and political development is of course preferable. The last four decades have not seen much of that in these countries, for reasons that cannot be explored here. Short of that, some elements of order and a more responsive state would help: such processes of democratization have not fared very well either (Sørensen, 1998a). Some commentators recommend secession as a way forward because that would separate conflicting ethnic groups from each other, but this also opens a whole new set of problems (Bartkus, 1999). In sum, there are no easy ways out, so the security dilemma of weak, postcolonial states will most probably be around for some considerable time. In a few cases, such as the current Musharref regime in Pakistan, the

United States will provide support in order to avoid a complete state failure that will let Pakistan fall prey to uncontrollable terrorism, but that is no general solution to the problems of weak statehood.

## CONCLUSION

States always change. When they do, it has implications for their security dilemmas. Specific security dilemmas are connected to particular structures of statehood. The classical Herz–Hobbesian security dilemma is relevant for the modern state. But the classical security dilemma is by no means an appropriate tool for a comprehensive understanding of security in earlier forms of state. Nor does it accurately depict security dilemmas in postmodern and weak, postcolonial states. Behind these problems is the one-sided fixation of the classical security dilemma on relations between states. The classical security dilemma does not make sense unless the increased power of states that is the driving force of the dilemma is meaningfully connected to the protection and safety of people inside the state. That premise is true for the modern state, but not for many other types of state.

Against this background, a further examination of security dilemmas in relation to different types of state is called for. Every state is of course unique, and in that sense every security dilemma has its peculiar features. I have suggested that in order to identify more general patterns, we look for major (ideal) types of states in the present international system. I zoomed in on two such types, the postmodern and the weak, postcolonial state.

Each of these types is characterized by particular security dilemmas. Between postmodern states, war is out of the question. But national security is much more difficult to define because in basic ways these states are no longer precisely defined in territorial terms. Furthermore, the notion of a risk society as well as the vulnerabilities exposed by September 11 constitute new serious challenges to security for the populations of postmodern states. Weak postcolonial states turn Hobbes on its head: the state, dominated by self-seeking elites, is the most serious threat to the security of the population. In addition, there is no external threat of extermination; to the contrary: the persistence of weak statehood is guaranteed by the international system.

States will keep changing, so new security dilemmas are bound to emerge. There are many and varied sources of changes in statehood: processes of economic and political modernization may be successful or may fail. Groups in society may be mobilized in new ways. When states change in major ways, their security dilemmas also change. Postmodern and weak postcolonial states are unstable types almost by definition because they contain various problematic features. But postmodern states are not about to amalgamate into some kind of federation, and weak postcolonial states will not swiftly become developed. Therefore, these states and their security dilemmas will be major elements of the international system for several decades of the twenty-first century.

## NOTES

1. I have discussed the subject of this chapter at length in Sørensen, G. (2001). Some formulations in what follows draw on that work.

# 6

# Anarchy Meets Globalization

## A New Security Dilemma for the Modernizing State

Ersel Aydinli

The mainstream of globalization and the state literature theorizes that state capacity is undergoing a transformation; however, it has been unable to operationalize the dynamics of the change. This chapter attempts to address that gap by exploring how states, which have been designed in reaction to the state-centric system and its primary demand of survival at home and abroad, respond to the pressures of globalization and localization.[1] The conflictual core of the transformation, therefore, is understood as occurring between the forces of power maximization and centralization, and the accelerating forces for power diffusion. To understand the transformation, we must ask: how is national power/capacity reconfigured when faced with the power diffusion impact of globalization and the power maximization demands of internal and external security dilemmas?[2]

The primary determinants of the traditional state-centric international system have been security concerns, both external and internal. These concerns kept states largely occupied with geopolitics and anarchic conditions in their immediate environments, as well as in the global system. In order to curb security threats and maintain a constant position of readiness, the national forces of a state had to be kept centralized and concentrated—though, of course, the degree to which this was true varied according to the acuteness of the nation's conceptualization of security threats. To achieve centralized and thus maximized power, a ruling elite not only had to keep security issues and rhetoric prominent on the public agenda, but it also had to seek to enhance the existing institutionalization of the security establishment. This process, which could be labeled as securitization, is one through which everything becomes linked to the idea of national security. National security becomes the primary directive when assessing the feasibility of any major political project requiring power reallocation at the national level. Ultimately, this led to the creation of security-oriented nation-states and, in extreme examples, to garrison states. The power pattern, securitization process, and resulting state type are shown in the first row of Figure 6.1.

The third row of Figure 6.1 outlines the new epoch of globalization. This new epoch has enabled a mobility of resources, ideas, and individuals, and thus empowered new actors above and below the state level. These new actors, with their varied agendas, produce demands for a sharing of national power and a consequent pressure for decentralization. The implication of this process in terms of security, can be labeled as desecuritization. This term should not imply an automatic minimizing of security issues, but rather a lowering of the 'prime directive' status of security over all other issues, and a reconsidering of security as one of several major needs to be satisfied by national governance. Achieving this involves increasing the transparency of and civilian control over the determining of threats and the implementing of national security policies. States that seem to be successfully managing this process can be identified as Western or globalized states, such as those of Western Europe and North America.

Many modernizing states[3] in particular, however, seem to fall somewhere in between these two worlds, as expressed by the middle row of the diagram. As such, these states are forced to try and balance contradicting patterns of power. The resulting conflictive process of power reconfiguration needs to be further explored theoretically in order to project its possible implications.


## THE GLOBALIZATION AND THE STATE DEBATE

### Hyperglobalists and Rejectionists

A first group of scholars, "hyperglobalists," claim that globalization represents a new epoch of human history in which traditional nation-states have become unnatural or even impossible business units in the new global economy (Albrow, 1997; Cox, 1997; Guéhenno, 1995; Luard, 1990; Ohmae, 1995; Strange, 1996; Wriston, 1992). Based mostly on economic globalization, this strand of the debate stresses the "denationalization" of national economics by the powerful transnational networks of production, trade, and finance.

As opposed to the champions of globalization, its skeptics (e.g., Hall, 1996; Hirst, 1997; Hirst & Thompson, 1996; Weiss, 1998) first make their argument that globalization is not new by drawing on statistical findings on world trade and on the level of economic interdependence in the nineteenth century. They imply that state capacity survived those periods and was perhaps even strengthened. They see intensification of interconnectedness as heightened levels of internationalization, which again emphasizes the key role of national capacities. This line of argument essentially rejects the popular under-

| | Pattern of Power | Resulting State Power Agenda | State Type |
|---|---|---|---|
| State-Centric world/security dilemmas | Power maximization centralization | Securitization | Security-oriented nation-state |
| Modernizing world | Turbulent balancing of the two | Conflictive power reconfiguration | Torn state |
| Multicentric world globalization | Power diffusion/decentralization | Desecuritization | Western/globalized |

FIGURE 6.1. A Taxonomy of State Power Configurations in the Modernizing World

standing that the power of national governments is being undermined in the current era by economic internationalization and global interconnectedness (Krasner, 1993; 1995).

## The Transformationalists

In between the total erosionist and statist arguments lies the transformationalist strand of thought regarding the fate of state capacity when confronted with globalization. The transformationalist approach is by nature closer to that of the hyperglobalizers than the rejectionists since it subscribes to the starting conviction that in the new epoch globalization is a central driving force behind the rapid social, political, and economic changes that are reshaping states, societies, and the world order (Giddens, 1990). According to this group of scholars, globalization dynamics may not be new, but they are certainly existing at unprecedented levels, and are creating a world of affairs in which no clear distinction exists between international and domestic lines to which every actor in world affairs feels the need to adopt and adjust (Cammilleri & Falk, 1992; Rosenau, 1990; Ruggie, 1993; Sassen, 1996).

While the direction of the globalization impact is not fixed within the transformationalist approach (Mann, 1997) and, therefore it does not include claims about future trajectories of globalization and its impact, these scholars' core emphasis is that globalization is a powerful transformative force that introduces a "massive shake-out" for the subjects—including the states.

The transformationalists' main argument regarding state capacity is that contemporary globalization is reconstituting and reengineering the nature and configurations of national governments. This argument does not claim that the territorial frontiers have no political or military significance, but rather it accepts that these issues have become increasingly challenged in an era of intensified globalization. The major basis for this conviction is that the world is not just state-centric or only state governed. Rather, as authority becomes diffused among public and private agencies at the local, national, regional, and global levels, nation-states are not the principal form of authority in the world (Rosenau, 1997).

States and national governments, being subject to these pressures, devise strategies to adapt to the new conditions. Distinctive strategies lead to different forms of states—from the neoliberal minimal state to varying types of developmental states to the "catalytic" state, in which the government is a facilitator of coordinated and collective action. What is proposed here, therefore, is that states adapt and transform to become more activist in determining their destinies (Rosenau, 1997).

There are several arguments why the transformationalist approach is the most appropriate to explain the dynamics of current world affairs. First, the hyperglobalist argument that a perfectly competitive global economy is emerging (or has already emerged) is an unlikely assumption since we have yet to achieve perfect national economies. In other words, a fully integrated global market with a minimized, if not completely diminished role for states, does not represent the true nature of the new epoch.

The rejectionist approach also has shortcomings. The empirical evidence on which this approach relies can easily be interpreted differently. For example, even if the trade/GDP ratios in the 1890s were higher than the ones in the 1990s, this reveals little about the social and political transformations to which this trade led. To draw an analogy, Chinese speakers may constitute a larger number worldwide than English speakers, but this does not make Chinese a global language (Held & McGrew, 1993). It is clear that the expanding liberal economy is also attached to the expansion of liberal democracy, which implies that the qualitative implications of these transformations must be studied in order to understand the phenomenon better.

As opposed to these two approaches, the transformationalist understanding does not see any fixed future in the globalization debate. There is neither a perfect global economy nor state-system dominated global changes. Moreover, contrary to the hyperglobalists and rejectionists, the transformationalists do not see globalization as a singular process (economic or cultural) or as a linear movement to a known destiny. The dynamics of globalization may include progress as well as retreat and reversals, and they can happen in very different ways in all major areas of life, including political, military, environmental, or public policy. Most important, integration and fragmentation, convergence and divergence, can all occur simultaneously in a highly interconnected manner, so that states, in particular, will have to find their way in adapting not only to globalization but to "fragmegration."

In addition to the previous arguments, the diversity of state types and of capacity levels in current world affairs requires a flexible approach, one that emphasizes the differentiated processes that are also influenced by other realities of life, such as security. The transformationalist approach is particularly suited for a study that is concerned with states of the modernizing world since the states and national capacities in this realm seem to be the most in transformation and also the most entrapped between the new world and the traditional one. The vast spectrum of the degree of development in these states is also an indication of transformation and of being subject to fragmegration.

Has the transformationalist approach achieved all that it could to explain the transformation of the state within fragmegration/globalization? The answer, quite simply, is no. Perhaps because they have been occupied within the debate by establishing their strand of the argument, but most scholars have tried to establish the approach in their work rather than to operationalize it. We are left still not knowing how the transformation actually occurs. We now know that there are different types of states—for example, neoliberal or developmental—we now know even that we can label different nation-states as security states, sovereign states, or democratic states, which are most of the time intertwined and overlapped (Clark, 1999). What we do not know is how these different characteristics of state identity and capacity coexist or compete and, most important, how they transform from one to the other. This leads to the core inquiry of this chapter: the dynamics of the transformation of the state capacity and identity at the domestic level.

What, then, are these important transnational phenomena that are subjecting state power to both integration and fragmentation and therefore imposing a need to transform its structure in order to better adapt? In the current age and for most modernizing world states, these phenomena are political globalization's reforming impact and the resilient forces of traditional security dilemmas. These two elements are particularly crucial to analyze since their ultimate impact is about national power—whether they are forcing it to diffuse or to maximize, to decentralize or centralize. Once the national power configurations and the nature of a state have been changed, one can then truly talk about a transformation of state identity and capacity and of global transformation.

## The Modernizing World

The so-called modernizing world is considered here as largely synonymous with the democratizing world since political globalization (i.e., pressure for democratization and liberalization) is one of the starting points for my arguments. The idea of a "democratizing world" stems from the postulation that the world political system can be divided into two or more spheres in which the rules of the game as well as the types and natures of the actors may differ from each other. By making such categorizations, we not only can present a more accurate picture of reality but can also provide a more convenient base for intellectual exercise to describe, explain, and possibly predict the external and domestic dynamics within these spheres (for similar views, see Ayoob, 1995, and Buzan, 1998).

A further and equally important advantage of such a classification is to help tackle better the problem of broad but unjustified definitions of the developing world. Since the end of the Cold War, the Second World is considered to have disappeared. Its subsequent incorporation into the traditional Third World exacerbated the problem of definition by widening the already existing degree of variation and diversity.

One common concept in the classifications of world political systems is the type and nature of the unit actor: the state. The concept of the state warrants further elaboration since a state-based classification scheme is another starting point of this inquiry. Since democratization as a way of responding to political globalization is another variable, not only the type of the state but the degree of its political development is also important for this research. This means determining how the relationship between the state and the society is structured; in other words, how are "power" and "consent" mixed? This question is significant because this domestic characteristic, which was emphasized by Hobbes and Machiavelli, has a strong role in the interrelationships between unit level factors and global processes (William, 1996). This link is also important when categorizing world spheres according to the type of the states because the management of power without the exercise of force has become the true measure of states' political capacity (Jackman, 1996).

The assumption here is that modernizing world states are not fundamentally different from Western ones (since we at least know that they want to progress into a similar 'successful' structure—the common nation-state) rather, they are located at different stages of a developmental process (Buzan, 1991). The criteria, therefore, for the differentiation is the level of development toward modern statehood. In terms of this research, the measurement of these criteria could be seen as the degree of ability to balance the needs of effectiveness (power) and consent (legitimacy).

Within this measurement, one could conceive of the world political system as follows: in the first sphere, also known as the core, the state is powerful enough to exercise force to gain consent, but does not and can not, due to the level of accountability it is subject to from society. What we have is a state that is weak in terms of accountability to society, and a society strong enough to exercise considerable power over its state. This category is similar to what Buzan and Segal (1996, 1998) or Sørensen (this volume) label the postmodern state, which has a much more tolerant attitude toward cultural, economic, and political interaction, and define[s] a much narrower range of things as threats to national security. In the postmodern state 'civil society' has, in a sense, more influence than the government—fitting with the criterion of high degree of accountability of the state to society.

This categorization also resembles somewhat Holm and Sørensen's (1995) "operational sovereignty," which refers to limits on sovereignty that states choose to place on themselves. In other words, state control over institutional or issue domains that they are willing to give up or trade in return for greater influence at the system level. If a state is currently in a strong position or if it carefully uses its bargaining power, it may be able to influence decisions/changes/trends at the system level.

At the opposite end of the spectrum it is difficult to speak of any type of accountability due to the poorly developed political entities and incoherent (sociologically and politically) societies. In these units, the state is so premature that, even if it wanted, it would not be able to use force to gain consent. This is also due to the level of fragmentation in the society. What we have in this sphere is a weak state and fragmented society (Ayoob, 1995). This is similar to what Buzan calls a premodern state, or what Holm and Sørensen refer to as negative sovereignty. While such a state may aspire to becoming a modern state, it is prevented by the weakness at both the political and societal levels. With essentially no room for a wide sense of accountability, there is more of an anarchy than a hierarchy within the state. Some examples of such states are located primarily in Africa and Central Asia (e.g., Afghanistan, Tadjikistan, Somalia, Nigeria, Sudan, and Zaire; Buzan, 1998).

In between these two groups is the third type of state in which the balance between effectiveness and consent/legitimacy is still biased toward effectiveness/power. In other words, the state and the representative governments continue to enjoy strong prerogatives, either constitutionally or not, and are able to use force to gain the necessary consent from society—a strong state and weak/fragmented society in which the state and power-holders are not highly accountable to society. Although there is some accountability, it is between weak political figures—for example, the products of imperfect elections—and society. The state itself is not accountable in a number of domains.

This is similar to what Buzan labels a modern state, or Holm and Sørensen categorize as a positive sovereignty. Such a state desires to become a postmodern one, but has not yet been able to overcome the improper accountability problem. According to Buzan, the major characteristics of this type of state is the "strong government control over society" (1998: 221). He adds that these modern states typically define a wide range of military, political, economic, and cultural factors as threats to national security. The aspirations of these states are not only to become postmodern states but also, and more important, to become great powers, or at least regional hegemons. Some examples he cites are Iran, Iraq, Russia, China, India, Turkey, and the two Koreas. These status-related intentions, combined with other unit and system-level sources, increase a high degree of vulnerability and pressure for the unit actors and their policies. Basically, in the regions in which these states are located, and the international relations in which they take part, classical realist rules remain valid since armed conflicts are still applicable as policy options.

## DYNAMICS OF THE TRANSFORMATION

The nature of power in security-oriented nation-states has been based on the idea of power maximization through power centralization. State security bureaucracies grew ever larger during the centralization process, primarily at the expense of a societal role or input. The primacy of state interests and national security reached such a level in some cases that these states can be argued to have become in fact giant security apparatuses, which possessed nations and societies. Thus, a model of a strong state and correspondingly weak society emerged. Global democratization and liberalization waves have targeted this particular state/society relationship by promoting, if not provoking, more societal input in the national governance. Nevertheless, the primacy of national security and the consequent steady securitization of the public agenda by these security apparatuses have been trying to resist against these powerful global liberalizing dynamics.

Due in part to its own internal inefficiencies and as well to the increasingly irresistible attractiveness of global liberalization dynamics, the lowering of the perceived levels of international anarchy and its accompanying vulnerability put the strong state/suppressed society structure to a serious test. Securitization of the public agenda has become much more difficult in these governance structures.

As long as securitization of the public agenda and the consequent allocation of material and psychological national resources remained relatively unquestioned, strong states were able to keep the society and its potential hazards under control. The primacy of national security and the exaggerated characterization of vaguely defined internal and external enemies and threats rendered the fragmented societal structure and its potential demands less relevant and urgent. Therefore, a strong state-fragmented society relationship was able to endure.

One of the major problems of the seeming resistance of the strong state-fragmented society model was that the fragmented nature of the society and its potential demands were only curtailed, but did not necessarily transform in a manner the state elite would like to portray to the outside world or even to their own domestic public opinion. The state elite, and in particular the giant security apparatuses, knew of the potential societal threats, and calculated for them as a part of the larger security dilemmas they perceived for their states. These considerations, however, viewed these domestic vulnerabilities as potential weak points that might be manipulated by others during the anarchic geopolitical atmosphere between nation-states. Such an understanding provided not only additional bases for the primacy of national security over other domestic public agendas, but also further provoked power centralization at the national level in order to weaken those fragmented societal elements deemed threatening. Most states with such governance structures appeared on the surface as relatively stable nation-states who were prepared to play by the rules of the realist anarchic world. In these states, certain types of gradual and carefully supervised modernization projects were implemented, also in an effort to minimize outside impact and thereby remaining national and protectionist.

In this overall picture, the strong state (centralized power) was the best possible response not only to handle external threats and security dilemmas, but also to cope with potential problems stemming from the fragmented nature of the societies. Relentless securitization was the order of the day.

## SECURITY VERSUS LIBERALIZATION

The emergence of the multicentric world, the significant rise in global liberalization (hereafter, political globalization) forces, and most important, the end of the Cold War and the impact this had on reducing the perception of external threats, have led to an environment in which, for many of the modernizing world states, the primary security agendas of the previous world order have become less able to function as determining instruments of public life. First, a general need for some kind of change—most often toward a more democratic form of state/society relations—now appears inevitable and unavoidable. Second, the capacity of security apparatuses to use external threat calculations for domestic securitization has shrunk. Large, strong security apparatuses no longer seem to have a definitive mission, and, moreover, societal interpretations of Western liberal democracies do not look favorably on large roles for states and security apparatuses. The strong state, therefore, is feeling not only systematic pressure from the external and internal environment to downsize and share some of its power or halt some of its functions, but is also facing a society that is more actively demanding a share from the centralized power structure. The weakening process of the strong centralized state has been put into action. Fragmented societal elements can no longer be considered merely potential challenges to national security; these potential threats are already politicized and empowered by economic globalization and are beginning to corner the state power structure.

What does a centralized state structure do to respond to such power demands? One can anticipate first an immediate reflexive move by elites to try

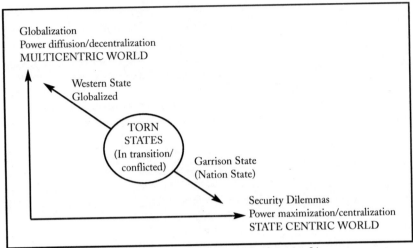

FIGURE 6.2. Locating the Torn States Along the Power Configuration Line

and hold on to their already established prerogatives in the name of stability and the survival of the state. Although this point is important since it can freeze or delay the budding power struggle for an uncertain period, it can ultimately be overcome when the sitting elites or administrators are replaced. Thus, some form of inevitable transformation will occur.

There is more to the story, however, than just power-holding elites resisting domestic power reconfiguration. Though designed to in fact overreact to security issues, the existing state structure now must find a way to, at minimum, preserve its centralized/maximized power structure in order to cope with the combined remaining amount of perceived external threats and the resurfacing of formerly suppressed domestic threats, such as power demands and potentially even secessionist efforts of segments of their fragmented societies.

Ideally, a centralized domestic governance structure should adapt to a decentralized power structure, perhaps even taking on a managerial or supervisory role in the transition process. However, most developing world state security apparatuses do not know how to adapt due to their inherent nature of overreacting to frightening situations of instability. Rather than an ideal response of decentralizing and downsizing while simultaneously maximizing its effectiveness for meeting new security challenges, the strong state structure reacts in its traditional manner of trying to even further maximize and centralize the power configuration at the national level. It is difficult to find an example of an old-world state structure (i.e., garrison states or a variant thereof) with the potential for such a rapid adaptation and transformation process. This is especially true because this new threat demands an immediate securing of the conflictive transformation process to avoid dangerous domestic instability.

There is not sufficient time, therefore, for the nation-state as a whole to produce a new, sophisticated functioning power structure to meet this new challenge.

Thus, security versus liberalization becomes the primary impasse faced by the national governance structure. The state is pressured by power diffusion dynamics that cannot be dismissed, yet there remains the need to preserve if not maximize its power at a time of (over)perceived insecurities. The position of such torn states is expressed in Figure 6.2, which is, in a sense, a dynamic representation of the middle row of the taxonomy in Figure 6.1. Can the necessary transformation for these states occur in a peaceful manner? In the course of such a transformation over issues of power, and in the absence of an overarching agency to manage this tumultuous process, the answer seems to be no. The dynamics of this new security dilemma will be even more acute in those countries in which societal fragmentation levels need significant time to develop cohesive national understandings and structures.

## HYPOTHESIZING ON TORN STATE TRANSFORMATIONS

### Bifurcation of the National Agenda

The taxonomy and discussion in this chapter suggest certain outcomes that we might expect of such a torn state structure, both at the macro and micro levels, and which can now be used to project certain implications. If power maximization leads to an agenda of securitization, and power diffusion leads to one of desecuritization, then the existence of both forces could lead to a bifurcation of the national agenda into two parts—one belonging to a relatively closed realm that might be labeled as hard politics and include issues such as state unity, sovereignty, geopolitical concerns, foreign policy, and domestic and external security issues. This realm would presumably be controlled by conservative security elite/bureaucrats, and nationalists among the public officials. The second half of the agenda, belonging to a relatively more open realm, might be labeled soft politics, and may include issues such as economic and political liberalization, and domestic links to global elements such as civil society and human rights groups. This realm would likely be run by, for example, political parties, the liberal elite, intellectuals, and the newly emerging, globally linked NGOs.

### Duality in Governance

A bifurcation of the national agenda, depending on the context, that is, the level and length of exposure to either or both of the external pressures, the particular qualities of the leadership, or the possible existence and strength of coalitions, may lead over time to a dual institutionalization of the two political realms. Since the powerful security-minded elite cannot ignore the political globalization impact due to international legitimacy needs and other factors such as IMF financial aid and often embedded modernization drives from within, they can be expected to allow the soft politics realm of civilian governments and political parties to expand—as long as it does not intervene in the hard politics realm. In the extreme case this might be anticipated to lead to a duality in the domestic governance structure that could be deconstructed as an inner state and an apparent state. While the former would remain to respond to the state-centric world demands, the latter would exist to meet increasing globalization pressures.

## Increasing State/Society Conflict and Resulting Chronic Governance Crises

One might anticipate certain implications of such a state structure on the level of stability at both the domestic and regional levels. With power relocation and resistance to it remaining the main ingredient of the domestic level agenda, repression and counterinsurgencies would be expected to occur, leading to bumpy transitions to democracy and conflictual domestic settings.

One of globalization's indirect pressures on the modernizing state comes about with the empowering of society in the sense that deepening political globalization can be considered as greater democratization and thus more input from society. Given that in the modernizing countries relevant to this discussion, the state is the existing power center, any empowerment of some other element logically means a reduction or compromising of the state's power—a situation bound to lead to conflict between the two. This confrontational positioning of the state and the societal masses may mean a base for indefinite domestic instability and authority crises in political affairs.

## Reemphasizing the Primacy of Internal Threats

An additional projection that can emerge from this research is evidence reemphasizing the primacy of internal security over external security in parts of the modernizing world. This does not mean that these countries are no longer concerned with external security threats. It also does not deny that internal threats are still partly of concern due to their external connections, that is, such threats cause instability and weakness that can be taken advantage of by external rivals and thereby weaken the country within the regional balance of power. However, the research does suggest that internal threat perceptions themselves are becoming more salient in provoking power centralization needs. In other words, the safety of the inevitable transformation is viewed as being most vulnerable to domestic challenges. As such, survival at home can be seen as almost a prerequisite even for just being an actor in the international system, let alone for playing power politics at the international level.

## The New Security Dilemma

Research projects that transformation from more centralized to more diffused state structures is inevitable in the new era. If it is inevitable, it must therefore be managed. Maintaining the stability of this unavoidable transformation when there is a simultaneous combining of power centralization and power diffusion demands can be considered as the source for a new security dilemma facing the state types under discussion in this chapter. In the process of managing this transformation, states must find a balance between the two pressures in which, first, neither influence is excluded to a point that it jeopardizes the stable transformation, and, second, the balance is maintained at a level at which the dynamism of the progress continues.

Once the powerful elite feels that the process of desecuritization has the potential of allowing instability to rise, the basic instinct remains to centralize power in order to most efficiently face these possible challenges. These elite's past practices and experiences of anarchical world understandings, along with existing 'realities' of geopolitical calculations, further facilitate power centralization instincts. If these instincts are materialized, however, the result is bound to clash with the power diffusion requirements of the current era. This clash, therefore, constitutes the new security dilemma with which modernizing world states must cope.

Since the power-holding elite in these states traditionally know how to manage power centralization, the emphasis in dealing with this transformation is understandably on how to manage the power decentralization/diffusion that the new epoch requires. Since power centralization in these countries was traditionally carried out through a securitization process—relying on security's primary role in public life—decentralization can generally be equated with desecuritization. The challenge becomes one of managing and stabilizing the desecuritization process without damaging the traditional mechanisms of power centralization and thus one's sense of national security in a particular country's context.

## Conclusion

The preceding theoretical analysis and implications suggest that the dualistic (state-centric and multicentric) structure of the international system generates certain inevitable transformations between the major forces of these world perspectives. It also suggests that these transformations lead to a type of torn governance structure at the national level. Such potentially unstable yet inevitable transformative processes appear as the major source for the new security dilemmas that these modernizing states face, due to the contradictory instincts of power centralization and power diffusion.

Providing concrete evidence of such turbulent transformations and dualities out of real-life experiences was beyond the scope of this chapter. Future case studies must therefore be conducted to explore in depth the internal nature of this new security dilemma and resulting institutional responses to it. Several countries appear to be facing this dilemma of conflicting globalization and security pressures, such as Russia, China, Turkey, and Iran. To accomplish this task effectively, and reveal the secrecies of the black box of the state in transformation, any research of this type must cross disciplinary boundaries between, at minimum, international and comparative politics. At a time when physical borders are reputedly becoming more transient, conceptual boundaries must be at least equally so for a fair reflection of reality.

## NOTES

1. These two forces and their corresponding pressures of fragmentation and integration have been suggested to express the transformative dynamics of a new era in world politics—one labeled fragmegration (Rosenau, 1997). This chapter focuses on pressures of globalization since they promote the potential for power diffusion and relocation. Localization pressures such as ethnic or nationalist unrest, on the other hand, may actually increase a state's security relevance, and not disturb the accordingly designed state power structure.

2. While various forms of globalization have been identified (Held et al., 1999), this research refers primarily to globalization in its political form. Political globalization is understood here as a consensus on the combined ideas of economic liberalism and liberal democracy and the pressure this creates on states for further democratization and liberalization, which in turn necessitate a diffusion of national power. Focusing on this aspect of globalization is crucial because it is the liberalization impact of political globalization in particular that leads to a reconfiguration of state power structures. Power maximization and centralization may, at least initially, coexist with, for example, economic globalization and liberalization—as evidenced by existing nondemocratic regimes with relatively liberal economies—but is incompatible with political globalization and liberalization pressure. Security dilemmas in the modernizing world are seen as based not only on external vulnerabilities, but also on domestic ones such as regime insecurity issues. This means that traditional states of the modernizing world have to protect themselves from both an external anarchy and an increasing internal one.

3. The modernizing world of Figure 6.1 refers here to those states of the developing world that have long-standing strong state traditions, a history of aspiring to modernize, and are highly concerned with traditional security dilemmas. Examples of such states can be as diverse as China, Russia, Turkey, Pakistan, India, Iran, to name a few. The definition is discussed in more detail in the next section.

# Part III

---

## Regional Reflections

# 7

# Global Challenges to Russia's National Security

## Any Chance for Resisting/Bandwagoning/ Adapting/Contributing to an Emerging World Order?

Alexander Sergounin

The term "globalization" has been a popular word among Russian politicians, academics, and journalists since the early 1990s. Even among academics, however, globalization remains a rather vague notion. Depending on their theoretical underpinnings or research objectives, Russian analysts offer quite different interpretations of this phenomenon. Following a brief overview of various prominent understandings, this chapter examines recent Russian national security doctrines to show how globalization has affected Russian security discourse. The chapter concludes with a more detailed look at understandings of globalization and security according to various paradigms of thought within Russian International Relations scholarship.

Some Russian authors tend to equate globalization with cosmopolitism (Timofeev, 1999). The term "kosmopolites" stood even in ancient Greece for "citizens of the world," individuals who considered the whole of humankind as more important than their own state or native land. Similar globalist ideas can be traced in the writings of Hugo Grotius and Immanuel Kant. The Marxist paradigm, with its emphasis on a world system and mode of production, the cosmopolitan nature of capitalism and class struggle, and universal historical laws, also offered a globalist vision of international relations. Russian proponents of this definition of globalization note that, in the current world, perhaps the most important manifestation of cosmopolitanism is the increasing acceptance of and concern for freedoms and individual rights irrespective of state or national boundaries. However, this argument provokes heated debates, since states can invoke their claim to domestic jurisdiction and block outside interference with the freedoms and rights of their own citizens.

Other Russian scholars understand globalization as a quantitative shift of several autonomous national economies toward a global marketplace for production, distribution, and technology (Neklessa, 1998). Similarly, globalization in terms of open-border relations has been associated with liberalization, while in terms of transborder and cross-border relations it connotes internationalization (Shishkov, 2001). For some authors, globalization may also be consonant with a number of other phenomena, such as the spread of liberal democracy, developments in the domain of information technology, and the worldwide impact of mass media. In describing these phenomena, such notions as "delocalization" and "planetarization" have been used (Makarychev, 2002; Molchanov, 1999).

The mainstream of Russian political thought, however, describes globalization as a worldwide spread of common patterns of production, technology, management, social structures, political organization, culture, and values—a process that leads to the rise of supranational institutions and, ultimately, a single society (Makarychev & Sergounin, 2000: 398).

## RUSSIAN SECURITY THINKING

### Conceptualizations and Threat Perceptions

Russian political and academic communities were caught off guard by globalization, even though this process did not occur overnight. It has taken much of the last decade to see a redefinition of national security concepts and a more or less thorough academic analysis of relevant issues. Several fundamental changes in Russian security thinking, however, have been brought about by the worldwide process of globalization.

First, in contrast with traditional security thinking that has emphasized 'narrow' or military security, Moscow has begun to accept a broader concept of security. According to the 1992 Russian Law on Security, not only military but also economic, social, information, and ecological aspects of security were given importance. Instead of a state-oriented definition of security, the new law singled out three levels of security: "security is freedom from internal and external threats to vital interests of the individual, society and state" (Yeltsin, 1992: 5).

Second, in addition to a new definition of security, there has been a growing understanding among Russian strategy planners that in the age of globalization the focus of national and world politics is gradually shifting from the hard (military) to soft (non-military) security domain. This understanding presents a dramatic change from Russia's traditional security policy, especially that of the Cold War period. The Soviet Union has always placed tremendous emphasis on the development of full-fledged armed forces (both nuclear and conventional) and the Russian military traditionally had a major say in decision making. In the post–Cold War era, hard security issues have lost much of their former importance and a completely new agenda looms ahead. Within this new desecuritized agenda, 'normal', nonsecurity issues have come to the focus of global cooperation. 'Grand' policy has retreated to the shadows and 'low politics' (economy, trade, societal issues, ecology, border infrastructure, migration, etc.) increasingly dominate the scene.

Consequently, the predominance of the 'soft' security agenda has led to a questioning of the role and capabilities of old actors (NATO, OSCE, etc.) in dealing with a new set of challenges.[1] It seems that newly created institutions, such as the Council of the Baltic Sea States (CBSS), the Barents-Euro-Arctic Council (BEAC), and the Arctic Council (AC), are often designed more to cope with new problems and actors than traditional ones. It has taken considerable time for Russian foreign and security policies to begin to accommodate such new realities.

Third, globalization has challenged Russia's traditional concept of national sovereignty and, subsequently, related security issues. Moscow's traditional position was that all Russian regions were integral and equal parts of the Russian Federation. Initially, Moscow feared that international collaborative projects could strengthen disparities and evoke an unhealthy competition between Russian regions. Russia insisted that it was able to solve its regional problems on its own, even in the most difficult cases, such as Kaliningrad or the Far East. With time, Moscow has come increasingly to the understanding that international actors are not set on challenging Russian territorial integrity and that by engaging Russia's border regions in cross-border and transregional cooperation, they aim at creating zones of stability and economic prosperity rather than breaking Russia apart. Gradually, Moscow's preferences have shifted from semi-isolationist, unilateral options to cooperative models and multilateral solutions (particularly demonstrated in the cases of Kaliningrad and Karelia).

Finally, there has been a dramatic change in terms of threat perceptions. The new Russian national security doctrines of 1997 and 2000 assert that Russia faces no immediate danger of large-scale aggression, and that, because the country is beset with a myriad of debilitating domestic problems, the greatest threat to Russia's security is now an internal one.[2] For example, the national security doctrine of 1997 reported that: "An analysis of the threats to the national security of the Russian Federation shows that the main threats at present and in the foreseeable future will not be military, but predominantly internal in character and will focus on the internal political, economic, social, ecological, information and spiritual spheres" (Yeltsin, 1997: 4). This is a distinct departure from previous doctrines. For example, the draft of the military doctrine of 1992 and the military doctrine of 1993 were still based on the assumption that the main threat to Russia's security was posed by external factors such as regional conflicts, territorial claims or violations of rights of Russian-speaking minorities in the former Soviet republics (Ministry of Defense of the Russian Federation, 1992; Yeltsin, 1994).

The recent Russian security doctrines clearly suggest that today's relatively benign international climate affords Russia the opportunity to direct resources away from the defense sector and toward the rebuilding of the Russian economy. This shift is particularly evident in the 1997 document, which underscores: "the development of a qualitatively new pattern of relations with the leading world states and the political absence of the threat of a large-scale aggression against Russia, while it preserves its nuclear deterrent, makes it possible to redistribute the resources of the state and society to address priority internal problems" (Yeltsin, 1997: 4). In general, it places this rebuilding effort in the context of continued democratization and the strengthening of Russia's markets.

These national security documents focus highly on the dangers posed by Russia's economic woes, such as the substantial drop in production and investments; the destruction of scientific-technical potential; disarray in the financial and monetary systems; the shrinking of federal revenues; the growth of the national debt; Russia's overdependence on export of raw materials and import of equipment, consumer goods, and foodstuff; brain drain; and an uncontrolled flight of capital.

The documents also point to internal social, political, ethnic, and cultural tensions that threaten to undermine both the viability and the territorial integrity of the Russian state. Among these, social polarization, demographic problems (in particular, the reductions in birth rate, average life expectancy, and population), corruption, organized crime, drug trade, terrorism, virulent nationalism, separatism, deterioration of the health system, ecological catastrophes, and disintegration of the 'common spiritual space,' are singled out.

It should be noted that the August 1998 economic crisis undermined to some extent the popularity of liberal concepts (including a positive attitude toward globalization) by exposing Russia's vulnerability to the international economy and financial markets. Some specialists believe that the fundamental sources of the crisis were internal policy failures and economic weakness, but it was precipitated by the vulnerability of the ruble to speculative international financial markets (Wallander, 2000). Moreover, because Russia's economy began to recover in the aftermath of the decision to devalue the ruble and implement limited debt defaults, the crisis reinforced statist arguments that a less Western-dependent, more state-directed policy of economic reform could be Russia's path to stability and eventual prosperity. One of the lessons of the 1998 financial meltdown was that globalization may be a source of threat to Russia's economic security.

Alongside the major internal threats to Russia's security, the documents do also identify a number of dangers stemming from international dynamics.

The doctrines highlight the following sources of external threat: territorial claims; attempts of foreign countries to use Russia's domestic problems for weakening its international positions or challenging its territorial integrity; local conflicts and military buildup in the country's vicinity; mass migration from troubled CIS countries; proliferation of weapons of mass destruction; international terrorism and drug -trafficking, and growing activities by foreign intelligence services. In the 1997 document, these threats, however, are awarded less significance than internal ones.

Although the previous paragraphs point to numerous similarities between the 1997 and 2000 national security doctrines, certain crucial differences also exist between the two. The most important aspect of the 2000 doctrine is that, in addition to still noting internal threats, it begins to once again elevate the importance of and expand on the types of external threats to Russian security. The document no longer states that there are "no" external threats arising from deliberate actions or aggression; rather, it provides a substantial list of external threats, including the weakening of the OSCE and the United Nations and a weakening Russian political, economic, and military influence in the world. It also notes the consolidation of military-political blocs and alliances. In particular, concern is expressed about further eastward expansion of NATO and the possibility of foreign military bases or deployment of forces on Russian borders. The document goes on to mention threats such as the proliferation of weapons of mass destruction and the means of their delivery, the escalation of conflicts along borders with CIS members countries; and territorial claims against Russia (Putin, 2000: 4).

In several places, the 2000 national security document emphasizes that the natural tendency of international relations in the wake of the Cold War confrontation is toward the development of a multipolar world, in which relations are based on international law, and on finding a proper role for Russia. It argues that the United States and its allies are working against this tendency, and, under the guise of multilateralism, have sought to establish a unipolar world outside of international law. The document warns that NATO's shift in policy to accept the use of military force outside its alliance territory without U.N. Security Council approval is a major threat to world stability, and that changes such as these create the potential for a new era of arms races among the world's great powers. The document links the internal threat of terrorism and separatism (clearly with Chechnya in mind) to external threats, arguing that international terrorism involves efforts to undermine the sovereignty and territorial integrity of Russia, with the possibility of direct military aggression. However, in terms of dealing with such threats, the document calls for "international cooperation" (Putin, 2000: 4).

In general, the shifts in Russia's threat perceptions in the post–Cold War era could be assessed positively. At least three main advantages can be distinguished. First, they represent steps toward a more realistic estimation of

Russia's domestic and international problems. Second, given Russia's limited resources, these doctrines help in setting up a proper system of political priorities. Finally, they diminish earlier xenophobic tendencies in Russia's relations with the West and thus lay the foundations for more intense international cooperation.

## International and Regional Dualities

The era of globalization has cast doubts on the key principle of the Cold War international security architecture that international security is indivisible. Under the new circumstances, it has become possible to make a region or subregion more secure without creating a security regime for the whole world or continent (Sergounin, 2002). This change in thinking has challenged the role of the traditional security organizations (OSCE and NATO) as the major security providers. As far as European security is concerned, developments of the last decade or so have undermined the pillar of traditional Russian-European security policy that aimed at making the OSCE a main pan-European security institution. Hence, Russia has had to redefine its attitude toward various international security organizations.

The post–Cold War period has also brought a new pattern in the globalization/regionalization relationship. It has become quite commonplace to assert that globalization and regionalization are two sides of the same coin, and to create different words (e.g., glocalization, fragmegration) to denote this complex phenomenon. The entire world faces processes such as the erosion of the nation-state and national sovereignty, and a shift of power from the national level toward supranational and subnational institutions. Russia is a part of these global dynamics and cannot ignore the rules dictated by them. In particular, however, Russia is affected by regionalization in the Trans-Atlantic space (NATO enlargement), in Europe (EU enlargement, Baltic and Nordic subregional cooperation), in Eurasia (the CIS), and in the Asia Pacific region (APEC, ASEAN Regional Forum).

Initially, Moscow underestimated the role of regionalism/subregionalism/transregionalism in 'soft' security cooperation. Russia saw regional/subregional cooperation as either a low priority (compared to grand policy) or as a space for diplomatic maneuvering in the event of grand strategy failures. For this reason, Moscow was quite suspicious about the subregional nature of a number of subnational/international initiatives such as, for example, the EU's Northern Dimension. The federal government was afraid of strengthening separatist tendencies in a number of Russian regions (especially in Kaliningrad, Karelia, and the Russian Far East) as a result of their deep involvement in subregional cooperation. With time, however, Moscow has begun to realize that subregionalism can bring more positive than negative results and has started to think of the Russian border areas as pilot regions (for more on changes in Russian thinking on regionalism, see Sergounin, 1999). As part of emerging new strategies, Moscow has begun paying serious attention to joining appropriate regional and subregional institutions and organizations. For example, Russia concluded an agreement on partnership and cooperation with the EU (1994) and now takes part in various EU programs on cross- and transborder cooperation. Moscow also participates in the activities of such subregional organizations as the Council of the Baltic Sea States (CBSS), the Barents Euro-Arctic Council (BEAC), the Arctic Council, the ASEAN Regional Forum, APEC, and the Black Sea Economic Cooperation regime. At the same time, Moscow tries to exercise its role as an economic and political leader in the CIS.

## Internal Regionalization as Decentralization

Global dynamics have also influenced decentralization in Russia. This has occurred in various ways, such as: promoting regionalization along Russia's borders; economic cooperation of Russian border regions with powerful neighbors such as the EU, China, Japan, and South Korea; instigating ethno-territorial and religious conflicts; encouraging cultural cooperation between related ethnic groups in Russia and foreign countries; and making public the need to stop further degradation of the environment (particularly in the Russian North West) (Sergounin, 2001). Many foreign countries and international organizations prefer to deal with Russia's various regions rather than with Moscow. They regard cooperation with subnational units as both a means for bypassing Moscow bureaucracy and as a good route for solving many of Russia's problems. For example, the EU established a special Interreg program to promote cooperation between countries along Europe's border regions, including Russia. The TACIS program, another EU initiative, is oriented to stimulate cross-border cooperation and local government within Russia as well. Various Western foundations and organizations specializing on education and research support programs have also emphasized regional priorities. In the late 1990s, for example, the Nordic Council of Ministers and the British Council launched special fellowship programs for the Russian Northwest. In 1998, the Soros Foundation launched its "Mega" project, aimed at supporting and developing Russian peripheral universities. Despite territorial disputes with Russia and the lack of a peace treaty between the two countries, Japan also cooperates with Russian regions such as the Kurile Islands, Sakhalin, and the Maritime Province.

Russia's decentralization (or internal regionalization) is a contradictory process that both poses challenges to and provides benefits for a federative state. Russia's regionalization carries with it certain negative consequences that are perceived by Moscow as a source of threat to Russian national security. These threats are seen as stemming from further disintegration of the single economic, financial, and cultural space; degradation of the party system and the rise of interest group politics answering to parochial interests; regionalization and privatization of security services and armed forces; and the rise of separatism and secessionism, which could result in disintegration of the country (for more on these, see Sergounin, 1999).

The separatist tendencies in various parts of Russia are clearly the most unpleasant implication of regionalization for Moscow. Not only Chechnya but other national republics as well have demonstrated their secessionist sentiments from time to time. In the early 1990s, Bashkortostan and Tatarstan were suspected of being separatist-minded. There was even an idea to create an independent Idel-Ural republic consisting of the Muslim peoples of the Volga region. The dean of history at Kazan University argued in October 1993 that "the idea of the Idel-Ural has become a necessity now." Yet another academician, the Dean of Humanities at Ufa State Aviation and Technical University, admitted that "if the dictatorship of Moscow persists with its demands for a unitary state, centrifugal forces may triumph and a new federation may be formed in the region of Idel-Ural and in the North Caucasus." The Head of the Bashkir Cultural Society, Robert Sultanov, was also willing to agree in October 1993 that "if the Russian Federation disintegrated," Bashkortostan, along with Tatarstan, "would become the subjects of a new confederation, while retaining their independence" (Petersen, 1996: 137).

The Russian Far East, another troubled region, has often over the last decade discussed plans of independent development. For example, in 1994, Viktor Ishayev, head of the administration of the Khabarovsk Province, announced that the Russian government "has done all it could to sever the Far East from Russia." That same year, workers of the Khrustalny tin-extracting company, who had gone for several months without pay, wrote in a declaration: "The government and the president don't pay any attention to our troubles. We have concluded that they have given up on us. Therefore we must also give them up and form our own republic with an independent government. There is no other way to survive" (Matveyeva, 1994: 13).

In the 1990s, secessionist movements could be found in Karelia, Kaliningrad, and the North Caucasian republics as well. To date, however, Chechnya is the only actual breakaway republic. Other potential candidates for secession have not officially pressed for independence. Two factors have prevented separatist-minded politicians from making such a declaration: first, the understanding that independence would lead to further deepening of various crises rather than improvement; and, second, as the Chechen example has shown, Moscow does not rule out the use of military force to stop Russia's disintegration.

## Positive Aspects to Decentralization

While most analysts focus primarily on the "dark side" of Russia's regionalization, the process of regionalization can also be seen as bringing about a number
of positive changes. First and foremost, internal regionalization encourages
further democratization of the Russian administrative system. The regions
themselves, not Moscow, are now responsible for decision making in many
areas. This shift facilitates the solving of local problems because regional governments are more competent in this sphere than the federal center. The introduction of representative governments, a multiparty system, more or less
independent mass media, and free elections in the regions have drawn millions
of people into political life and have made democratic reforms irreversible.

Decentralization has helped to discredit the Soviet model of federalism.
Prior to the economic crisis of 1998, the idea of regionalism was mainly
understood as Moscow's policy toward the members of the Russian Federation as based on the redistribution of resources between regions via the federal budget and subsidies (so-called budgetary federalism). This "top-down"
model of state intervention in a region proved inefficient in light of the systemic crisis in Russia.

New understandings of regionalization, on the other hand, have paved the
way for new models of federalism in Russia. Contrary to the old top-down
model, a new interpretation of regionalism as a basic characteristic of civil society ("bottom-up" model) is gradually taking root in the country. Interestingly,
because of the crisis of 1998, many Russians discovered that civil society really
exists in the country (albeit in an embryonic form) and that it is much more
reliable than the state—which failed in its commitments and once again
deceived its citizens. The crisis stimulated individuals, groups, and organizations to begin forming a system of horizontal networks and connections—the
basis for civil society. Subregional, interregional, and transregional cooperation
can be considered part of this endeavor.

The division of labor within regions and cooperation between various
regions have helped many members of the Federation—particularly remote
and border regions—to survive the transition period. In 1992–1994, the Russian Far East managed to cope with shortages of food and other consumer
goods thanks to barter trade with China (Portyakov, 1996: 80). In the fall of
1998, Poland and Lithuania provided Kaliningrad with humanitarian assistance, while at the same time Japan launched a similar program on the Kuriles.

Decentralization of power in Russia has also boosted certain regions' foreign relations and made them true international actors. For example, in
1991–1995, the Russian regions signed more than 300 agreements on trade,
economic, and humanitarian cooperation with foreign countries (Matvienko,
1996: 91–92). Agreements such as these help to undermine Moscow's

monopoly on foreign relations and reorients diplomacy from grand policy issues toward the pressing needs of the Russian periphery. Moscow can no longer make decisions concerning the international status of the regions without at least consulting with them first. For example, with assistance from the Russian Foreign Ministry, the local governments of Kaliningrad, Karelia, and St. Petersburg actively participated in negotiating and concluding a number of agreements on cross-border and transregional cooperation with EU member states and some Baltic and Nordic countries. Interestingly, these developments have, in turn, resulted in fundamental institutional changes. The Russian Foreign Ministry has established a special unit on interregional affairs, along with offices in those regions engaged in intensive international economic and cultural cooperation.

Yet another positive side to regionalization has been how it has in some cases served as an instrument for problem solving with respect to Russia's relations with neighboring countries. For example, Kaliningrad's close cooperation with Lithuania, Poland, and Germany helped prevent the raising of territorial claims on their part, and dampened their concerns over excessive militarization of the region. Cooperation between Finland and Karelia also eased Finnish–Russian tensions on the Karelia issue, while cross-border cooperation between the Kuriles, Sakhalin, and Japan led to a quiet Russia–Japan dialogue over the disputed territory. These examples show how regionalization can help open Russia to international cooperation and facilitate its participation in a worldwide process of intensive transregional cooperation. In this regard, regionalization also has a very important integrative function: it prevents Russia's marginalization or international isolation, and helps to bridge different civilizations.

## GLOBALIZATION AND SECURITY IN RUSSIAN POLITICAL DISCOURSE

Globalization as a universal phenomenon can be viewed along the lines of the paradigm debate in post-Communist Russian International Relations (IR). Three alternative perspectives of international relations—*state-centric* (realist), *multicentric* (idealist/liberal/pluralist), and *global-centric* (structuralist/radical) (categorization devised by James Rosenau, 1982: 1–7) exist in Russia, and each school has developed its own vision of globalization processes.

### State-centric Realists

Currently, realism is the dominant paradigm in Russia. This group of theorists regards states as the key unit of analysis. Russian realists on the whole are rather skeptical about globalization and believe that its implications for international relations are overestimated. Power politics, balance of power, and national interests are still their most valued theoretical categories. These scholars view globalization mostly as the militarization of the international system and the emergence of patterns of political control and domination that extend beyond borders (such as hegemonic control or spheres of influence), but they reject the idea that globalization is accompanied by a deepening sense of community (Klyuchnik, 2002; Sekatskiy, 2002).

The Russian realists are also skeptical about global governance as a product of globalization. They prefer to speak of world power distribution, world leadership, concert of powers, alliances, coalitions, and so on. In their opinion, multilateral institutions are little more than vehicles for powerful states to establish rules and norms of action that are in their interest. Participation in an international institution does not mitigate the anarchic nature of world politics—states remain interested in survival at the very least, and in pursuing power at the most. Even those neorealists who understand in principle the need for managing global problems believe that such governance is possible only when it is exercised by a superpower or by a coalition of the most powerful states (Klyuchnik, 2002; Kozhinov, 2001).

It is also argued that the term "globalization" frequently is used to define something fairly similar to a process of worldwide colonization. In some cases they refer to particular and widespread economic strategies that aim to draw the greatest immediate gain, often extremely standardizing economies and cultures in the various countries in the world (Globalizatsiya—eto kolonizatsia?, 2002; Klyuchnik, 2002; Kozhinov, 2001).

Since Russia is no longer able to play the role of a superpower (see Buzan, this volume) the United States is the only single country that is able to exercise global governance. This fact is unacceptable to Russian realists, who tend to interpret globalization as an Americanization of the world. Russian realists view globalization and global governance as a manifestation of an eternal geopolitical rivalry between Russia and the West. In contrast with the past, however, the West now prefers economic rather than military instruments for putting pressure on Russia (Kozhinov, 2001). The aim of Western policies is seen as securing Russia's status as the West's "younger partner" and as a source of cheap labor and natural resources. Some radical versions of realism believe that the final goal of the West is to divide Russia and turn it into a sort of American "colony" (or colonies) (Khlopetski, 2000: 111).

Russian realists' greatest fear about globalization is that countries might be unable in the future to control their development. In this sense, globalization refers to the denationalization of politics, markets, and law (Klyuchnik, 2002). Fear of globalization is also used by realists and conservative politicians in Russia as an argument for government aid to Russian national industries. The argument's claim is that transnational/global corporations erode the ability of nation states to regulate their own economies.

In seeking a response to the global challenges, these realists suggest that the Russian political leadership should be more assertive in ensuring Russia's national security and resist any encroachments on Russia's national interests (Klyuchnik, 2002; Zadokhin, 2001). They articulate several alternatives to global leadership in the field of international security, including greater reliance on regional security organizations and the creation of spheres of influence or regional balance-of-power arrangements. Particularly, they pay special attention to bilateral and multilateral security arrangements such as the Tashkent collective security system (between CIS countries), the Russia–China strategic partnership, the Shanghai organization, Russia–India security cooperation, and the military alliance with Belarus (Klyuchnik, 2002). They warn Russian leaders that security arrangements with the United States and NATO should be taken with a grain of salt, should strictly correspond to Russian national interests, and should be short term and nonbinding.

The most pessimistic version of Russian realism suggests that if Russia is unable to resist the challenges of globalization, it should consider joining the world leader(s) (the United States or the EU or China) and becoming its (their) younger partner. Such bandwagoning, the argument continues, should be made on certain conditions that, in turn, should be negotiated and fixed in a series of international agreements (Klyuchnik, 2002; Kozhinov, 2001). The realists recommend dealing mainly with states (e.g. the United States, Germany, China) rather than with multilateral institutions (including NATO) because in the context of bilateral cooperation Russia could gain from them more than it could from international organizations. To support this recommendation they point to such examples as the quite successful U.S.–Russia cooperation on fighting international terrorism, nonproliferation, the new strategic arms control regime (even after having scrapped the ABM treaty), and Russia–China strategic cooperation.

## Multi-centric Idealists

For the multicentric Russian theorists, nonstate actors are seen as important entities in international relations, and the state is not a unitary, and often not even a rational, actor. This group of theorists view multilateral institutions, along with the states, as crucial actors in world politics. Moreover, Russian idealists believe that international institutions and law can be safeguards against anarchy in international relations and bring order and justice to world politics.

Russian liberalism emphasizes globalization trends in the world economy, which strengthen the trend toward global management of economic and political developments and generally increase the relevance of international legal frameworks, thus reducing global anarchy. Although the idealist/liberal perspective does not completely dismiss the trend toward a multipolar world, it does generally argue that future development of the international system is no longer predominantly determined by the shape and outcome of rivalries among the major centers of economic and military power, but increasingly by the dynamics of their common development and interdependence (Bazhanov, 2002; Khrustalev, 1992; Zagorski et al., 1992). The Russian liberals argue that the geopolitical drive for control over territories does not matter anymore, and suggest that it should be replaced by geoeconomic thinking (Zagorski, 1995: 5–8).

Russian liberals also tend to view globalization and global governance as both an objective process that is impossible to resist and, at the same time, an opportunity for Russia (Bazhanov, 2002; Znachkov, 2001). They believe that globalization is a chance for Russia to join with the most developed parts of the world and in doing so to reform its economy and sociopolitical systems with the help of the international community.

According to the liberals, global governance comprises the complex and highly varied ways in which national or international actors reach understandings and solutions of all problems they need to resolve collectively to achieve their goals. Specifically, this school singles out six main aspects of global governance (Videman, 2002; Zimin, 2002). First, the global governance architecture is seen as polycentric. There is no a single decision-making center or world government. Global governance is an end result of a collective decision-making process based on mutual trust and shared sovereignty. Second, global governance is conducted both by governmental and nongovernmental actors (NGOs, transnational corporations, international pressure groups, etc.). Governments play a central role in global governance, but the significance of nongovernmental actors is steadily growing. Third, global governance is grounded on public–private partnerships and cooperation because resources for dealing with global problems are scarce and scattered among different actors (both public and private). In this sense, global governance is seen as the pooling of resources and expertise with the aim of solving problems of common concerns. Fourth, global governance arises where states realize the need for collective action and give up (at least partially) their national sovereignty to address global problems. Fifth, global governance implies not only multilateral cooperative efforts but also multilevel ones. Liberals emphasize that global governance is a part of multilevel governance (that includes, regional, national, and subnational levels), which is necessary in a world of sovereign states. Finally, global governance results in a fundamental transformation of world politics, including an institutional change. It should be noted, however, that this change takes the form of a horizontal and vertical networking rather than hierarchical and formal institutions.

Despite the general positive attitude to globalization, Russian liberals do not ignore the challenges that it is seen as posing to Russia and other countries. Among these challenges of globalization, the foremost one is that of ensuring that globalization's benefits extend to all countries (Kuzminov & Yakovlev, 2000; Znachkov, 2001). Also present is the fear that the growth brought about by globalization is inherently and dangerously destabilizing (Znachkov, 2001). There is as well the concern that increased global competition is driving down wages and siphoning off jobs. Russia is especially vulnerable to these developments because its economy is very weak (Bazhanov, 2002). For example, powerful industrial (automobile, metallurgical, machine-building, and electronic companies) and agrarian lobbies put pressure on the Russian government to take a firm position on negotiations with the United States and EU on conditions of Russia's joining the WTO (Sas, 2002: 3).

Turning to problems of globalization at particular levels, there is the global level problem of how to harmonize approaches and coordinate the activities of numerous international actors to make global governance more efficient. At the subnational level, globalization has in some cases inspired separatist tendencies, leading to a number of dangerous conflicts between regional and central authorities. For example, some Russian observers are afraid that Russian regions deeply involved in cross- and transborder cooperation (e.g., Karelia, Kaliningrad, and the Russian Far East) may secede from the rest of the country and thus undermine the unity of the Russian Federation. The Russian liberals differ on this point with Russian realists, in that they do not tend to attribute this possibility to any Western conspiracy. They instead blame the Russian federal government for being unable to provide conditions for a sustainable development of all Russian regions.

In terms of globalization's implications at the state level, the results are also contradictory. Many governments (including Russia's) continue to violate human rights regardless of the processes of globalization. Even in democratic countries, governments are unable to encourage people to actively participate in policymaking or provide them with some voice in global politics. The nation-state does not offer the means to secure the popular will in relation to such issues as global capital, global ecological problems, or arms control.

As a final note, Russian liberals have argued that global governance agencies are also far from the democratic ideal. Most of these agencies make decisions behind closed doors and do not consult citizens about their day-to-day work (Znachkov, 2001). These agencies have thus been accused of being instruments of techno-politics and technocracy, in which economists, bankers, managers, lawyers, and other experts are exempted from public scrutiny. Some procedures widely accepted in global agencies, such as the reservation of permanent membership and veto powers in the U.N. Security Council to five great powers, and quota-based votes in the IMF and World Bank, are democratically unjustifiable.

## GLOBALISTS

Contrary to the state-centric (realist) and multicentric (idealist) schools, the Russian globalists' starting point is the global context—within which states and other entities interact, and supranational structures are more important and influential than nation-states. Some Russian globalists question the very existence of the nation-state in today's world. National governments are seen as unable to resist or control global processes and have to submit to universal laws dictated by global dynamics.

As is well known, the globalist paradigm is not monolithic and consists of several subschools. In terms of Russian understandings, the following sub-schools can be identified. First, Russian Marxists and neo-Marxists tend to characterize global governance as a system of world capitalist domination exercised through various international institutions. This form of capitalism is viewed as distinct from the old, classical model of capitalism in that global capitalism prefers more sophisticated and less violent forms of domination and exploitation. Nevertheless, the new form of capitalism does not preclude man-ifestations of classical imperialism in numerous ways, as attested to by such cases as the Falklands/Malvinas war of 1983, the US/Western invasions of Lebanon (1982–1984), Grenada (1983), Panama (1989), and Iraq (1991), in addition to NATO operations in former Yugoslavia in the 1990s (Podberezkin, 1996; Shapinov, 2000; Veber, 2001).

Yet another perspective of Russian globalists includes theories that por-tray the emerging global society as an enlarged copy of the national society. Hence, global governance has the same functions as national governments but at a different, higher, level. For those globalists, effective global governance requires a world government. Suggestions on how to establish a world gov-ernment range from the soft option (the United Nations assumes this role) to extreme versions (a centralized governmental structure with attributes similar to the national government) (Afontsev, 2001). However, proponents of this view have largely failed to realistically explain how such a government could be provided with legitimacy and how it could govern countries with drastically different economic, social, and political organizations.

Other Russian globalists adhere to a more moderate version of global gov-ernance and interpret it as a system of organizations, arrangements, mecha-nisms, and regimes emerging in the globalizing and postsovereign world and aimed at managing global processes. They stress the fact that global gover-nance is resulting from the inability of national governments to cope with new types of problems and thus there is a growing need for new structures (Sokolov, 2001).

Finally, there is the environmentalist version of Russian globalism. This group of globalists was one of the first to redefine the concept of security in the post-Soviet period. As one leading Russian environmentalist said at a conference on Russia's foreign policy doctrine in February 1992, "National security is no longer purely military. I am sure that Russia's national security is environmental by at least one-third" (Yablokov, 1992: 98). As has been pointed out by environmentalist scholars, ecological threats differ dramatically from military ones. While military or geopolitical threats can be seen as mainly hypothetical, ecological threats directly affect the nation's economy, health, and climate.

Under environmentalism's pressure, nearly all leading schools of foreign policy thought now include an ecological dimension in their concepts of security. A special section on ecological security was put into the National Security Concepts of the Russian Federation of both 1997 and 2000.

The environmentalists believe that traditional diplomatic methods are not sufficient for resolving ecological problems, which have now tended to become global rather than national or regional. They believe that Russia, along with the rest of the world, should develop "new thinking" based on a common interest in survival in the face of global problems (Plimak, 1996: 42–52). Some environmentalists are quite radical in their recommendations regarding solutions to global problems. They have recommended, for example, a dissolution of political boundaries and a de-ideologizing of international relations (of course, with the exception of environmentalism itself). In order to cope with ecological problems, they point to a need for humankind to be able to forecast both the near and distant future and consider all the components of ecological problems in their historical and physical developments. Since only scientists are able to make good forecasts, this stratum of society should be elevated and charged with political management as well. National and international economies should be based on new technologies targeted at the rational exploitation of natural resources. Contrary to public and private properties, these globalists argue that cooperative property will be the best form of ownership to deal with environmental issues. They also point out that transnational rather than national bodies should be in charge of global problems as nation-states are unable to cope with them any longer (Burlak, 1992: 16–24).

## CONCLUSION

Globalization has dramatically changed post-Communist Russian security thinking. New, broader, definitions of national and international security have been adopted, and a greater priority has been given to soft security issues. New operational models of international security have also been suggested, and the role of various international security organizations and arrangements has been reassessed. A new strategy on regional and subregional cooperation has been developed and, in connection with this, Russia has also been forced to adjust the center-periphery balance to cope with new challenges to the subnational level of Russian security. The era of globalization has required new approaches to national sovereignty and necessitated a combination of national and multilateral solutions to Russian security problems.

Despite differences of opinion among various Russian IR schools about the definitions, explanations, and implications of globalization, they almost unanimously acknowledge the fact that globalization has dramatically changed, and continues to change, the nature of world politics and Russia's place within them. The focus of debate in Russian scholarship is gradually shifting away from questions such as whether globalization exists toward questions of how to manage practical problems. In other words, the emphasis has shifted to coping with the challenges of globalization, minimizing its negative consequences, and better utilizing its advantages and achievements. Despite the continuing realist dominance in Russian political thinking, national security discourse is slowly moving from one of resisting/confronting globalization toward one of adapting/contributing to this worldwide process.

## NOTES

1. On the changes of security arrangements in Europe, see Ole Waever's chapter in this volume.

2. A similar increase in focus on internal threats was noted in roundtable discussions on the Turkish case at the Ankara conference during which the works in this volume were first presented.

# 8

# Globalization and (In)Security in AMENA

## A Contextual Double-pronged Analysis

Bahgat Korany

### Analyzing AMENA Security in the Global Era

Current debates and issues within security studies are bypassing the Arab Middle East and North Africa (AMENA) in the sense that the major countries of the region seem to be remaining victims of traditional security issues and have not yet woken up to newer security aspects. According to these debates, the Middle East is an exception to what is taking place elsewhere in the world. This Middle East "exceptionalism" in terms of security is similar to what is happening in the analysis of democratization, the third wave of which—according to the assumptions of the majority of the literature—barely touched the region. In the voluminous and rapidly growing literature on democratization we rarely have an analysis of an AMENA case. Are critical security studies repeating this exceptionalism phenomenon? Admittedly, the dominant pattern of interstate interaction in the region is very Hobbesian. This observation could perhaps explain why security studies of the region deal almost exclusively with old threats, but it is not an adequate justification for them to exclude new ones. Even if we are singularly interested in classical interstate warfare, where would we fit in potential water wars? If globalization is about the blurring of barriers between conventional high politics and low politics, then doesn't the continued neglect of this overlap in AMENA ultimately mean that we are removing the region from global-era analyses?

In an era of global societal interconnectedness, it has been argued that the term "security" should not be limited to state/national security and thus dissociated from the complexity and richness of human life (Booth, 1991). In this perspective, the centrality of the state in the global system is more of an assumption than a prevalent reality. When we look at the state itself in the global south—of which AMENA is a part—we see an entity that is increasingly fragmented, if not failing and even collapsing (eg., Sudan, Somalia). Even before the onset of globomania, concepts like "security community" and "security regimes" had begun efforts to reformulate—if not revise—security studies. The aim was to get away from the blind alley of military security and purely external threats. These early restructured visions of security were debated in various international reports such as the 1982 Palmer Report, the 1987 Brundtland Report, and the 1980 Brandt report: "an important task of constructive international policy will have to consist of providing a new, more comprehensive understanding of security, which could be less restricted to the purely military aspects" (North-South: A Program for Survival, 1980: 124). The result of this revised (if not yet revisionist) outlook is that in response to the question about who or what is to be secured, the answer cannot then be limited to the state.

On the other hand, security should not exclude the state either, for the state—despite its weakness—is nominally and symbolically still there (Ayoob, 1993). Are not the Palestinians, for instance, blowing themselves up in order to have their 'state', and are not the Israelis mobilized to face up to suicide bombings to keep theirs? Any discussion of security must therefore necessarily embrace traditional aspects of state/national security as well as the new globalized ones. The focus has to be the defense of not only the state but also, and arguably primarily, the society and identity (Kaldor, 2001). Alongside such a paradigmatic shift, it follows that analytical tension, concepts, and methods of an enlarged securities field cannot be limited to geostrategy and high politics, but must also embrace political economy, sociology, cognitive sciences, and an emphasis on low politics (Korany, 1986, 1989).

To deal with this dualistic view of security in the era of globalization, this chapter chooses to first emphasize the generally overlooked aspects of societal security before turning to much more familiar traditional threats of high politics. Thus, the first section gives an overview of the relationship between globalization and (in)security as it applies to the AMENA region.

The emphasis of the discussion in this chapter is on nonconventional threats, dubbed as societal/identity issues, but including economic ones as well. The discussion draws attention to globalization threats and the impact of a particular type of polarization, and links this bipolar pattern to the South's earlier experiences. It then focuses in detail on the cases of two principal countries in the AMENA region, one from its Asian part and the other from its African one. The first case deals with the incarnation of Holy Islam, Saudi Arabia, toward which the majority of the world's 1.2 billion Muslims turn five times a day in their prayers. The second case looks at a paradigmatic case of Third World national liberation movements and independence wars: Algeria. Despite dramatic differences in history, state-formation experiences, ideological vision, elite socialization, and socioeconomic structure, the debate within these two countries over societal security and identity threats is found to be strikingly similar.

The last section of the chapter returns to more traditional issues in security. It deals with the persistent war-proneness of the region, which serves to remind us of the lingering relevance in this part of our global system of traditional military threats as emphasized by established "national security" studies. This part concentrates on the post–Cold War period and the second intifadah era, and attempts to show how, notwithstanding the general decline of the state in the era of globalization, a great deal of bloodshed, destruction, and human suffering continues to prevail in the name of state-creation and state-preservation. The section also explores how globalization's technological sophistication is being harnessed to promote these traditional objectives. Such observations are reminders of the importance of not succumbing to a one-dimensional analysis, whether a singular obsession with formal and narrowly defined state security or the opposite extreme of its utter omission.

## GLOBALIZATION AND (IN)SECURITY: AN AMENA OVERVIEW

Globalization, understood here as time and space compression leading to societal interconnectedness and daily consciousness of it, can be seen as beneficial in some aspects. However, the provisional balance sheet, as far as the global South is concerned, is on the whole rather negative (Scholte, 2000: 232–233). This is even the case at the economic level, which has usually been seen as the least negative aspect of globalization. For instance, in relation to economic subsistence, the globalization of capitalism has contributed to the spread of welfare and the rise of Newly Industrialized Countries (NIC). None of the AMENA countries, however, has reached NIC status. On the contrary, economic restructuring in the face of globalization has often increased poverty in the region (Henry & Springborg, 2001). Many Middle Eastern countries have crippling trade deficits,[1] and most are hurt as well by the gap between gross domestic investment and gross domestic savings (Richards & Waterbury, 1998).

One might consider current global financing as a kind of casino capitalism, in the sense that despite large sums of capital for investment being moved around, not much has moved in the direction of AMENA. Hopes were raised in 1997 when, with the collapse of the Asian markets, MENA (i.e., AMENA, plus Turkey, Iran, Israel, Greece, and Cyprus) attracted 7.8% of the world investment in emerging stock markets, but the overall picture is still negative. The region's stock markets accumulated less than $10 billion in foreign capital between 1990 and 1998, less than sub-Saharan Africa, and almost half of that went to Turkey (Henry & Springborg, 2001: 49). Moreover, the volatility of global financial markets has added considerably to feelings of economic insecurity. The Egyptian pound, for instance, has been officially devalued twice in a year, leading to a rapid loss of about 35% of its value in the face of the dollar (slightly more on the informal market). Since Egypt's imports are four times the volume of its exports, and the country's trade deficit with the United States is five to one, however, the pressure on the Egyptian pound is bound to continue.

Generally, currency devaluation could be argued to improve a country's competitiveness, but in AMENA at present it is instead reflecting financial instability and leading to corporate relocation. This in turn leads to job loss and job insecurity. This job insecurity is accentuated by the fact that global capitalism is generally less labor-intensive and is diverting investment from the "real" economy. Consequently, in many AMENA countries, the unemployment rate is on average 20% and rising. Among young graduates (including medical doctors and engineers) it may reach 50% in the first two years after graduation. Even those who finally find work must then face up to deteriorating working conditions with the undermining of the Fordist social contract and the absence of adequate guarantees for workers' rights. Indeed, the prevalence of cutthroat competition and survival policies (at both the individual and collectivity levels) as well as the decline of socially responsible global business are resulting in deteriorating social capital and social cohesion. What we are faced with is the rise of exclusionary nonterritorial communities whose negative impact is greater than the development of transborder solidarities or socially oriented NGOs.

Even information technology (IT) is being used more to shore up failing state systems and increase governmental control of individuals rather than to empower citizens. Meetings among Arab ministers of the interior have been the most regular and effective means of information gathering and data exchange to heighten "national security" (i.e., regime maintenance) regionwide.

The result of this negative impact of globalization is that people and governments alike tend to look back at the global system as favoring some countries at the expense of others. Such an imbalance is indeed reminiscent in their collective memory of a particular type of bipolarity.

## GLOBALIZATION AS PERPETUATION OF BIPOLARITY

This particular type of bipolarity is different from the conventional East/West one, but, even at the height of the Cold War, usually marked people in the global South at a disadvantage. We can witness a precursor militant view of the international system in such countries as Castro's Cuba, Nkrumah's Ghana, or Sukarno's Indonesia, at the first summit of nonaligned countries, in Belgrade in 1961 (Korany, 1976: 188–189). The moderate group at the summit held a benign view of the international system, emphasizing a mediating role for nonaligned countries in the East/West conflict—a role represented by Nehru as an example of "India losing its revolutionary spirit." Sukarno, on the other hand, perceived this same international system as a hostile one. For him, the root problem was not the East/West conflict but:

> a conflict which cuts deeper into the flesh of man, and that is the conflict between the new emergent forces of freedom and justice and the old forces of dominance, the one pushing its head relentlessly through the crust of the earth which has given it its lifeblood, the other striving desperately to retain all it can, trying to hold back the course of history.

International theory analysis also captured this "structural conflict" in which "the Third World [is] against Global Liberalism" (Krasner, 1985) and vice versa. Though the capabilities are unequal, this asymmetric conflict is both endemic and normative. This conflict is not about material issues, such as goods distribution, but about meta-power as distinct from relational power. Krasner specifies that whereas relational power:

> refers to efforts to maximize values within a given set of institutional structures; meta-power behavior refers to efforts to change the institutions themselves. Relational power refers to the ability to change outcomes or affect the behavior of others within a given regime. Meta-power refers to the ability to change the rules of the game (1985: 14).

Since current international regimes were perceived as pitted against the global South (Krasner, 1986), these countries of the South were not able to advance within them but were forced to move beyond them. Is this structural conflict continuing in the globalization era? Is globalization still having the same negative impact on AMENA? For Islamists and Nationalists, this is indeed the case (Abdel Mo'ati, 1999; Mabrouk, 1999). Their views are substantiated by the findings of international organizations. According to the United Nations Development Program (UNDP) 2000 report, globalization and the primacy of market dynamics have widened the economic gap between countries. The income gap between the top fifth of the world's population and the bottom fifth reached 74 to 1 in 1997, in contrast to 60 to 1 in 1990 and 30 to 1 in 1960 (UNDP, 2000: 343). This huge gap is due to rapid global integration that benefits the developed at the expense of the less developed. The same trend prevailed in the nineteenth and early twentieth century (a period of intensive global integration), when the gap between the top and bottom countries jumped from 3 to 1 in 1820, 7 to 1 in 1870, and 11 to 1 in 1913 (UNDP, 2000: 343). At the end of the twentieth century, the picture is quite frightening. The UNDP report of 2000 points out that by the end of the 1990s, the fifth of the world's population living in the highest income countries had:

- 86% of world GDP—the bottom fifth just 1%.
- 82% of world export markets—the bottom fifth just 1%.
- 68% of foreign direct investment—the bottom fifth just 1%.
- 74% of world telephone lines—the bottom fifth just 1.5% (UNDP, 2000: 343)

Globalization, in the form of structural adjustment and economic reform programs, leads to a wider gap between social classes in any given country. In AMENA, globalization has exacerbated societal inequalities, thus leading to more social frictions between the haves and the have-nots. Sporadic actions confirm that proposition. In 1977, in Egypt, for instance, shortly after the *infitah* or opening (the first step of integrating Egypt into the global economy) was applied, food riots erupted. Similar chaos broke out in 1986, revealing— at least partially—a manifestation of underlying tensions between the rich and the poor. In both incidents, symbols of wealth and the wealthy (five–star hotels, fancy cars, nightclubs) were fiercely attacked. Islamic militancy reached its peak in 1992–1993, just after the Egyptian regime concluded a deal with the IMF that implied serious cuts in subsidies and an enormous rise in the prices of basic services. This militancy was also an expression of social protest over the sense of economic deprivation felt primarily by the educated middle class, who could not find decent jobs and, at the same time, faced a serious decline in their social status. The Berber minority riots in Algeria (April–May 2001) likewise were seen by many as triggered more by economic reasons than the everlasting identity dispute with the Algerian state. A recent standard liberal analysis cannot help drawing a parallel between colonial legacies and globalization legacies.

These different analyses, coming from different interdisciplinary and normative backgrounds, seem to indicate that although the actors and means of domination have changed, the structure of the relationship has not. Instead of Great Britain and France, it is the United States and the IMF (dubbed by some the International MISERY Fund), and instead of geostrategic dictat, it is Washington's consensus.

This multidimensional threatening situation fuels the antiglobalization campaign of the "moralizers" (the "traditionalists" of the colonial days, and the Islamic fundamentalists of the present day). Their continuing success is due, however, not only to the strong appeal of their message, but also to the fact that the peculiarities of the globalization/insecurity complex give credibility to this message and back it up. This can be seen more clearly by focusing on the specific case of societal security in one of the most orthodox—but also influential—societies in AMENA: Saudi Arabia.

## SOCIETAL INSECURITY IN HOLY ISLAM

The case of Saudi Arabia is revealing since it shows the overlapping multidimensional aspect of security in the global era, especially the salience of societal security. In a classic analysis of security issues, societal security has been defined as "the sustainability within acceptable conditions for evolution, of traditional patterns of language, culture, religion and national identity and custom" (Buzan, 1991: 19). A key word here is identity (Bell, 2000; Crothers & Lockhart, 2000; Harrison & Huntington, 2000; Johnston & Sampson, 1994). The inclusion of this concept is an indication of a shift—even within the mainstream tradition—from material to cognitive structural resources and from state to human subjects of security. Identity is thus no longer simply a "soft concept" suitable for novelists and sociologists (McSweeney, 1999: 69). Rather, it is becoming a bridge toward social constructivism, a perspective focusing on "the process and practices by which people and groups construct their self-image" (McSweeney, 1999: 69), as distinct from the dominant positivist tradition in established security studies.

It is in the European context with the end of the Cold War that research on societal security and identity has been brought to the fore (Waever et al., 1993). Whereas state security was related to state sovereignty, societal security is held together as a concept and practice by concerns about identity (Waever et al., 1993). More important, societal security is no longer subordinated to state security, but has become an object of inquiry and analysis in its own right, inseparable from the analysis of identity: "The key to society is that set of ideas and practices that identify individuals as members of a social group. Society is about identity, about the self-concept of communities and of individuals identifying themselves as members of a community" (Waever et al., 1993: 6). Consequently, societal security concerns "the ability of a society to persist in its essential character under changing conditions" (Waever et al., 1993: 23); in other words, the preservation of "us" against existential threats (Waever et al., 1993: 26).

Obviously, society is in trouble when it faces intense competing identity claims, as in ethnic wars. With the exception of peripheral areas of AMENA (e.g., Sudan, Somalia, the Kurds in Iraq, and potentially the Berbers in Algeria), this region suffers more from ideological civil wars—especially in relation to the rising appeal of "political Islamism."

It might come as a surprise to many that the Saudi Arabian political system not only faces domestic opposition, but that its most virulent opposition forces are Islamic. The surprise is all the more justified since Saudi Arabian state-formation is based on a 1745 alliance between the Al-Saud family and Sheikh Mohamed Abdel Wahab, a strict Islamic revivalist who aimed to purify Islam from innovation. Accordingly, the country is modeled on the original Islamic state of the seventh century. It has no legal political parties, its constitution is the Koran, and its source of laws and regulations is the sharia'a Islamic law (Korany, 1991: 316). The official title of King Fahad is "custodian of the holy places" of Mecca and Medina. Moreover, 'Ulama and Islamic scholars are among the most prestigious social elite and influential decision-making groups (Korany, 1991: 329–330). Indeed, before making any crucial decision, the Saudi king is sure to formally enlist 'Ulama support, usually through fatwa or religious verdict. This was the case in 1979 when governmental forces had to storm one of the biggest mosques to dislodge Islamist opposition rebels, and in 1990–1991 when U.S. troops were to be stationed in the kingdom to dismiss Iraqi troops from Kuwait.

Yet different writings on the politics of dissent within the avowedly Islam-incarnating kingdom (Fandy, 1999; Teitelbaum, 2000) list no less than six major Islamic opposition groups, including Osama Bin Laden's Advice and Reform Committee. One shared point between these groups is the perception of the Saudi government as contributing to the emergence of an infidel state:

> "Islam" and its values are under attack both globally and locally . . . and the Saudi government has failed to protect Islam and Muslims. According to Al-Shamrani, the [opposition] group used to meet and discuss whether the Saudi state conformed with Islamic teachings, how the state followed secular law and supported the United Nations, and how the Ulama such as Bin Baz and Bin Otheimein were conspiring with the state to undermine Islam (Fandy, 1999: 3).

Both the Saudi government and the opposition groups are part of the local-global nexus, in terms of means, values, and dilemmas. Thus, global links and technologies of globalization are empowering both government and opposition. Indeed, both count very much on the communication revolution, networks, and netwars (Arquilla & Ronfeldt, 2001) that globalization has put at their disposal. Consequently, Saudi Arabia lives divided between time and space. Officially, the date used in all official communications is the Islamic year (now the year 1423), separated by seven centuries from the Christian one. Laws applied reflect the Orthodox Wahabi interpretation of Islam. The struggle to educate women was waged only in the 1960s, and still no mixed schools are allowed and women are forbidden to drive cars. Yet at the same time, airports and cars portray the latest technological gadgets, often ahead of New York and London. These global symbols have sometimes collided with and provocatively threatened traditional culture. Even when individuals are able to successfully cope and adapt to such clashes, the ambiguities and contradictions of a multidimensional self can be unsettling (Scholte, 2000: 233).

The importance of this new compressed time and space, especially through the worlds of television and finance, embodies for Saudi society the paradox of homogenizing and fragmenting impulses. As a result, a television viewer in Saudi Arabia can watch an animal rights demonstration in London a so-called homogenizing experience—yet at the same time be angered by Westerners' apparent greater concern for animals than for mal-nourished children in Gaza—a "fragmenting experience" (Fandy, 1999: 8). The experience could occur as well with such issues as sexual permissiveness or gay rights. This continuous hybridity and oscillation between "here" and "there," "now" and "then," "tradition" and "postmodernity," "us" and "them" can be very tiring and disturbing. The state tries to make the best use of technology by being more present on the television screen than in reality, and is hence very vulnerable to opposition groups. These groups use the same IT means to cap-ture both domestic and world alternatives to reveal the government's lack of consistency, credibility, integrity, and faithfulness.

In Saudi Arabia, where politics and culture are intermingled and insepa-rable, the dilemmas of an interdependent world are also reflected in the econ-omy. Saudi Arabia was until relatively recently a sandbox, a holy one because of Mecca and Medina, but a sandbox nevertheless. It could have, however, continued as a sandbox, if it were not for oil. Oil represents the quasi-totality of Saudi exports and the basis of its geostrategic worth and financial power.

The country's arid and barren soil has almost one-third of the world's oil reserves. The country's oil revenues soared from a little under $3 billion in 1972, the year preceding the oil embargo, to $113 billion in 1981, before again plummeting to around $23 billion in 1987 (Korany, 1986: 141). As a result of the unsettled and unsettling world oil market, the rentier-welfare state, or what I call the Bakshish state, could no longer maintain financial largesse. The crisis started in the Ministry of Finance and then filtered out to society. The Ministry's generous subsidies could not continue to placate and buy off oppo-sition forces. For instance, in 1981–1982, governmental subsidies for food, agriculture, social security, and electricity peaked at more than $10 billion Saudi Riyal. By seven years later, they had gone down by 80%, to reach just over 2 billion Saudi Riyals (Chaudhry, 1997: 130). The sudden recession was so deep in this period that King Fahad went on national television to declare the government's inability to produce a national budget. About 35% of the fac-tories funded by the Industrial Development Fund declared bankruptcy. Moreover, in this commerce-based country, the number of merchants, retail-ers, commission-holders, agents, and industrialists in Riyadh declined in this period by 80% (Chaudhry, 1997: 273).

As a result of economic woes, underlying societal insecurity could no longer be camouflaged and had to come out in the political arena. The peculiar social contract of the unavailability of political representation in return for no taxation could no longer be maintained. In this situation, political conflict comes to the forefront and legitimacy deficit increases. Hence, we face the rise of the apparently contradictory phenomena of an Islamic opposition in an orthodox Islamic country. Moreover, this opposition can spill over beyond borders (*la Premiere Guerre du Siecle*, 2001). This has been the case with the Afghan Arabs (Faraj, 2002; Mokaddam, 2002) and Osama Bin Laden (deprived of his Saudi citizenship in 1994), both of which constitute extreme and bloody examples of uncivil society contesting global governance (O'Brien et al., 2000)

Nevertheless, Saudi Arabia, despite its crisis of governance, is a fortunate country. It enjoys Islamic prestige and its 'Ulama's words have a great impact on Muslims worldwide. More important, it has voluminous oil resources and—despite price fluctuations—it masters worldwide investments and cash. The great majority of AMENA countries, on the other hand, cannot marshal either needed resources or liquidity. Their dilemma is much more one of dependence rather than interdependence. Though not as poor as Yemen or Sudan, Algeria is a good case in point.

## SOCIETAL (IN)SECURITY AND IDENTITY IN A STRONGHOLD OF GLOBAL SOUTH REVOLUTIONARISM: ALGERIA

Parliamentary elections at the end of May 2002—partially boycotted by some major political forces—gave a slight majority to the historical and presently governing National Liberation Front (FLN). The results were soon to be contested by almost all other parties, amid accusations of widespread police intervention in the voting process, irregularities in ballot counting, and outright hijacking of election results. Earlier controversies over elections in 1990 helped to derail the nascent democratic process, bring the army explicitly into the political arena, put major Islamist leaders in prison, and intensify the sociopolitical rift. After being qualified as the Japan of Africa in the 1970s, Algeria has, since the early 1990s, moved from an ideological war to an undeclared civil war.

At the beginning of the third millennium, Algeria also shows the havoc of an identity debate and the failure of the bakshish state. During a visit to Algeria on the eve of the 2002 elections, I was offered revealing data on the primacy of the threat emanating from a virtual civil war. I was told that, during the last ten years, just over 100,000 individuals had been killed, including 150 university professors, 52 journalists, and just over 100 foreigners. The latter had to be 'physically liquidated'—according to the *Group Islamique Arme* or

GIA—because they promote secularism and disseminate wordly indeterminate knowledge. Collective massacres occurred in 299 cases. As another sign of the failure to guarantee individual security, evidence also shows how the kidnapping of women became common currency: 197 cases in 1993, 582 in 1994, 550 in 1995, 144 in 1996, and 180 cases in 1997.

Economic losses have been no less than the human ones. Just over 350,000 have lost their jobs (and the number of the unemployed could have been higher if internal security bodies were not hiring). Destruction has replaced any attempt at sustainable development—930 school buildings, 8 university institutes, 16 training institutes, 120 administrative buildings, and 630 factories were destroyed. Thus, despite territorial/political differences with neighboring Morocco on the status of the Western Sahara, the major threat to security in Algeria remains primarily domestic.

The focal issue of conflict between the militant Islamists and the political authority is related to issues of identity and society's political evolution. In this sense, the significance of what is taking place in Algeria at present and its denouement go beyond the case itself. Indeed, Algeria has been and continues to be a paradigmatic case in the analysis of Third World politics and society. Until 1962, Algeria was not only a French colony but officially a part of France, a *departement d'outremer* (DOM). While many French-speaking African countries accepted Charles de Gaulle's offer of "independence," Algeria fought a national liberation war that by 1962 had cost it a "million martyrs." After independence, Algeria aspired to be a *montreur de conduite*—a behavioral model—and exemplar for the rest of the Third World to follow. Internally and externally, in both its domestic and foreign policies, it incarnated a revolutionary state bent on showing the serious inadequacies of the status quo and indicating the road ahead. Many Third World statesmen and prominent world intellectuals looked to the Algerian model as a hopeful alternative.

Both this hope and its basis in reality crumbled in the late 1980s. Yet even in times of crisis, Algeria continued to be paradigmatic. It showed the failure of monolithic, authoritarian, one-party rule in the Third World, a rule that shortchanged its people. The implicit social contract between state and people—based on offering social welfare in return for deprivation of some basic political rights—collapsed after the continuous decline in oil earnings and the state's consequent lack of resources to keep buying off its people. The state's inefficiency became apparent, and its legitimacy eroded. A political vacuum, a quasi-anarchy in a Hobbesian state of nature, followed while negotiations continued about a new "governing formula".

This state of virtual civil war motivated a policy-oriented Rand study to concentrate on possible scenarios of future governance in Algeria. Starting with the question of "not so much whether the FIS will come to power, but how, and to what degree," the Rand study compares two scenarios: the possibility of a democratic alternative (through elections) and a nondemocratic "deal" (between the military and the Front Islamique du Salvation, or FIS). If President Bouteflika (elected in November 1999) cannot manage the crisis of governance, Algeria could then be the first Arab state to have Islamists in power. Is this indeed the wave of the future? If so, how does democratization fare in this respect? In both questions and answers about the crisis of governing and the future of democratization, the analysis of the Algerian experience thus goes beyond being a mere case study and continues to be paradigmatic (Korany, 1998: 11–12).

A recent estimate by the Economist Intelligence Unit (May 2002) describes Algeria's political outlook as bleak, because of the state of domestic insecurity. Unemployment and poverty, as well as a crumbling infrastructure, have led to riots in recent years, including some outside the traditionally restive Berber-speaking area of Kabylia (which has been going through unrest for the last few). Moreover, there has been an upsurge in Islamist violence, and with the main Islamist groups refusing to articulate a political platform, the chances of any accommodation between them and the government is remote.

After more than three years in office, President Bouteflika appears to be no closer to ending the Islamist violence that has plagued the country for ten years. Despite the amnesty deal struck with the Armée Islamique du Salvation (AIS, the armed wing of the banned FIS) in mid-January 2000, "Islamist" violence continues, returning to urban areas in recent months, and killings in the hinterland of Algiers have increased in frequency and brutality. The killing by the army of a leader of the militant GIA in February 2002 provoked a ferocious backlash of revenge killings. A political compromise between the avowedly secular military-dominated regime and the amorphous GIA is unlikely and violence is set to continue.

The economy expanded by only 1.7% in real terms in 2001. Economic reform, which Bouteflika had pursued as a means to reduce civil unrest, is also unlikely to gather pace owing to opposition within the military to privatization, the linchpin of the reform program. The appointment of Noureddine Boukrouh, a man with close ties to the military, as minister for privatization in June 2001 reinforced the perception that reform would be gradual and even patchy at best. This change was forced on Bouteflika, who has had to accept a more circumscribed role in the Algerian power structure than he had at first, to avoid being crushed as happened with the two former presidents (even though they came from military ranks). Since his participation in the 1965 Boumedienne coup d'etat against Algeria's first president, Ben Bella, Bouteflika has been adept at exploiting the myriad personal jealousies and suspicions within the military and continues to be an assured diplomatic performer, an asset that the generals appreciate. Could these qualities and maneuvers reduce the ideological war and favor domestic security?

These ups and downs are related to the process of governance, but the structure of threats themselves hardly changes. They are primarily societal in nature and at variance with traditional external and military threats singled out by conventional "national security" approaches. These conventional threats, however, have not yet disappeared in the "zone of turmoil" (the Global South, as opposed to the northern "zone of peace") of which the Middle East is a significant part.

## FROM A PERSISTENCE OF CONVENTIONAL MILITARY THREATS TO A JEAN MONNET APPROACH?

The conventional vision of national security as based on state primacy, systemic anarchy, and war-proneness seems to apply to the Middle East. Indeed, in the war annals of the last 50 years, the Middle East will occupy a very distinctive place. It seems to be the embodiment of the proverbial Hobbesian world of the war of all against all. It has fueled both arms trade and arms sophistication, including nuclear proliferation and biological-chemical weapons of mass destruction. About three-quarters of developed countries' arms sales are consumed in the region, and rich oil-producing countries in the Gulf allocate, on average, 20% of their annual budgets to arms purchases (Henry & Springborg, 2001: 104).

But arms acquisition and sophistication seem to be correlated—not with greater security, but rather, with conflict escalation (Utgoff, 2000). In the last two decades the region has witnessed the longest war in post–Second World War history (the war between Iran and Iraq), and also the most sophisticated one (the Gulf War of the coalition against Iraq). It is also home to the Israeli-Palestinian conflict, which seems to defy any attempts at control, let alone at resolution. Peace treaties have indeed been signed (e.g., between Egypt and Israel in 1979, and between Israel and Jordan in 1994), but events seem to forever bring us back to square one.

This regression is due to the fact that the region exemplifies a security complex (Buzan, 1991: 190; 1983: 106). Basically a security complex is a continuum that ranges from chaos at one pole to security community at the other, and has as its essence security interdependence among its members. Though Buzan seems to limit it to states, a security complex can include nonstate or prestate communities like the Palestinians.

The traditional perspective of Middle East security has to be accompanied by newer perspectives that include an emphasis on nonconventional security issues. One could propose the importing of a Jean Monnet approach (the founding concept of the European integration process) to the Middle East region to reorient it from an economy of strife to an economy of peace. Two prime beneficiaries of this economy that would target peace are tourism and water.

It is true that many sites of the Middle East make the region a magnet for tourism. It is also true, however, that when the region is dominated by a balance-of-power approach and saber-rattling, tourists will turn elsewhere. The Gulf War was very instructive in this respect, as bankruptcies in the private sector as well as crippling governmental budget deficits resulted. An atmosphere of peace, however, would not only lure these tourists back, but could even increase their numbers through "open borders, a sophisticated transportation and communication infrastructure, joint marketing of popular tour packages and a well-developed tourist industry" (Peres, 1993: 153).

A second beneficiary of changing the mind-set from balance of power to interdependence would be the water shortage problem in the Middle East. The challenge is first to halt the browning process (desertification). While the Arab world controls 13 million square kilometers of the earth, roughly 90% of it is desert (Peres, 1993).

Since wars have not managed to solve anything, least of all water problems, and since water flows do not follow state frontiers, water issues need to be regulated regionally. Given the importance of the water issue in this arid region, it needs to be emphasized. The Middle East "is the most arid of the world's major regions" (Shapland, 1997: 1). The rising demand of water in the twentieth and twenty-first centuries caused by economic development, rapid urbanization, and population growth has led to a further scarcity of water, with no major opportunities for increasing the supply. Therefore, "the water problem" has imposed itself on the national security agenda of many AMENA states.

A potential regional water regime would deal with water distribution from areas of plenty to areas of scarcity and would study the possibilities of making desalination technologically and economically feasible. Such transformation necessitates huge capital and technological infrastructure (i.e., international cooperation—both regionally and internationally).

## Middle East Security after September 11

The events of September 11 and their repercussions have worsened the AMENA insecurity context. In fact, these events have increased both traditional state (in)security as well as societal (in)security. Threatened by accusations of terrorism and/or of harboring terrorists, many AMENA states feel even more insecure since the events of September 2001. The fear, in particular, of post–9/11 American military schemes has produced a remarkable shift in the policies of some AMENA states who have subsequently felt obliged to give concessions to avoid potential American economic—or military—punishment. Sudan, for example, signed an hitherto unconceivable agreement with the Southern rebels. For the first time, southerners were granted right of self-determination, a step that might lead to the disintegration of the Sudan.

Yemen also succumbed to the demands of the U.S. administration on combating terrorism to absorb the rising American criticisms, and agreed to allow direct intervention to liquidate physically those suspected of terrorist activities.

American military retaliation post-9/11 did indeed focus on the Middle East. Afghanistan—a non Arab Middle Eastern state—was, just a month after 9/11, subject to a massive American military attack, and subsequently a change in regime. Iraq—on allegations of possessing weapons of mass destruction—was the next candidate. A change in Saddam Hussein's regime may fulfill, from the American perspective, other objectives (access to oil fields, grand geostrategic plans, etc.) but it is, no doubt, the global context of post 9/11 that enabled the United States to get out the old plans and embark on implementing them.

September 11, however, was not seen as a security threat by all AMENA states. Some countries, for instance, Algeria, perceived it instead as an opportunity to enhance their own domestic security. They thus seized that opportunity to crush their Islamic opposition, in the name of fighting terrorism. The outcome has been a grave erosion of civil liberties and a serious encroachment on human rights. As such, state security has been pursued at the expense of societal security. Consequently, civil society forces have been highly concerned about the widespread human rights' violations by AMENA regimes.

Societal insecurity was further accentuated by the global trend of associating terrorism with Muslims and Arabs. The AMENA populations, predominantly Muslims, were terribly offended by the West's media campaigns that have constantly suggested that Islam condones—or even encourages—violence. The irresponsible announcements on Islam made by some key Western figures (e.g., Italy's prime minister, the U.S. Attorney General John Ashcroft) convinced many that the current Islam–West confrontation is not due to sheer misunderstanding. Hence, xenophobia and obsessions of a conspiracy under way became ubiquitous in AMENA. Moreover, the recently imposed American regulations on Arabs' entrance to the United States added humiliation to insecurity. Feeling that they are the prime suspects in any crime on earth, the AMENA populations will not likely divorce their sense of insecurity in the foreseeable future.

Whether seen as a threat or an opportunity, AMENA states, generally speaking, are, post-9/11, more amenable to American pressure. In some cases, fear was exaggerated. For example, the late Yasser Arafat, Chairman of the Palestinian Authority—a victim of state terrorism himself—hurried to donate blood in public to the victims of the September attacks, though he, ironically, never did so to thousands of his own people injured by the brutal Israeli use of force (Amin, 2002: 87). It seemed as if Arafat, in the words of Galal Amin, wanted to say: "I swear, I have nothing to do with it" (2002: 88).

Even Egypt and Saudi Arabia—the closest allies of the United States in the region for decades—are not exempt from the fear of future American plans. Talks of a potential change of regime or, at least, strong pressure to reform their ailing and "undemocratic" political systems after the Iraqi problem is settled are widely circulated. Those fears partially explain the strong Egyptian opposition to the American strike against Iraq. If the American plan in Afghanistan is successfully repeated in Iraq, Egypt will be exposed to immense pressure to make hard decisions.

## CONCLUSION

In the ongoing debate on the analysis and practice of security in the era of globalization, this chapter has adopted a dualistic view. It emphasized in the AMENA region the primacy of the overlooked societal-identity threats without neglecting, in this conflict-ridden region, the importance of traditional military threats.

According to the two-world dichotomy of "zone of peace" and "zone of turmoil," the present Global South is facing a myriad of security threats to both its state security and this security's societal infrastructure. Rather than being mutually exclusive, state and societal security are mutually reinforcing (Rosenau, 1997) as the events of September 11 clearly indicate. These events as well as potential water wars show that not only the line between domestic and interstate security is blurred, but so also is the line between low and high politics. Briefly, insecurity is multidimensional rather than (militarily) one-sided as it has been conceived (Heydemann, 2000; Sick & Porter, 1997). Consequently, both analysis and policy have to deal with warfare (and its management through, for instance, peacekeeping forces and arms control regimes) and welfare (and its enhancement through, for instance, empowerment schemes by means of sustainable development and democratization).

## NOTES

1. External debt in 1998, expressed as a percentage of GNP, was 12% for Iran, 29% for Egypt, 41% for Lebanon, 49% for Turkey, 54% for Morocco, 56% for Tunisia, 66% for Algeria, 79% for Yemen, 128% for Syria, 128% for Jordan, and a crippling 172% for the Sudan (Henry & Springborg, 2001: 57).

# 9

# The Constellation of Securities in Europe

Ole Wæver

A chapter on European security written in the shadow from the terrorist attacks on New York and Washington on September 11, 2001, easily turns into a search for the European reaction, the place of terrorism in European threat perceptions and the impact of 9/11 on conceptions of security in Europe. Similarly, a conference on globalization and security seems to ask for an elaboration of those security problems that are related to globalization. However, the result would in both cases be misleading. Yes, terror *is* on the European security agenda, and so is globalization. But no, they are not the major issues and they have not recast more long-standing patterns. Therefore, they are not the place to start. It is necessary first to understand the structural conditions and the constellation of primary security issues. Then, the analysis can return to these starting questions and show *how* terror and globalization are approached as security issues (or not) in Europe as a result of the security agenda onto which they have to be attached. Otherwise, the questions themselves lead one to assume a close link between globalization and security as well as a centrality of terror, where the more interesting point might be their absence.

Developing states face particular security problems due to an immature political apparatus and particularly severe challenges from globalization. However, a closer look at Europe also reveals that one of the most posttraditional regions is marked by new complexities and confusing interactions of state-centered and nonstate-centered dynamics. At the same time, Europe explicitly confirms expectations about the decline of traditional security problems: the most striking feature of present-day European security is *how* marginal the classical security issue of state-threatens-state has become.

Since Europe in some ways experiments with developments that IR theory otherwise knows only from its dreams, there is a tendency to jump to idyllic and premature conclusions. For instance:

- Europe has moved beyond interstate security concerns among its main powers. One tends then to expect a stable interstate security system. However, this is not the case for two reasons. One is that this removal of security problems happened by the indirect approach, that is, not by setting up a security system, but by pulling the states into other activities, through the Jean Monnet strategy of desecuritization. The other is that as interstate concerns fade, the system increasingly moves in a postsovereign direction and therefore a multitude of new cross-cutting units become referent objects for new security dynamics. Notably, it is no coincidence that this postsovereign development appeared just as the states were about to celebrate the end of security concerns, because their pacification was largely driven by the process of European integration that includes supranationalism and a general complication of political structures. Or, in Deutschian terms, the security community could not be realized in purely pluralistic form—it had to include elements of the amalgamated type (Deutsch et al., 1957; Wæver, 1998).

- With this decrease in traditional security concerns, one might expect that Europe was 'free' to take up new challenges and, for example, act more unrestrained and decisively in relation to global challenges. However, new security issues do not reach an empty page because European developments are structured by a host of nontraditional security issues. Again, this is no coincidence: the process of stable peace among the states is partly built on a security constellation, on fears variously on behalf of or against Europe. The region is far from free to pick new themes. Europe too is in the grip of security, even if in unusual forms.

The aim of this chapter is to map the security problems of present-day Europe and how they tie together into a regional formation. The first section presents some theoretical tools, security complex analysis, and securitization studies. The second section offers a brief outline of the structure of the European security complex, whereas the third section investigates the complex in more detail by surveying the main types of securitization (i.e., what are the issues that are acted on as security issues in Europe). The fourth section shows how this conditions the European approach to global security issues including terrorism post-9/11.

Thus, the first purpose is to understand why Europe does not securitize global threats to a much larger extent. This is done by mapping the European security constellation, which is also of interest in itself and therefore the second purpose. Third, it makes a theoretical and methodological point by doing that. In the first parts of the book, the traditional picture was modified in one way: to allow for variations in the state, which implied changing conceptions of security. This is extremely useful and important, but there is another part of the debate, which these first chapters held back from: to introduce other referent objects than the state. I will argue that doing this is absolutely necessary when trying to understand the European situation. If you look only for concerns about *state security*, it seems that Europe is beyond security, desecuritized. While it is true that changes are drastic, it would be wrong to ignore the new forms of security that dominate in Europe today.

However, it is particularly important to be conceptually clear when moving beyond the traditional agenda. There is a risk of widening the meaning of the concept to the useless point of "everything is security." This risk in turn is used by traditionalists as an argument for not widening at all, which creates an arbitrarily delineated concept because no substantial, noncircular case can be given for the narrow meaning. The result is an analytical choice that increasingly gets separated from practical reality. Reconnecting concept and reality can be achieved by using the theory of "securitization." When I coined that term, it was to a large extent an attempt to find a structured way of looking at the wider security agenda, a middle position between "everything is security" and "keep it narrow or you get confused."

This chapter shares much with Korany's chapter in this part. As he states, we look at global context, regional dynamics, we are interested in nontraditional, nonstate security; and we both emphasize the importance of *identity* as the object experienced as threatened.

## REGIONAL SECURITY—TWO BRIEF, THEORETICAL INTRODUCTIONS

This analysis will be assisted by the theory of regional security complexes and the concept of securitization, two of the pillars of the so-called Copenhagen School.[1]

### Security

In order to assess what actually counts as security in Europe, I will apply the method of securitization analysis (Buzan et al., 1998; Wæver, 1995). When something is constituted as a security issue (i.e., securitized), it means that somebody (a securitizing actor) argues that this (the threat) poses an existential threat to something (the referent object) that has to survive (e.g., the state, the nation, or the environment). Because this threat is too urgent or for other reasons cannot be trusted to be dealt with properly through normal procedures, extraordinary measures could be used. Thus, by securitizing an issue, it is lifted above normal politics and given priority. This can not be done arbitrarily on just anything because not everything has a socially recognized claim for survival—for instance, not a normal company in a capitalist economy, because its possible bankruptcy is part of the logic of the system. Nor can every actor do it with equal ease, and official representatives of a state are typically in the best position to succeed. Still, the theory is open to the possibility that those who have a formal role in securitizing might fail (as, e.g., the communist regimes in Eastern Europe in 1989), and those who have no official position might succeed (as some environmental groups).

Generally, this theory of securitization serves to create an open theory of security. It is not for the theorist to define a priori that security either is the narrow thing with state and military, or to widen in the direction of everything is security. If we should be able to study *empirically* changes in what counts as security, our *analytical* concept has to be an open one that registers such change. By pointing to a specific rhetorical structure as defining for security, the theory allows security to be recognized in new fields. And it equally allows for the possibility that empirical reality conforms to the most conventional and narrow understanding. The theory is not state-centric, but it allows for the possibility that our reality might be so.

There has been a tendency to assume that a broader concept was good. Often, this question is presented as one about narrow, military definition versus a wider and allegedly more humane definition. However, to widen the concept of security could actually mean more militarization because wider security means that more issues are approached according to a logic of security, that is, framed in the way traditionally reserved for military issues (e.g., with a presumption that threats are external, that society has to present a 'defense' against such threats, and that the state it the appropriate agent for this). Securitization justifies extreme measures—whether politicians limiting democracy "for security reasons" or animal rights activists shooting politicians.

In the longer history of what "security" has meant throughout the centuries (Wæver, 2002), the concept has been relatively stable for the last half-century. The general sense of the concept has been the same since the idea of national security was launched in the early to mid-1940s in the United States. Before that, the concept had taken many twists and turns since its Roman origins. It had changed between subjective and objective, between individual and collective, and even between positive and negative several times. Mostly, it had been a meaningful but far from central concept. Only in the 1940s did it become an organizing concept and a rallying cry in foreign affairs. Partly for peculiarly American reasons (related to the difficulties of legitimizing standing armies and long-term military efforts as well as achieving close integration between military and civilian affairs), the concept became the vehicle for a claim that had been known in previous periods as raison d'etat or necessity, but had fallen out of fashion with democratization and liberalism. "Security" became the place to continue the argument that when facing particularly threatening possibilities, the state has a right to transcend normal rules. Traditionally, this effect is seen as a secondary side effect by security studies. However, it is the main effect of labeling something a security issue and the political struggles around security are, to a large extent, fought because of this powerful effect. Then it should also be put at the center of analysis. The definition of security is what the concept does.

Originally (1940s), the introduction of this particular meaning of security, and the singular attachment of the term to the state (national security) only, were two sides of the same move. However, the concept has gradually detached itself from this particular object and therefore the debate on wider concepts of security has become one over the legitimacy and fruitfulness of accepting securitization on behalf of other referent objects. The core meaning of security was kept constant while the demand on the referent object was loosened.

On the basis of this key idea, a theory has been constructed made up of a set of interconnected concepts (securitizing actor, referent object, audience, existential threat, extraordinary moves, etc.). This theoretical apparatus will not explicitly and systematically be used in this chapter and even when employed, the analytical terms will not be flagged excessively. Instead, the aim is to tell a story that is meaningful on its own and only informed by the theory as a general perspective more than a slavish application.

## Regional Patterns

Regional security complex theory (RSCT) points out that the world to a considerable extent is made up of regional chunks of security.[2] The world is not homogenous—we are not all equally connected to everybody else. Looking at the world through the lens of security produces a regional pattern. A regional security complex is defined as: "a group of states whose primary security concerns link together sufficiently closely that their national securities cannot reasonably be considered apart from one another" (Buzan, 1983: 106). Or if the language of securitization theory is made explicit, this becomes: "a set of units whose major processes of securitization, desecuritization, or both are so interlinked that their security problems cannot reasonably be analysed or resolved apart from one another" (Buzan et al., 1998: 201). (The basic idea is the same in the two definitions, only the newer one sheds the state-centric and military-political focus and rephrases the same basic conception for the possibility of different actors and several sectors of security. The original one is contained as special case—although a fairly common one—within the newer, general definition.)

The regional patterning of security is a product of geography. Despite globalization, it is still the case that most threats travel more easily over short than long distances. This is clearly valid for military threats, often also for identity, migration, and many political threats, but not nearly as much for economic security. From the perspective of RSCT, deterritorialization is the most important long-term effect of globalization.[3] On the one hand, a number of leading scholars of globalization agree that deterritorialization is the defining feature of globalization (Scholte, 2000; Held et al., 1999), and, on the other hand, territoriality is a necessary assumption of RSCT. Thus, far-reaching globalization will eventually undermine RSCT, but it does not seem reasonable to depict the situation today or tomorrow or in 20 years in terms of that much deterritorialization. In lieu of this radical change, globalization will nevertheless have effects that can be studied *within* RSCT. The effects defined in terms of relative deterritorialization will show themselves partly as an increase in nonterritorially defined referent objects, partly as an increasing importance of great powers with region-transcending military power and thereby the formation of more supercomplexes (like the Asian one today). In the context of this chapter that looks at the present and near future, more important effects are related to the kind of units to be studied. Cha (2000: 397), Clark (1999: 107–126), Guéhenno (1998–1999) Scholte (2000: 207–233) and Zangl and Zurn (1999) all argue that globalization is responsible for complicating the security agenda, while at the same time reducing the elements of control that underpin the security strategy options of states. This aspect of globalization is sufficiently far progressed that it is necessary to include more than states as referent objects. As with deterritorialization, the process is far from complete, nor does the theory assume anything close to obsolescence for states. Much security theory implicitly assumes a state monopoly on security and radical deterritorialization—the opposite choice regarding the two kinds of globalization effects seems much more reasonable: the current degree of globalization is enough to supplement states with other referent objects and enough to add nonterritorial patterns to the territorial ones, but neither the state nor territorializing dynamics have evaporated.

The globe is not tightly integrated in security terms, and except for the special case of superpowers and great powers, only a limited amount can be said at this level of generality that will reflect the real concerns in most countries. The region, in contrast, refers to the level where states or other units link together sufficiently closely that their securities cannot be considered in separation from each other. The larger picture of international security is best seen as the conjunction of two levels: the interplay of the global powers at the system level, and clusters of close security interdependence at the regional level. Each RSC is made up of the fears and aspirations of the separate units (which, in turn, partly derive from domestic features and fractures). Both the security of the separate units and the process of global power intervention can only be grasped through understanding the regional security dynamics.

The pattern of amity and enmity is normally best understood by starting the analysis from the regional level, and extending it toward inclusion of the global actors on the one side and domestic factors on the other. The specific pattern of who fears or likes whom is generally not imported from the system level, but generated internally in the region by a mixture of history, politics, and material conditions. For most of the states in the international system, the regional level is the crucial one for security analysis. For the global powers, the regional level is crucial in shaping how they project their influences and rivalries into the rest of the system. The regional level thus matters most for the states within it, and matters a lot for the global powers. Security features at the level of regions are durable. They are substantially self-contained, not in the sense of being totally freestanding, but rather in possessing a security dynamic that would exist even if other actors did not impinge on it. This relative autonomy was revealed by the ending of the Cold War, when enmities such as that between Israel and Syria, and Iraq and the Gulf Arab states, easily survived the demise of a superpower rivalry that had supported, but not generated, them.

The exception to this is the extreme case of *overlay* in which global powers enter in such a dominant way that local dynamics are suppressed. This was done to much of the world by the colonial powers and the superpowers did it to Europe during the Cold War.

In the post–Cold War world, it is absolutely necessary to analyze both global and regional patterns (which implies some conception of how to keep them apart) and to study their interplay. It is necessary to distinguish regional and global levels, not because they are unrelated, but because it is crucial to capture their interaction in a systematic way. (On the global level, see Barry Buzan's chapter in this volume.)

A key element in the theory is to define different types of RSCs. It is not necessary for the present case to outline the full range, but only to notice some of the major distinctions:

- RSCs can vary along the spectrum of enmity and amity—that is, from conflict formation through security regime to security community.
- A major distinction is between standard complexes with two or more powers defining their polarity and the security dynamics played out between the actors, and on the other side centered complexes in which the region is dominated from a center in line with the historical importance of empires as the organizing form of systems (Watson, 1992).
- Within centered regions, a major distinction is between those that have at the center a power (so far always a great or superpower, but potentially a regional power) and those that are integrated by institutions and thus with an 'artificial' center like the EU and early United States.
- The presence in an RSC of a great power should be noticed because it naturally spills over into neighboring regions (witness China–South Asia relations) and this can create asymmetrical relations among regions, and it can tie two or more RSCs together in a supercomplex as seen today in Asia.

A final concept to introduce is that of insulators. Most often the borders between regions are—often geographically determined—zones of weak interaction, or they are occupied by an *insulator* (Turkey, Burma, Afghanistan) that faces both ways, bearing the burden of this difficult position but not strong enough to unify its two worlds into one.[4]

The theory demands a conception of regions as exclusive and not overlapping (as an analytical conception, not an empirical question). The result is therefore a world made up of global powers, regions, and insulators.

## Method

The study of securitization can be the way to map an RSC, because ultimately an RSC consists of the constellation of interlocking security concerns. In practice, it is not possible to fully trace the processes of competing securitization and desecuritization in relation to each referent object and thus consistently mapping a whole region (not to talk about the globe; Buzan & Wæver, 2003). Ideally, the long-term answer to this is the interaction between micro and macro studies, detailed case studies and integrative analyses at the regional and global levels.

In this chapter, the presentation occasionally becomes somewhat impressionistic. I have to abstain from documenting in detail how various securitizing actors have attempted to securitize this or that and to what extent they have succeeded. Some of it is more fully documented in Buzan and Wæver (2003), and I would especially like to point to the high number of emerging studies (not least PH.D. dissertations) from many countries employing the theory in detailed case studies (e.g., Christensen 2002; Kazan 2003; Wagnsson 2000).

In the following section, the larger picture is outlined in more structural terms, while the third section tries to capture the nature of the constellation by surveying the different main forms of securitization in the region.

## THE EUROPEAN SECURITY COMPLEX

Throughout its history, Europe has experienced a limited number of decisive structural changes. In various periods the continent has tried out many of the forms a region can take: centralized, fragmented, overlaid, and itself overlayer of most of the world. Furthermore, it has been through processes of mergers of and redifferentiation into several RSCs. During the Cold War the Soviet Union moved up to the global level, becoming co-constitutive of the 2 + 3 world (two super powers plus three great powers). Thus, Russia was lifted out of Europe, and had no RSC around itself (due to its direct dominance of potential members). In the current 1 + 4 world, Europe has two of the four great powers, but in contrast to Asia as members of separate RSCs. After the end of the Cold War, Europe has wavered between a formation as one, two, or three complexes. In the first post–Cold War years, a large OSCE Europe began to form, which included Russia, but increasingly Russia drifted off to become the center of its own RSC. The Balkans for a while looked as if it formed a distinct RSC. This development ultimately did not materialize, and Europe now consists of two centered RSCs, which have decisively curbed its traditional power balancing and friction. The geographical closeness of Europe's two great powers (EU and Russia) makes a reunification of the two complexes a possibility and today they form a loose supercomplex. The Baltic States are the most important zone of contact, but generally the EU and Russia are not enough involved in each other's security issues to turn 'Europe' into one large RSC.

The present chapter only covers the Western, EU-centered complex, not the Eastern, Russia-centered one. For simplicity, it talks of this as "the European complex," which is, on the one hand, in accordance with much convention, but, on the other, incorrect as there is another European complex to the East.

In addition to the boundary questions related to the separation of the Russia-centered complex and the nonseparation of the Balkans, two particular powers have to be dealt with: Turkey and the United States. Turkey, because it is a key insulator at the meeting point of three RSCs (EU-Europe, ex-Soviet space, and the Middle East). Insulator is not the Turkish self-perception, which is understandable given the unattractiveness of this role, and Turkey prefers (like Russia) to project an image of a larger Eurasian region in which it would itself be very central. However, in practice, Turkey has after the Cold War cultivated a regional policy of a very different kind that reveals the actual location much better (Kazan, 2003): a policy of regionalized security in the sense of stressing and exploiting a position of relevance to four or five of the most important 'regions' today: the Balkans, Caucasus, Central Asia, the Eastern Mediterranean, and the Middle East (most of which are subregions seen from the systemic perspective). Thereby, Turkey has become an unusually active insulator challenging both our traditional (implicitly more passive) concept of insulator and Turkey's own traditional policy. However, there is nothing in the basic theory that precludes this role, as long as it remains impossible for Turkey to tie together the different regional arenas, because the main actors of each relate to their separate settings. The—for Turkey negative—scenario of its main rivals or problems in each region allying due to their common opposition to Turkey is the main challenge to the theory, but here for once, the theory is kind to Turkey and predicts that this will not unfold on a large scale. Should Turkey eventually join the EU, it would probably move into the EU-European RSC.

The United States is the other main actor with a complicated location in relation to the RSC. The American view is that the United States is a member of the region as expressed in membership of key institutions like NATO and the OSCE. This is in line with a general American inclination to define itself into a number of regions (Europe, Asia, and pan-America) that politically serve to blunt attempts to form regions without the United States and to play the regions against each other (swing power position). Interestingly, this is also the inclination of U.S. theorists of the matter (Lake & Morgan, 1997). According to RSCT, the United States is not a member of the RSC as such— it makes a difference whether you are located in a region and thus without choice of participating, or you have chosen to participate but with the possibility not to. The United States is the only superpower in today's world, and due to the global reach of its power it can enter (as seeming-to-be-member) almost any region it chooses to. Analytically, it is important to analyze this in terms of global-regional interplay instead of membership.

During the Cold War, the area that would become EU-Europe was overlaid and the dominant security concerns in the region were defined externally. Especially since the Cuba missile crisis in 1962, security politics involved mostly struggles over how intensely to securitize superpower rivalry versus to desecuritize as a product of détente or deterrence. By definition, the main threat was seen to be the East–West conflict. The most thorough securitization on either side was the other side as threat. Western oppositional forces securitized the nuclear confrontation itself either because it could run out of control and lead to nuclear war, or because the East–West conflict dominated Europe and repressed other possible identities. Overlay was complete with alliances, stationing of foreign troops, and a suppression of older intra-European conflicts. On the Western side, international cooperation took a unique form as the North Atlantic alliance developed into an *organization* (NATO), uncharacteristic for alliances.

During the Cold War, Western Europe went through periods of insecurity (i.e., threat and no sense of sufficient defense) in the 1940s and 1950s, security (i.e., a threat but also a reliable defense) in the 1960s, desecuritization in the 1970s, to reach a situation in the 1980s and especially 1990s of resecuritization (Wæver, 1998).

Desecuritization was a result both of the success of the neofunctionalist strategy of solving security problems by focusing on something else and of the paradoxical stability of the nuclear balance of terror. Security arguments underpinned both the integration project and the military mobilization of the Cold War, but it all became stabilized as a kind of normality. In addition to the marks left by division, the Cold War gifts to EU-Europe were desecuritization and reconciliation internally in Western Europe, dense institutionalization, including far-reaching multilateralization of the military sector (NATO), and a consolidation of the EU to the point at which it became a great power from somewhere in the 1970s.

In the categories of RSCT, the European RSC is a centered complex and notably the type without a power at the center but constructed through institutions. Europe is not being unified because 'somebody' is strong enough to conquer it from the center (as in previous attempts in modern time—Hapsburgs, Napoleon, Hitler), and the driving force is rather a 'will to center' more akin to early American history—and explicable through Adam Watson's (1992) concept of legitimacy: Europeans have gradually changed their view about what is the appropriate position on the line between extreme fragmentation of multiple independences and centeredness. A balance of power system was for centuries celebrated as not only a technical remedy but a European value connected to liberty and freedom of religion; today it has become seen as a threat, as a pattern Europe should not be allowed to fall into again. While not wanting any power external to themselves to dominate, Europeans increasingly accept the idea that Europe should be organized in some mixed form combining independent states and a center.

This explains the superior importance of the EU, compared to, say, NATO; it is European integration that decides the structural question whether Europe will continuously and maybe increasingly be a centered complex. Even in terms of security, where seemingly NATO is the main 'security' institution, the EU should be recognized as key because the structural question of what kind of region and general coherence of the regional powers comes before the more instrumental one of who can do what in a certain crisis.

The question whether the European complex contains a great power is a tricky one because the EU is such an unusual and inconsistent power. In some respects, the EU is a global power (and then a tier two one, neither a superpower nor a regional power, but a great power). In other respects, the 'old' powers—France, Germany, and the United Kingdom—appear as powers still and complicate the picture. Because of the salience of the center-periphery pattern, it is most helpful to take the picture with the EU as the power as the starting point of analysis and only remember the complexities created by the dual nature of powers in Europe.

The European RSC has three defining features: it is centered, it is the kind of center focused on institutions (and legitimacy, a will to center) not a single power, and third: it is shaped as concentric circles. Specifically, the EU operates as a security institution through three distinct mechanisms that are layered in the shape of concentric circles (Wæver, 1996a; 1998; 2000).

First, it keeps the core intact by its identity effect on the overall foreign policies of the European main powers (Wæver, 1990, 1994, 1998). A concept and vision of Europe have become critical to each nation's vision of itself and therefore since it is very hard notably in Germany and France to construct convincing narratives of where we are heading without presenting or drawing on a project for European integration. It is not that the countries agree on one concept of Europe or that European identity comes close to outcompeting national identity, but in each country the concepts of nation, state, and Europe have become closely intertwined—'Europe' is colored in each case by national traditions of political thought, but the meaning of 'Germany' and 'France' has become inseparable from some sense of Europe.

Second, the EU has a silent disciplining effect on the East-Central European countries due to their applicanthood. This magnetism allows for both implicit and explicit demands and anticipated effects that have dampened potential conflicts such as those related to Hungarian minorities.

Third, direct interventions occur further out in the periphery where the nicer nonmilitary factors do not work strongly enough to avoid conflict. Here, the EU has so far been secondary to NATO, but there is no doubt about the aspirations from both EU countries and the United States to see such tasks increasingly shifted toward the Europeans.

All these elements are structural only. The content of an RSC is the constellation of actual securitizations. Therefore, it is necessary in order to assess stability, trends, and pressures, to map these securitizations, and this is the task of the following section.

## SECURITIZATION IN EUROPE

### Securitizations in Post-wall Europe: The EU Core

What kinds of security problems do actors in the EU-part of Europe articulate?[5] After 1989, several new elements were added to the security discourse in Europe: environment, migrants, ethnic conflict, organized crime, and terrorism. The list in Europe achieved maximum breadth, covering all sectors and almost all levels. The issues were mostly not new but with the end of the Cold War they became articulated as *security* problems. At first increased diversity was easy to see; a new pattern was not. The atmosphere was one of insecurity again, contrasting strongly with the asecurity of the 1970s but even with the security of the 1960s. Of the ten elements listed below, the first two increasingly came to organize the whole field.

*1. The threat to Europe from its own past.* At the European level, one security discourse is patently dominant, even if not always recognized for its centrality. Some years ago, I analyzed the major general debates or speeches during 1995 from the different EU institutions (Council, Parliament, and Commission), searching for anything that was phrased in security terms (as previously defined). In all three places, one discourse was clearly dominant: Europe has to avoid a return to its own notorious past of wars and power balancing, and integration therefore is a necessity (Buzan et al., 1998: 176–189; see also Wæver, 1996). This is phrased in security terms, because it is argued that a self-reinforcing process of decline would set in if power balancing and classical mutual security concerns were to return; Europe would then be pulled apart, integration rolled back, and Europe would return to its own habits. According to this discourse, it is not a question of a little more or a little less integration/fragmentation because the power of the old configuration poses an existential threat to integration and thereby security in Europe. Therefore, a point of no return exists and it is mandatory to ensure enough integration to avoid crossing this point. Integration is thereby invested by a security quality, which is actually mobilized (not least in Germany, but also to some extent France) whenever a change of policy direction is considered.

While discourse analysts often search in official texts for instances of NATO, the United States or EU 'othering' somebody like Russia, Muslims, or Turkey, it is actually striking that the most powerful Other in relation to which Europe's identity is constituted is Europe itself. Interestingly, this means that European historical identity is largely constructed as something negative—not through a celebration of European heroism but through defining wars and bloodshed as characteristic for Europe and therefore a break with this as necessary and as the European vocation of our age. This in turn, of course, becomes heroic and something to be displayed and maybe even exported as a European triumph. However, it still installs a basic modesty and self-limitation into European identity that it is a negative past from which to break rather than a classical nationalist story of a great past to be reconquered in a great future.

More recently, I have checked major speeches from the leaders of France, Germany, and the United Kingdom[6] to see if this discourse continues to be as powerful as it used to be or is in decline either due to generational change (the departure of leaders who experienced the Second World War) or because of the end of the immediate post–Cold War situation. The result is that in Germany we still find the direct argument about a possible return to a past of wars and destruction and the necessity of integration. The centrality of the Franco-German couple in overcoming this past is underlined as least as much as in the past.[7] In France and the United Kingdom, the outright possibility of war is not used, but the dichotomy between a Europe of wars and a Europe of integration is still the basic figure. It is both a temporal dichotomy (past and present in EU Europe) and a spatial one of Western (EU) Europe versus Eastern Europe and especially the Balkans. In British discourse, this is used partly to present a hard choice, especially to people in the Balkans, and partly to argue the importance of EU (and NATO) enlargement. In France, it becomes an argument for the construction of EU-actor capability in foreign and security policy being the crucial issue: this is what decides whether the Eastern part of the continent will be saved along with the Western part and not least it is necessary for the Western countries to save their own soul and civilizational obligations.[8]

The strongest security discourse in post-wall Europe has been the argument that Europe needs more (or at least continued) integration to avoid a return to the past. This argument qualifies as a security argument because it posits an existential threat and a possible point of no return: 'Europe' is the referent object, and will be lost in a fragmentation scenario.

*2. The other main security argument is the reverse of the first. European integration itself is presented as a threat, primarily to national identity.* Various—mostly nonstate—actors have mobilized a resistance against EU integration based on the security claim that integration threatens national identity.[9] Often, this converges with nationalist or xenophobic reactions against foreigners (immigrants and refugees), but also in some cases against globalization/Americanization (especially in France). The two scenarios produce an overarching conflict not so much between *different* particularisms as between the universalism of internationalizing elites on the one hand and particularism in general—that is, the reaction of "mass politics" on behalf of different cultures against cosmopolitanism (Hassner, 1993; Reich, 1991).

The security argument about Europe's past has experienced and will experience various developments that respectively strengthen and challenge it. First, the wars in the Balkans have generally served to strengthen this discourse. They reintroduce the idea that war in Europe is possible, and "one of the main clichés about the Balkans [is] that they are the part of Europe which is haunted by the notorious 'ghosts of the past', forgetting nothing and learning nothing, still fighting centuries-old battles, while the rest of Europe is engaged in a rapid process of globalization" (Zizek, 2000: 3). The Balkans have served as Europe's ghost, reminding it of the risks and defining Europe's own identity in terms of no longer being like that. Second, Eastern enlargement has more ambiguous effects. On the one hand, the growing of the EU is likely to mean that the Franco-German tandem, which has been the main home of this discourse, becomes less dominant simply because it becomes a smaller fraction of the whole. On the other hand, the project of enlargement reinforces the historic sense of the EU project, of what it has done to Western Europe and now is to do in Eastern Europe. How these two will balance out is hard to predict.

The total European security landscape is extremely complicated, exhibiting almost all imaginable forms of insecurity except the classical military one. In addition to these two dominant and reciprocally opposed ones, I will list others more briefly, though most of these increasingly tie back into the two basic ones.

*3. Some local conflicts are intense without tying much into the European whole: Northern Ireland, the Basque region in Spain, Corsica, and (more peacefully) South Tirol.* Although not enacted as state-to-state conflicts, these are quite traditional conflicts in being territorial and in some sense state-centered ("we want to be one," or "we belong to the wrong state"). Cyprus (and thereby the general Greco-Turkish conflict) also has a domestic conflict at the core, but here the antagonistic involvement of the states is much more direct and unrestrained (see later). With the exception of Greece–Turkey–Cyprus, these local conflicts do not have or threaten to have repercussions beyond the local setting. A European dimension to these conflicts emerged in the 1980s when it was widely expected among the leaders of some of the regionalist movements (Scotland, South Tirol, Catalonia) that European integration would solve the conflict with the central state. Sovereignty would become an irrelevant goal as the old states also lost it. However, the 1990s disconfirmed sweeping prophecies about a solution beyond sovereignty to these conflicts.

Although they are major security issues locally, it is striking that these conflicts are rarely even mentioned in general rankings of security issues in Western Europe. In contrast, more often Western Europe is seen as threatened from the Eastern neighbors.

*4. One the most talked about issues especially in the early 1990s has been ethnic conflict in Eastern Europe, sometimes referred to as regional stability or the Eastwards export of stability.* Especially in NATO contexts, the first securitization (fragmentation/integration) is for obvious reasons less prevalent and often modified, and this other discourse has been central.

This has been depicted as a concern and a task, but it gets its main security importance when connected to the first discourse. Ethnic conflict in Eastern Europe (especially the wars of former Yugoslavia) are a *threat* to the West primarily when it threatens to have a rub-off effect of dragging Western powers into local conflicts and thereby triggering classical power balancing and geopolitical thinking in the core. Thus, the first discourse is still the master discourse in most cases because the radical version of the second only materializes when the two are combined.

Ethnic conflict is bad enough in itself, but it is primarily a *security* threat to Western Europe if an ethnic conflict drags Western powers in on opposing sides and thus triggers the return to power politics among the EU core states. (Sometimes, the threat of refugees functions similarly as accelerator of the threat, making it directly relevant to the member states in a way, which the conflict itself is not.) Thus, the reflections on conflicts (e.g., in the Balkans) gets overpowered by the calculation of effects on EU integration/fragmentation dynamics. Western Europe's (non)actions during the 1990s can best be made sense of through this lens: yes, Balkan developments were very important, but it was necessary to think "EU first" even for the best of people in the Balkans in the long run.

East Central Europe has a special status in European security discourse because it is depicted as potentially "us" (Hansen, 1995)—security problems here can potentially be resolved in the ideal and complete way of becoming part of the Western integration project(s), thus the centrality of enlargement.

This defines a separate category for other instabilities in neighboring regions: Russia, the Caucasus, and Northern Africa.

5. *Instability in Russia and the Mediterranean has a different status from Eastern Europe*, because Eastern Europe is supposed to become part of the EU self very soon and thus threats are both more problematic (if they block enlargement and might send the EU into crisis) and less likely (because they are not radically different from us) (Hansen, 1995; Larsen, 2000: 225). Russia and the Mediterranean are usually not presented as military threats or radical Others either, but they are more unreliable.

Whenever reluctantly moving beyond the preferred strategic space of Europe itself (which can be dealt with by the logic of integration and enlargement), priority has been given to the areas directly adjacent to Europe. Lacking a global strategic vision, and driven by the internal security problem due to the unfinished character of the regional project, other regions are approached in a way that differs from the American one. For the United States, regions link *via* the global level on which the United States is present. This will probably increasingly become the case for Europe, too, as it becomes a more fully global actor. But, for now, other regions are approached on the basis of their interregional connections to Europe. The mechanism that regulates this is the lack of securitization of the global distribution of power and therefore the priority of direct security effects on Europe. Such effects can easily be projected for Russia, possibly for other parts of the CIS (like the Caucasus), clearly for Turkey (if not already counted as part of Europe and the space of enlargement), and not least for the Maghreb.

6. *Globalization and immigrants securitized as threats to national identity increasingly merge with no. 2, and integration becomes the scapegoat for all effects of globalization*, but also direct action on a threat from foreigners is powerful in many countries. The rise of a sometimes xenophobic and usually nationalistic new Right in several European countries testifies to the persuasiveness of such arguments to wide sections of the public.

Increasingly, globalization appears in a second function in European politics. Whether this has reached the point of securitization is more doubtful, but flirtations have certainly appeared: the argument is that the European welfare state model is particularly threatened by globalization, more than many other societies. This becomes a threat to identity—national and European—as well as welfare and independence. In this version, the pro-integration argument is used strongly to argue the necessity of paying a price in terms of additional integration to defend ourselves against globalization. What appears to the ordinary citizen as sovereignty losses due to the EU are rephrased in this discourse as countergains of sovereignty via the EU against the onslaught from globalization. The security potential in this argument is mostly related to the identity and independence argument for the classical reason that welfare is harder to securitize because of its gradualist nature. On the countermeasure side, it is used to justify integration one would otherwise not tolerate.

7. *Terrorism, international organized crime, drug trafficking, and illegal migration are often presented as a security problem especially in specific EU sources* (Larsen, 2000: 226). Notably, these questions have become a standard package, which implies that immigrants are at the root of these problems and the solution is to tighten the regime of policing in depth and other compensatory mechanisms related to the removal of internal borders in the EU (Bigo, 1996). Thus, it partly channels back into the package with ethno-national fear of foreigners, and partly it supports practices of internal security. (Terrorism was, prior to September 11, mostly placed as part of this package. Whether it stays here or moves toward item 9 is not clear yet.)

8. *Environmental security is high on the agenda in many places,* partly because of the high density and smallness of units in Europe that make more environmental issues than elsewhere border-crossing and therefore lead to more dramatic politicization, for example, the Danube dam, nuclear power plants in the former East, air pollution mostly blowing eastward, and upstream pollution (such as that of Swiss medical giants), threatening downstream areas along the Rhine. This one does not so far tie much into the two master discourses, although the EU has made some attempts to merge integration and environmentalism (Buzan et al., 1998: 163–194; Jachtenfuchs & Huber, 1993; Jachtenfuchs, 1994).

9. *Global terrorism, regional conflicts, extra-European environment, and infectious diseases.* When approaching security issues further away from Europe—regional conflicts in all other regions, including even the Gulf, and new global threats like the environment and AIDS—it is striking how Europeans are inclined to define these in two characteristic modes that are distinct from the American approach. One is a developmentalist discourse in which all conflicts from intrastate to major regional wars are ultimately caused by problems of resources and lack of development. Thus, while Europe participates in American-led efforts like the Gulf War, the characteristic profile of its own efforts is not a military one but attempts at redefinition. The other characteristic European angle is to export its own regionalism—that is, emphasize against American attempts to see all conflicts in a global perspective, along with the necessity of allowing indigenous dynamics to evolve in the particular region.

Even in the reaction to the terrorist attacks on the United States in September 2001, the debate in Europe showed clear signs of the inclination toward developmentalism. The argument was heard in the United States, too, but in Europe public debate has to a much larger extent established almost as common sense that terrorism is attributable to socioeconomic causes, and official statements hint in this direction.

Other global threats, like AIDS, are also largely defined as problems of development.

*10. Traditional state-to-state securitizations play a surprisingly marginal role on the European security agenda.* The most important presence is in the form of a worry about Germany, which is then politely rephrased more structurally as securitization-1. Political security on behalf of the sovereignty of the states, the usual core agenda, has been displaced partly to the societal sector (identity), and partly to the EU level (protection of the European order and the European project). When state security appears, it is almost always in *vertical* conflicts, that is, articulated as threatened from *above* (EU) or *below* (minorities), but not *horizontal* threats between states.

Security in Western Europe is a uniquely complicated constellation (probably only rivaled by sub-Saharan Africa), but it does have a core dynamic and a discernible pattern. The two first securitizations stand out as dominant and most of the others tie back to these two. This shows how central the EU has become for security—the driving security issues are security concerns either for or against European integration.

## Securitization in the Eastern Circles

The overall pattern of European post-wall politics is of a center-periphery nature. Almost all nonmembers aspire for membership in the EU and, with a few more exceptions, in NATO as well. To them, the relationship to the EU (and, to some extent, NATO) is both a solution to security concerns and a source of insecurity in itself. The West is their anchor of stability—the source of security guarantees as well as prosperity. However, the relationship is also a source of security concerns, especially with far-reaching intrusions of Western organizations into domestic decision making in the applicant countries. This is particularly problematic in countries that combine economic and political reform with a national revival. The countries that became independent with the end of the Cold War, but also to some extent the former Warsaw Pact allies, have had a dual agenda of returning to Europe and returning to themselves—that is, rediscovering their allegedly repressed nationality. The two seemed perfectly compatible in the immediate liberation perspective: both Europe and the nation were opposites of Soviet oppression. But as adaptation to the new realities becomes concrete, the two conflict more often. Europeanization implies opening and internationalization, which is often resisted by nationalist politicians (e.g., see Jurgaitienè, 1993; Miniotaite, 2000.)

The Eastern half of the RSC articulates most of the same security issues as do EU members, but some are either added or accentuated (and one downplayed): classical interstate fears are relevant in the Baltics, sometimes between Hungary and its neighbors, in the Balkans, and between Greece and Turkey.

Societal security problems and political security link up the classical way because it is in many cases (the above plus, e.g., Polish and Czech relations to Germany) a matter of debate within 'host' countries to what extent the striving for regionalism among minorities should be seen as an alternative or a prologue to secessionism.

Economic, broadly social, and law-and-order issues sometimes come close to constituting a security threat to society not in the identity sense of our societal sector but to the coherence and functioning of society as social order. One case of *less* intense securitization than in the West is the environment. Only in a few, more local instances, like the areas in Poland and the Czech Republic where air and soil pollution are most acute, do local (i.e., substate) actors dramatize the issue.

In some of the easternmost countries, Russia is presented as a threat. When it was played up in order to gain Western attention as by the Baltic States, they learned that the West did not want trouble spots and therefore it was better to downplay the threat and become 'normal' (Joenniemi & Wæver, 1997). The Russian threat seems unlikely to become directed toward anybody in the RSC in any reasonable future. Due to historical experiences and the domestic usefulness of a Russian threat, it will probably continue to be invoked for a while, and as in all securitization an unlikely threat can have effects, but given the decreasing power of Russia and its preoccupation with its own RSC and the global level, this is unlikely to become a driving issue in East Central Europe.

To sum up, East Central Europe has local security issues related to minorities and other historical and ethnic issues, but the overriding pattern is structured by EU integration. Still, it is not identical to the dilemma in the Western part of the continent. It is a dilemma of dilemmas. In Western Europe, EU integration generates two contradictory security issues: a fear of fragmentation and a fear of integration. As participants in the EU-based security order—formal members or not—the East Central Europeans join this dilemma, but they add another to it: due to their asymmetrical relationship to the EU, the EU is both a source of security and insecurity, a disciplining force that dampens local security problems but also an intruding and demanding *external* threat to national independence and sovereignty.

## The Outer Circles of EU Europe

Most of the attention regarding the EU-dominated parts of Europe goes to East Central Europe. However, the RSC of which the EU is the center is larger than this. In the southeastern part of the continent, there are countries not usually discussed as Central Europe, but involved in the enlargement process nevertheless: Cyprus and Turkey. One member country, Greece, is involved in a conflictual relationship with Turkey—partly over Cyprus—that has many features uncharacteristic of the rest of the RSC and therefore deserves special attention. The other—often forgotten—periphery is the southern one, the Maghreb. Because they are less fully shaped by the processes of the EU-core, these cases require more detailed examination (Buzan & Wæver, 2003: ch. 11). For more on the case of the Maghreb, see Korany's chapter, this volume.

Greece and Turkey have been in varying degrees of confrontation since the Second World War. Increasingly, the conflict over Cyprus has moved to the center of the relationship. The EU gambled that opening enlargement negotiations would function as some kind of catalyst. But how exactly this was to work given its entanglement with the difficult question of Turkish membership remained unclear (Diez, 2002). This part of Europe is influenced very strongly by the relationship to the EU, but here the dynamics of a centralized complex interact with a classical interstate conflict not characteristic of the European RSC at large.

The Maghreb is a large southern periphery to the EU. The relationship to Europe is historically as strong as the link to the Middle East, and the weakening of inter-Arabic cohesion during the 1990s, plus a new dynamism in Europe, caused the Maghreb to drift toward Europe. Based on security reasoning about threats of immigration and regional instability on Europe's doorstep, the South European members of the EU have tried to raise the Maghreb on the agenda. Unlike in the other concentric circles, the EU cannot use the promise of eventual membership to influence politics in the Maghreb. Whether the Maghreb becomes a part of the European RSC, an overlaid neighboring mini-complex, or yet another independent African complex like West Africa and the Horn of Africa, is too early to say.

## Beyond the European Constellation and the Future

Europe is a security community, which is rare in a global comparative perspective. The way Europe has become and remained a security community is even more intriguing. Although the classical security community theory (Deutsch et al., 1957) envisioned that states would become gradually more confident in each other and thus a regional state-based order would stabilize in a nonwar mode, the actual development in Europe contains two surprises. One is that the states establish a peaceful order at the same time as they start to blur, merge, and fade, and numerous nonstate forms of securitization enter. The other is that this security order does not take the form of a direct security system—like collective security—solving the security problems of the region. To a large extent, the order is built on desecuritization, but it only works by mixing in a strong dose of resecuritization in the form of a metasecuritization:

a strong narrative of the historical development of Europe, past, present, and future.

Objections will be raised to this interpretation that a Europe returning to its past is no longer a real possibility. It was in early EU history, but today it is only a myth invoked by elites to legitimize the project. Maybe—but this is very difficult to know for certain. Theories of democratic peace, interdependence, and trading states insist that war is irrevocably ruled out among the states of Western Europe irrespective of the degree of integration. But in the light of centuries of wars, the last doubt will be difficult to erase, and maybe the fear might be the major force preventing this. The constitutive uncertainty about the possibility of a return to balance of power behavior and possibly war is thus central to both European political reality and the present interpretation. This threat operates in a curious way as the replacement for the Cold War reasoning around nuclear deterrence where a breakdown of deterrence and actual usage of the weapons should be highly unlikely but could not be allowed to become totally impossible if deterrence was to function (Tunander, 1989). As long as war is possible, it does not happen. If it becomes impossible, it might happen.

## THE EUROPEAN APPROACH TO INTERNATIONAL TERROR AND GLOBAL SECURITY; OR "WHO SAID GLOBALIZATION?"

EU-Europe is the most institutionalized part of the world. Although the exact nature of the EU is hotly debated, its experiment in postsovereign politics undoubtedly pushes peaceful, regional integration to new limits. Europe develops unique forms of political organization not by either replicating the state form at a higher level, or by annulling the old order, but by mixing a continuity of sovereignty with new forms (Rosenau, 1990; Ruggie, 1993; Wæver, 1995a). Consequently, the European *security* landscape becomes distinctive. The traditional nearmonopoly of the state on security status and security action is challenged in Europe, where numerous other referent objects from mini-region to the EU itself, from environment to 'universal' political values are acted on in a security mode. Securitization theory facilitates this opening to a different picture from the one of only states (while allowing also for *that* possibility).

Among the EU members a security community has formed based on the integration project. Largely, this takes the form of desecuritization, which is natural, given the original Deutschian definition of a security community: that the parties no longer can imagine war with each other (Deutsch et al., 1957). However, this project is ultimately built on a metasecuritization: a fear of Europe's future becoming like Europe's past if fragmentation and power balancing are allowed to return. The integration project itself, however, generates securitization, which is largely 'societal security'—that is, fear for (national) identity. Traditional interstate security concerns only exist beneath the surface. Their effects are most often in the form of the generalized fear of back to the future, rather than the concrete fear of a specific Other.

EU-Europe has a center-periphery structure: Central Europe organizes itself as concentric circles around the Western core. Because these countries are included in the EU-centered order, security issues in this part of the continent partly follow the same pattern as in the West but have additional complications because the dependence on the West is both an anchor of stability and line of intrusion. 'Central' refers to the Cold War's 'Eastern Europe'. The security agenda is today very different in those countries that were market democracies during the Cold War (and formed nation-states early on) and those now engaged in transition economically and politically (which were until the twentieth century mostly contained within the Austro-Hungarian, Russian, and Ottoman Empires).

What does this tell us about the way Europe will and can approach global challenges like globalization and the global (war on) terrorism? Three things are clear:

1. Priority to 'internal' European matters
2. Priority then to neighboring regions
3. Specific approach to global security: economic and political (and often conceived of in terms of how it strengthens the actorhood of Europe)

While this might at first look like simple parochialism and free-riding, one has to point out two things. First that it can be justified in relation to the global issues to give a certain priority to the core question of shaping Europe, as it was, for example, argued in relation to the Balkans in the early 1990s. If there is no core, there is also no actor to do those other things that some want to be prioritized over the internal order question. Second, it is not only a question of not taking a fair share of the work, it is also a question of how global issues are interpreted; this is where the European experience leads to an approach very different from the American one.

This has been noticed quite often recently (cf. e.g., Kagan 2002), but whereas this is usually phrased in terms of a European inclination to try to recreate its own eternal peace order for everybody else, the analysis in this chapter has shown how the logic emerges at the microlevel through the task of connecting and thereby sorting and prioritizing security issues. In the United States, new threats are only accepted as security when they merge with the military agenda. "Defense" is still the defining criteria for "security." In Europe, in contrast, issues with a military component are ultimately subsumed into political-economic framing—within Europe in terms of integration/fragmentation and outside Europe as development and regionalism.

In Europe, the criterion that almost takes the role that the military factor plays in the United States is integration. It is the master variable that regulates the ability of an issue to reach top-rank. Thus, everything becomes colored by a politico-economic interpretation in contrast to the military framing in the United States. The threat can be in itself nonmilitary as can the reply, whereas in the United States, security problems can have nonmilitary origins—they only become 'security' when they meet the military agenda.

However, the main lesson from this chapter is probably that Europe is far more security driven than it is assumed in the usual depiction of a Europe at peace, free to do its share of global work or lean back in regional complacency. Europe is extremely low on traditional interstate security problems, and especially so on military ones. In the traditional optic this means then no security problems, and leads to the picture of relative freedom to choose how to engage in new issues. However, the present analysis has shown how Europe is far from free of security dynamics. There are major security issues that drive politics and threaten to escalate and send Europe as a region in completely new and not least old directions. These different securitizations have been tied together quite tightly around some master-narratives and the resulting constellation is therefore understood by participants of various fronts to be invested with far-reaching implications. It is only natural that in a region that we in so many other contexts accept as having moved beyond the usual sovereignty game, we should also find postsovereign security patterns, nonstate and nontraditional. Thus, Europe, despite all its peculiarities, reconfirms the basic expectation that usually regions are driven by their internal security problems and global links are fitted in as they can be, according to the internal logic of the region.

## NOTES

1. In the spirit of post-Maastricht Europe, the Copenhagen School is a three-pillar construct. The third one, sectors of security (economic, political, military, environmental, and societal), will only be used in an ad hoc way here, not as structuring device (cf. primarily Buzan, 1991, and Buzan et al., 1998).

2. Some paragraphs in this section are adopted from Buzan and Wæver, 2003.

3. As Cha (2000: 391, 394) notes, not much has been written about the links between globalization and security, probably because the security effects of globalization have been hard to distinguish from the more dramatic effects of the ending of the Cold War.

4. The concept of *insulator* is specific to RSCT and defines a location occupied by one or more units in which larger regional security dynamics stand back-to-back.

This is not to be confused with the traditional idea of a *buffer state*, whose function is defined by standing at the center of a strong pattern of securitization, not at its edge.

5. Most parts of this section are adapted from Buzan and Wæver 2003—sometimes shortened, sometimes elaborated.

6. Speeches during 2000–2001 by Chirac, Fischer, Schroeder, and Blair, analyzed in Buzan and Wæver, 2003: ch. 11.

7. See, in particular, Foreign Minister Joschka Fischer, *From Confederacy to Federation: Thoughts on the Finality of European Integration* (Berlin: Speech given at the University of Humboldt, 2000).

8. Jacques Chirac, *Our Europe* (Berlin: Speech to the German Bundestag, 2000); Tony Blair, *Speech by the Prime Minister, Tony Blair* (Warsaw: Polish Stock Exchange, 2000); Tony Blair, *Speech by the Prime Minister, Tony Blair* (Zagreb: EU/Balkan Summit, 2000); Robin Cook, "It is fascism that we are fighting 'Ours is the Modern Europe of the Human Rights Convention'," *The Guardian Newspaper*, May 5, 1999; Joschka Fischer, *From Confederacy to Federation: Thoughts on the Finality of European Integration* (Berlin: Speech given at the University of Humboldt, 2000).

9. In a Copenhagen School perspective, this where the concept of societal security shows its importance; these concerns are not primarily articulated in terms of threats to the state (its official representatives usually push for integration), but as fear for the nation and its identity (cf. Wæver et al., 1993; Wæver, 1996b).

# Part IV

---

Emerging International Patterns

# 10

# The Security Dynamics of a 1 + 4 World

Barry Buzan

This chapter[1] addresses the question: After bipolarity, what? Contrary to the prevailing mode of polarity theory in neorealism, the argument is based on a distinction between *great powers* and *superpowers*, with *regional powers* as the most useful way of designating the next rank down. The basis for the differentiation between superpowers and great powers is that superpowers operate globally, whereas great powers typically have their main influence in two or more regions, but not globally. *Regional power* is argued to be a much more important classification than the traditional *middle power*. Regional powers refers to the much larger and, in international security terms, much more significant, category of states that define the power structure of their local region: India and Pakistan in South Asia; South Africa in southern Africa; Iran, Iraq, and Saudi Arabia in the Gulf; Egypt, Israel, and Syria in the Levant; and so forth. Regional powers may not matter much at the global level, but within their regions they determine both the local patterns of security relations and the way in which those patterns interact with the global powers.

The chapter focuses on the present and possible future global power structure when seen as a mixture of superpowers and great powers. The current system is presented as one superpower plus four great powers (China, EU, Japan, Russia), and, if that is accepted, then there are three main scenarios that define its most probable future. At the global level, changes in the number of superpowers are more important than changes in the number of great powers. A 1 + 3 system may not be all that different from a 1 + 5 one, but 2 + 3 will be quite different from 1 + 4. The key exception is when the number of superpowers falls to zero, and this is significant because there is a historical trend for the number of superpowers to decline.

- The first, and most likely, scenario is for relative continuity with 1 + *x* (where *x* = 3, 4, or 5), which means that the United States remains the sole superpower, and the number of great powers either stays the same, or rises or falls slightly (perhaps India makes it into the great power ranks, perhaps Russia drops out).

- The second scenario, a move to $0 + x$ (where $x$ = 4, 5, or 6), is argued as a distinct possibility. Here the United States either loses, or steps down from, its superpower status, leaving a system composed only of great powers with no superpowers. This view rejects the neorealist assumption that a single type of great power defines multipolarity, and displays the benefits of making the distinction between superpowers and great powers. It opens up the previously unexplored idea of an international system that has no truly global powers in it, but only a collection of superregional great powers. This possibility is the main alternative to the present $1 + x$ structure, and it has been rendered invisible by the assumption in polarity theory that *great power* is a single category.
- The third possibility is a reversal of the secular decline in the number of superpowers in a move to a $2 + x$ structure (where $x$ = 3 or 4). This scenario is not explored at any length, both because it is seen as unlikely for at least a couple of decades and because a $2 + x$ structure is familiar from the Cold War. A move to $2 + x$ would require either China or the EU to attain superpower status, or for Russia to stage a miraculous recovery, or Japan to undergo a remarkable internal transformation. Notwithstanding fashionable talk in Washington about China as a peer competitor, I share the widely held view that the emergence of a second superpower within the next two decades is unlikely (Hansen, 2000: 79; Kapstein, 1999; Waltz, 2000: 29–39). Russia's problems of redevelopment are deep and do not seem likely to be solved soon. Japan would require massive political and economic reforms, along with a major change of attitude and self-perception among both people and leadership, to bid for superpower status. The EU, like Japan, has little will to seek superpower status, and will have to overcome a whole series of difficult issues in its own development before it could bid for superpower status. Despite its recent progress, China is not yet close to the level of economic and technological development, let alone political cohesion, that would be required to support superpower status. If I am wrong, and the future is a $2 + x$ system, then we return to a structure made familiar by the Cold War. If the second superpower was a nationalist, authoritarian China, a replay of the first Cold War would be likely, and the neorealist idea that two superpowers must be rivals would probably be supported. If the second superpower was the EU, then the neorealist hypothesis would have a harder test. Would two closely interdependent democracies securitize each other, or would the outcome be something more Kantian (Cronin, 1999; Wendt, 1999)?

If the most likely development is continuity at $1 + x$, then the imperative is to understand how a $1 + x$ structure shapes the processes of securitization within it. This is the subject of the next section. If there is a shift to $0 + x$, then we are in theoretical waters that have not been charted, but need to be anticipated. This is the subject of the second section, which also looks at how anticipation of $0 + x$ acts to reinforce the $1 + x$ structure. The third looks at the impact of a $1 + x$ structure on regional security.

In thinking through these scenarios, I interrogate some of the understandings that follow from neorealist assumptions by using securitization theory (Buzan, Wæver, & de Wilde, 1998; Buzan & Wæver, 2003; Wæver, 1995; and see Wæver, this volume), which departs from the neorealist assumption that material factors determine the nature of political relations. The question is not whether a certain issue is in and of itself a threat, but whether securitizing actors can successfully convince some community to treat it (or stop treating it) as such.

## SCENARIO 1: 1 SUPERPOWER AND 4 GREAT POWERS

How valid is it to talk about the post–Cold War global security structure as $1 + 4$? Given the disparity of capability, role, and status between the United States and the next group of great powers the system clearly cannot be described as multipolar. Just as obviously, the United States is nowhere near powerful enough to have eliminated the possibility of great power balancing, let alone being able to transform the international system from anarchy to hierarchy. If all the great powers aligned against it, that coalition would hugely outrank the United States in all resources except immediately available high-tech military capability. But the deeply institutionalized role of the United States in so many parts of the system, and its residual universalist ideological assets, have meant that it has not yet inspired a counterbalancing coalition fearful of its power. Despite the worrying drift toward unilateralism in U.S. policy, its two richest and most advanced potential rivals, the EU and Japan, remain firmly tied to the United States both in formal alliances and an informal security community. Indeed, in the decade following the Cold War, inability to identify a credible global level rival was something of a problem for foreign policymaking in the United States. In the absence of an obvious enemy or crusade, it had to struggle against its own inward-looking tendencies, leading to recurrent rhetorical attempts to construct Japan, China, rogue states (most recently manifested as the Axis of Evil), fundamentalist Islam, or international terrorism as a new global challenger. If this was unipolarity, then it was a far weaker construction of it than anything envisaged by Waltz's theory. Whether the war against terrorism declared in September 2001 will provide a durable foundation for a more engaged unipolar role is an open question. The war against terrorism has certainly facilitated the U.S. government's ability to securitize a wide range of things as threats, and also underpinned the Bush administration's unilateralist inclinations. But as the disagreements over how to handle Iraq suggest, it remains unclear just how far this rationale can be pushed without opening serious differences of opinion. Whatever happens as a result of September 11, the United States is neither a potential suzerain core of a world empire, nor is it about to construct a global federation. Whether it will reclaim its role as the leading constructor of international society, end up leading one side in a clash of civilizations, or sink into a unilateralism that alienates its allies remains to be seen.

Despite the weakness of the U.S. position by any serious standard of unipolarity, several attributes mark it as a superpower, distinct from the ranks of great powers. In aggregated power terms, it had a substantial edge over all the members of the great power group individually in one or more key attributes (military, economic, political). Despite its increasingly unilateralist tendencies, it still had some, albeit weakening, status as an acknowledged global leader, an asset not yet possessed to any significant degree by any other actor, with the possible exception of the EU. But perhaps its most striking, and in the longer run most important, attribute is its strongly embedded position in four regions additional to its home base in North America: Europe, East Asia, the Middle East, and its traditional backyard in South America. In the first two, it retains the main Cold War arrangements that institutionalized its hegemony (NATO and the United States–Japan alliance), and it continues to play a central role in politico-military developments (Bosnia, Serbia, Korea, Taiwan). The Americas have for long been linked in a military-political sense by the Monroe Doctrine and the Organization of American States, and the proposed extension of NAFTA into a Free Trade Area of the Americas would be a way of consolidating this link. In the Middle East, the United States took advantage of the ending of the Cold War to strengthen its position both by imposing its military presence in the Gulf and attempting to manage the turbulent peace process between Israel and its Arab neighbors. By 2001, both strategies were coming unravelled in their own terms, and the U.S. reaction to September 11 has both intensifed its presence and sharpened the contradictions generated by that presence. If nothing else, this demonstrated how world events are filtered through the specifics of regional settings, and vice versa. More on this in scenario 3. The United States has no similarly embedded position in Africa, South Asia, or the CIS, though it is, of course a strong outside player in all of them, and the first round of the war against terrorism pulled it strongly into South Asia. On the basis of these considerations, depiction of the current system structure as either unipolar or multipolar risks serious mispresspresentation, and 1 + 4 + regions seems both descriptively accurate and theoretically supportable.

The case of a single superpower facing several great powers is quite different from having two or more superpowers (or none). Neorealist theory never developed a coherent image of unipolarity (Hansen, 2000: 1), so there is no theoretical template against which to assess the post–Cold War development. Until recently, Waltz (1979, 1993a, 1993b) didn't consider the possibility, because, by his definition, an anarchic system requires a minimum of two great powers for balancing to occur. In his earlier reflections, the number of great powers can only go up from two, never down. In Waltz's game of strict number polarity, actual unipolarity would, by definition, eliminate the possibility of balancing, and therefore threaten a deep structure transformation from anarchy to hierarchy (Buzan, Jones, & Little, 1993: 53). Waltzian neorealism therefore sees unipolarity as unlikely, unstable (because of balance of power countermoves), and undesirable. More recently, Waltz (2000: 5, 24, 27–28) acknowledges the post–Cold War system as unipolar, and finesses the problem of the absence of balancing by saying that the balancing mechanism will restore itself, but that his theory cannot say when. Waltz (2000: 13, 27) has managed to tweak his theory to deal with the apparent fact of a type of unipolarity, but still argues, contra Hansen (2000: 80), that "unipolarity appears as the least durable of international configurations" on the grounds that "unbalanced power is a danger no matter who wields it," and because unipoles will be tempted (as he thinks the United States has been) into foolish policies of overextension.

An alternative, and less negative, view of unipolarity has for long been available within International Political Economy (IPE). Hegemonic stability theory (HST) had neorealist roots, and was de facto about a kind of unipolarity (Gilpin, 1981; 1987). Because its main concerns were about the stability of liberal international economic orders, it did not really consider balance-of-power issues, emphasizing instead the role of a hegemonic leader in the world economy, which combined power and elements of consent. No attempt was ever made to reconcile the apparent contradiction between HST's unipolarity assumption and mainstream neorealism's rejection of that possibility, but the existence of the two positions offered quite different ways of understanding unipolarity. Gilpin's more IPE-pitched view saw unipolarity as desirable (hegemonic leadership) and historically demonstrated (by Britain and the United States), but difficult to sustain in the long run (because costs of leadership undermine the hegemon). This contrasts with Waltz's more strictly political-military view that unipolarity was undesirable (unbalanced power), and unlikely to be more than a short-lived transitional structure. More recently, Kapstein (1999) has used HST to explain how unipolarity could in fact be stable, and Kapstein and Mastanduno (1999) also note the trouble for Waltzian logic in the mounting evidence that the great powers are not balancing against the United States. This seeming contradiction within neorealism can be understood in terms of the different conditions affecting processes of (de)securitization depending on whether one factors in or leaves out the existence of a strong international society based on shared economic values.

What is clear is that no version of neorealism ever seriously contemplated the type of 1 + 4 condition in which we now find ourselves. Nor could it, for, as Hansen (2000: 18) notes, "neorealism makes only one stratification of states: into great powers and other states." As a consequence, neorealists have explicitly theorized about neither great nor regional powers as understood here. Nevertheless, despite its shortcomings in relation to both unipolarity and the 1 + x scenario, neorealism does offer the only relatively firm image of a global-level international security structure. The view from the globalist perspective does not give much concrete guidance. As Cerny (2000: 642–646) sums it up, this envisages a world of "chronic but durable disorder, riddled with uncertainties" in which states of any sort play a decreasingly central role. Neorealism is therefore a convenient foil against which to start thinking in securitization terms about the effects of a 1 + 4 system, noting, as Hansen (2000: 5) rightly points out, that one must distinguish between the turbulence of a structural change and the ongoing effects of a settled structure. Neorealist-style reasoning suggests the following six hypotheses about the rules of the game for a 1 + x structure.

For the superpower:

1. That the lone superpower will securitize challenges to its status.
2. That it will want no superpower rivals and will thus act to delay or prevent the elevation of great powers.
3. That it will give priority to preventing the great powers from aligning against it.

For the great powers:

4. That their primary (de)securitization concerns will be with the superpower.
5. That the interdependence of (de)securitizations among great powers will vary with distance.
6. That the great powers will collectively securitize the unipole or, in Huntington's (1999: 44–46) words, that a counterpole coalition is "a natural phenomenon in a uni-multipolar world."

It is worth taking a closer look at each of these hypotheses, both in the light of the evidence available from the first decade of operation of the 1 + 4 system and with the more open, less deterministic perspective of securitization theory in mind.

*1. That the lone superpower will try to securitize challenges to its status.* Interestingly, this hypothesis is under question in the current debate about U.S. grand strategy. Some writers, most notably Wohlforth (1999), are strong advocates of a unipolarist strategy for the United States, but others, most notably Layne (1993, 1997) and Kupchan (1998), and also Waltz (1993a: 61, 75–76; 2000) and Huntington (1999: 37), either advocate, or see as inevitable, a multipolar world with the United States as one pole. This debate suggests that lone superpowers (especially ones favored by geography as the United States is) are not compelled to securitize their status. If they try to maintain their status (as most of the participants in the debate believe the United States is trying to do), then they generate the necessary securitization. If they seek to drop out, avoid the dangers of overstretch and free-riding (Carpenter, 1991; Layne, 1997: 96–112), and configure themselves as one great power among several (as many of those just cited advocate), then more things open up for desecuritization. Quite a few commentators make the point that the United States is more likely to be driven out of its superpower status by the unwillingness of its citizens to support the role than by the rise of any external challenger (Calleo, 1999; Kapstein, 1999; 468, 484; Lake, 1999: 78; Mastanduno & Kapstein, 1999: 14–20; Spiro, 2000). This interpretation could be either reinforced or countered by the U.S. response to September 11.

But the debate about U.S. grand strategy is being conducted without a clear distinction between superpowers and great powers. Consequently, the effects of the United States dropping out do not stand out as clearly as they should. As Waltz (1993a: 72) puts it: "the US will have to learn a role it has never played before: namely to coexist and interact with other great powers." But the result would not be a multipolar system structure as envisaged by his version of polarity theory. That would require three or more superpowers. It would be a global system with no superpowers and several great powers $(0 + x)$, an arrangment as suggested earlier that lies almost wholly outside the realm of existing theoretical speculation. Waltz (2000) believes that no lone superpower can succeed for long in maintaining unipolarity because some combination of overstretch and counterbalancing will undermine it. The view from HST would suggest that balancing reactions might be held at bay for quite some time by shared interests in an international economic order, but that in the long run overextension and free-riding will bring down the hegemon. Material factors may indeed shape the outcome in the long term. But as I will argue, in the short term the key will be what kind of (de)securitization process dominates within the United States. It is not unprecedented in U.S. history for engagement with the balance of power to be securitized as the main threat to American values, rather than threats from outside powers.

*2. That the lone superpower will want no superpower rivals and will thus act to delay or prevent the elevation of great powers, and (3) that it will give priority to preventing the great powers from aligning against it.* If the sole superpower decides to defend its status, then its strategies for dealing with these two hypotheses are broadly the same. For rising great powers, the superpower can oppose, suppress, coopt or encourage. Neorealist logic rules out encouragement because that would help create a superpower rival. In the case of a falling superpower rival, the superpower can try to support and bolster or encourage the fall. Neorealist logic more or less rules out that a superpower should try to prevent the demotion of its rival, but is open about whether it might try to sustain its ex-rival as a great power or allow it to free-fall to regional power level. HST logic suggests that the sole superpower will try to convert others to its views about how to run the global economy. The behavior of the United States since 1989 tends to support these assumptions. The United States has not sought to restore Russia as a superpower, but has supported it as a great power, conditional on reforms to make it more compatible with a liberal international economic order. By maintaining its alliances with Europe and Japan, the United States has coopted the two wealthiest great powers and thus both cemented an ideological consensus on the basic principles of the world economy, and prevented any really serious great power coalition forming against it (Job, 1999; Layne, 1993: 5–7). It has sought to deal with a rising China by a combination of containment and ideological conversion to at least liberal principles on economic practice.

The two most likely great power opponents to the United States, China and Russia, are the poorest and most technologically backward of the great powers, and have a long history of mutual antagonism as an obstacle to any serious anti-U.S. alliance. If the war against terrorism turns out to be a durable and dominating securitization, both are likely to be on the U.S. side. As Layne (1997) and Kapstein (1999b) argue, the United States has it relatively easy here. The potential challengers are no match for it, and its geographical position is favored: because the four great powers are all clustered in Eurasia, they are more impelled to balance against each other than to coalesce against the United States. Layne's argument rightly reintroduces geography into the equation, whereas neorealism tends to ignore it as a factor. Layne promotes the extreme version of this argument, which is that the United States could safely abandon its great power alliances because balancing within Eurasia would automatically cancel out the rise of any superpower capable of threatening the United States. This vision contrasts with those of Nye and Rosecrance who worry about the dangers of a return to balancing in the absence of U.S. primacy and engagment. The current U.S. strategy of primacy is based on a combination of coopting potential rivals, and promoting 'universal' values congenial to itself (and many of its allies) (Mastanduno, 1997: 51–52). It gives the United States a strong role as balancer in Eurasia, and helps to suppress the development of balancing behavior among the Eurasian great powers in relation to each other as well as to the United States.

The securitization perspective suggests interesting tensions within the United States. Even before September 11 there was not much sign that the United States was moving to Layne's position, which would require that it desecuritize the great powers. But, in defending its status, the securitization processes within the United States sometimes work at cross-purposes. The securitization of China causes no contradictions. But the securitization of Japan during the late 1980s and early 1990s set against each other the need to respond to a potential superpower peer and the strategy of preventing a counterpole coalition by keeping the strongest great powers on side. Similar, but less acute tensions could be seen between the United States and the EU over the latter's attempts to create a European military force. Only if the war on terrorism pushes the United States toward extreme unilateralism does Layne's scenario look likely.

4. *That the primary (de)securitization concerns of great powers will be with the superpower, and (5) that the interdependence of (de)securitization among great powers will vary with distance.* The behavior of the current four great powers and the leading aspirant (India) broadly confirms these hypotheses, as does the behavior of many regional powers from Israel and Turkey to Pakistan and the two Koreas. The EU is concerned primarily with the United States, secondarily with Russia, much less with China and Japan, and hardly at all with India. Russia is concerned primarily with the United States, secondarily with the EU and China, and rather less with Japan and India. China is concerned primarily with the United States, secondarily with Russia, Japan, and India, and rather less with the EU. Japan is concerned primarily with the United States, secondarily with China and Russia, and rather less with the EU and India. India is concerned primarily with the United States, secondarily with China, and aside from the residuals of its Cold War relationship with the Soviet Union, not that much with the others.

6. *That the great powers will collectively securitize the unipole.* This hypothesis is in line with classical and neorealist views of balancing in which materialist logic dictates that all will fear any power whose capability threatens to transcend the possibilities of balancing. The reasoning is nicely captured in Waltz's often-repeated refrain that: "Countries that wield overwhelming power will be tempted to misuse it. And even when their use of power is not an abuse, other states will see it as being so" (Waltz, 1993b: 189; 2000: 13, 29). Huntington (1999: 44–46) also asserts that a counterpole coalition is "a natural phenomenon in a uni-multipolar world." What logic makes it natural? Huntington acknowledges that cultural barriers and the temptations to bandwagon with the United States work against the formation of a counterpole coalition, but it is not clear why such a coalition would occur even with those restraints removed. For one thing, if war, whether hot or cold, is itself securitized, then the incentives to pursue desecuritization in relations with other global powers will be strong. For another, a counterpole coalition would

make sense if, and only if, *all* of the great powers felt that the superpower threatened their status and their independence. Given that most of the great powers share at least some 'universal' values with the United States, and the EU and Japan share quite a lot, the necessary sense of threat does not get generated. Even if one or two of the great powers do feel threatened by the superpower, the great powers may well be more concerned with securitizing neighboring great powers than with challenging the distant superpower. Fear of such securitizing dynamics among themselves may even give some of the great powers incentives to prefer the existence of a relatively benign superpower capable of holding the ring among them. This logic is still visible even within so well-developed a security community as the EU, where "keeping the United States in" remains important to the management of EU domestic politics.

If securitization is going to occur, the key question is whether the great powers will securitize each other or the superpower? This is a rather trickier question than simpleminded assumptions about balancing in traditional polarity theory. The fact that all of the great powers give priority to their relationship with the superpower skews the picture considerably, as does the well-developed institutional position of the United States in Europe and East Asia. Another distorting variable is the relatively removed geographical circumstance of the current single superpower. The United States has options to engage or withdraw (securitize or not) that are not available to the Eurasian powers. In Eurasia, both propinquity and a shortage of shared values increase the incentives for the Eurasian great powers to securitize each other rather than the United States. With the sole exception of a unity of all of them, the Eurasian great powers would find it difficult to form coalitions amongst themselves without triggering securitizations against each other. A serious Sino-Japanese alignment, for example, could easily trigger securitizing responses in Russia, and a serious Sino-Russian one would have the same effect on Japan. What this boils down to is an argument that counterpole balancing is far from automatic or natural, but that the United States could bring it about by working hard to undermine its own leadership assets and alienate the other powers.

Another way of questioning Huntington's hypothesis is to focus not on the imperative of balancing against the superpower, but on the aspirations of one or more great powers to rise to superpower status. Pursuit of such an aspiration is much more conditional on domestic developments (the ability to pursue internal balancing) than it is on forming coalitions against the existing superpower. In order to establish their credentials and status, aspirant superpowers are more likely to have to break any alliance they may have with the existing superpower than to form coalitions against it. Any moves toward coalition formation with other great powers would be likely to trigger anxieties among the remaining great powers, thus offering opportunities for the existing superpower to play balancer to its own advantage. And while some great powers may harbor aspirations to become superpowers, there is no reason to assume that this will be a universal trait. Some (such as Japan and possibly the EU) may have historical disinclinations to take up that kind of political role. Some might fear the popular theories of overstretch and decline that are said to be the price of global leadership (Kennedy, 1989). Some might want to avoid the pressures on their domestic politics created by global responsibilities and engagements. Notwithstanding the assumptions of traditional *machtpolitik*, it is far from clear that an aspiration to superpower status is a general feature of contemporary great powers, whatever may have been the case in the past. It seems safe to assume that all great powers will be concerned with maintaining status and avoiding demotion to regional power, but, in the twenty-first century, desire for superpower status may be exceptional rather than normal. The scenario for "benign tripolarity," based on centered regions in North America, Europe, and East Asia (Gilpin, 1987: 394–406; Kupchan, 1998), can be read as assuming that a system of great powers with no superpower(s) could be stable (see also Buzan, 1991: 174–181, 261–265 on mature anarchy). Looking at the behavior of the EU and Japan, and to a much lesser extent China, it is also possible to conclude that most, if not all, of the great powers that have risen up into that rank (rather than falling into it, like Russia) are happy to remain where they are and do not aspire either to superpower rank for themselves or to challenge the existing superpower. Calls for multipolarity by Russia, China, and others are not so much about making themselves into superpowers (a 2 or 3 + $x$ system), as about the United States giving up its superpower pretensions (0 + $x$).

Taking stock of this discussion of the six hypotheses, one can conclude that a 1 + 4 structure might well be stable for quite some time. The material logic of neorealism suggests that potential challengers for superpower status have a lot to do to get the necessary material and political requirements in place. This material logic gets tempered in two ways. First, by domestic considerations in some of the great powers that make them disinclined to bid for superpower status. Second, by globalist/HST/institutionalist reasoning—or in the English school version by international society—in which the U.S.-led international order carries considerable legitimacy, and rests on shared values that are fully internalized by some, though more the product of instrumental calculation or coercion in the case of others. These factors work powerfully to desecuritize relations between the sole superpower and the great powers. They suggest that continuation of a 1 + 4 system is a real possibility, provided that the United States does not itself work to bring it down.

## SCENARIO 2: SHIFTING TO 0 SUPERPOWERS
## AND $X$ GREAT POWERS

While a $1 + x$ structure looks the most likely for the next few years, it is not chiselled in stone. As previously argued, it is hard to envisage the number of superpowers growing to two or more before 2020, if then. It is easier to imagine the number of superpowers dropping to zero. There are two routes to this end, one material and one social. The material one is a simple extension of the declinist, imperial overstretch arguments from the early 1990s. The United States steadily loses relative economic, military, and ideological power and at some point becomes unable to sustain its superpower roles. It is noteworthy how much this logic has dropped out of the current debate, despite huge elevations in U.S. military expenditure relative to its competitors. The social route is about the loss of ability to lead, and there are two obvious, and potentially interlinked, ways for this to happen. The first is that the United States takes the initiative to abandon its leadership roles and alliance commitments, thus laying down the mantle of superpowerdom. This could take place either as a conscious strategic decision—a political victory for those arguing that the US should pull out of Eurasia—or as a result of neglect by U.S. governments dominated by inward-looking agendas, the arrogance of power, and a loss of will to create and maintain the institutional machinery of international society. The second way is that the United States loses its followers because it ceases to represent the set of shared values that legitimated its leadership during the second half of the twentieth century. It is easy to see how these two aspects of the social route could play into each other. Increasing U.S. unilateralism driven by domestic imperatives corrodes the loyalty and trust of allies, which, in turn, makes it more difficult for U.S. governments to justify the expenditure of resources abroad.

Either, or both, of the material and social routes to the loss of U.S. superpower status are possible, but the material path would probably be quite long, whereas the social one could, in principle, be quite short. It is not difficult to spin a quite plausible scenario that would lead to this result by 2010. The main elements in such a scenario could include:

- Increasing difficulty in the US in maintaining a coherent foreign policy posture and a commitment to overseas responsibilities in the absence of any clear and overwhelming external threat to legitimise securitization, and the failure of the war against terrorism to do this.
- A U.S. shift to more unilateralist military postures, including some version of ballistic missile defense, and the cultivation of long-range strike capabilities to reduce dependence on overseas allies and bases.
- Unilateral U.S. pursuit of unpopular polices abroad such as those

already in place regarding Cuba, Iran, Iraq, Libya, and Israel, and possible extensions of the war against terrorism.

- Exaggerated claims to sovereignty and special rights such as those already visible in relation to the World Criminal Court, the CTBT, various environmental agreements, and its use of controversial extraterritorial legislation (note that Huntington, 1999: 41, sees such a development as an expected feature of sole superpower status).
- Withdrawal from existing international regimes and institutions and/or refusal to adhere to new regimes widely supported in international society, as illustrated by U.S. attitudes toward the land mine agreement, the ABM treaty, and the United Nations.
- A drift apart on key domestic values that underpin international society of the type already visible in relation to capital punishment, abortion, gun control, drugs, and food.

China and Russia are already conspicuously uneasy about U.S. leadership. Japan could easily become so if it feared that U.S. policy was going to drag it into confrontation with China. Europe would be the most reluctant to let go of U.S. leadership, but might eventually come to that if the erosion of shared values became severe. In the upper ranks of the regional powers, India and Brazil also manifest conspicuous unease about a world in which the United States has too much of a free hand to intervene in all parts of the world. As many authors observe (Bobrow, 2001: 6–8; Bergsten, 2000: 22–24; Huntington, 1999: 42–43), echoing Waltz's more general worry about excessive concentrations of power, there is already a disjuncture between a U.S. self-perception of benign leadership, and a widespread image of it elsewhere as a threat whose foreign policy is driven overwhelmingly by a domestic politics in which corporate interests are strongly represented. This could be moderated if the war against terrorism comes to be seen as a general defense of civilization against extremists, but it could easily be exacerbated if that 'war' comes to be seen as an extension of U.S. support for Israel and for whatever governments in the Middle East are willing to be pliable on the question of oil. Superpower status in the twenty-first century hangs much more on the ability to create and sustain international societies (at which the United States proved remarkably talented during the Cold War), than on warfighting ability (now relevant mostly at the margins, no longer in head-to-head world wars). Consequently, the growth of U.S. hostility to many of the IGOs and regimes that it led in creating suggests a distinct drift away from leadership. This drift could prove central to determining whether the United States sustains or abandons its sole superpower role. Kupchan (1998: 66) notes that "the U.S. lacks the societal commitment to self-binding present in Germany and Japan," but it isn't clear whether the explanation for this comes from system structure (i.e., its sole superpower status) or from the unique and long-standing domestic character of American state and society. Both explanations make sense, suggesting that the behavior is overdetermined. A 0 + x scenario in the near future is thus not implausible, though neither is it a necessary or determined outcome. Its probability remains largely contingent on political choices made in the United States. Huntington (1999: 42–43) also notes a perceptual disjuncture between a U.S. self-perception of benign leadership and a widespread image of it elsewhere as a threat whose foreign policy is "driven overwhelmingly by domestic politics." This disjuncture seems likely to afflict most sole superpowers.

More difficult to calculate is the political character of a 0 + x system. As noted earlier, this is uncharted theoretical territory. In a 0 + x system there would be no truly global powers, only a series of great powers projecting their influence into adjacent regions. A realpolitik view would suggest that in an all-great power system, one or more of the powers would bid for superpower status. Any expectation of such an outcome would be a constraint on U.S. options to abandon the sole superpower slot. While the United States might well feel comfortable in a stable 0 + x system, it is much less likely to feel comfortable in a 1 + x system in which it is not the 1. But if all of the great powers in a 0 + x system remained content with their great power status (neither aspiring to superpowerdom, nor feeling obliged to take on the role of providing international order), then the result would most likely be a decentered system that the United States could live with. In its benign version, this would be something like that envisaged by Kupchan (1998), where one or more great powers serve as the center for macro-regional orders: the Americas, some form of EU-centered greater Europe, East Asia. In its most benign form, such a system would have a relatively strong international society, with the different regions sharing some key values, and maintaining an array of institutions to act at the global level. Whether the United States in great power, as opposed to superpower, mode, would support such institutions or oppose them is an interesting question, particularly concerning the maintenance of the liberal international economic order. If the United States's departure from the sole superpower role was accompanied by a wrecking of international institutions, they could be difficult to replace. A less benign version would have each macroregion going its own way, with fewer shared values and fewer global institutions, but no inclination to conflict or intense rivalry either. This would be the benign mercantilist scenario from IPE, reflecting the inability to sustain an international economic order in the absence of a hegemonic leader.

The most malign version of the 0 + x system would occur when one or more of the great powers seeks to assert itself as a superpower. Unless such a power was projecting widely acceptable values, the most likely outcome would be preemptive counterpole securitizations, probably involving both competitive military buildups and alliance formation. If this development was seen as likely, it might be the key consideration that prevented the United States from abandoning the present 1 + $x$ arrangement. A more moderate malign version of 0 + $x$ would be one in which one or more macroregions become the arena for rivalry among the local great powers. At present, the most likely candidate for that is Asia, where, in the absence of the United States as a ringholder, a stark choice would emerge between accepting Chinese hegemony and organizing some form of counter-China coalition based around Japan, India, and Russia.

In the long run, the power structure at the global level rests on material capabilities, but in the short run there is quite a bit of scope for political choice about what does and does not get securitized, and what roles are or are not sought. In the realm of choice, the two key players are the United States and China. After the loss of the Soviet Union as a clear and easy focus for securitization, the United States has real choices. It could decide to rest on its geostrategic advantages, desecuritize the global power structure, withdraw from its leadership responsibilities and forward deployments, leave the Eurasian powers to sort out their own relations, and step down from the role as the sole superpower. On the other hand, it could seek a new focus for securitization to support and legitimize its continued sole superpower role. This new focus would have to be something more plausible than North Korea or Iran. Before September 11 there were two likely, and mutually reinforcing, candidates: China as an emergent peer competitor, and the potential instability of a 0 + $x$ system. After September 11 the war against terrorism became a third. This situation gives China some political choices as well. An abrasive and assertive Chinese stance toward its Asian neighbors and the United States would ease the U.S. path toward choosing securitization, while a milder and more conciliatory one would facilitate the desecuritization choice. But, at the end of the day, China does not hold all the strings. If it chooses to play challenger to the United States, it probably could guarantee a U.S. choice for securitization. But, if it takes the more cautious route it by no means guarantees a U.S. choice for desecuritization. The behavior of the United States since the end of the Cold War suggests that it wants to find a focus for securitization. If that inclination is being internally driven, then there is probably not much that can be done by China, Russia, the EU, or Japan to stop it. If it becomes driven by the war against terrorism, then a great deal will depend on the specific way in which that war plays out.


## REGIONS AND GREAT POWERS IN A 1 + $x$ WORLD

In the short term 1 + $x$ is likely to remain the security structure at the global level. For the reasons argued previously, this makes the United States the most critical player, both in maintaining the 1 + $x$ structure or pushing it toward $0 + x$. But it does not all lie in U.S. hands. China, as suggested, is the most likely to challenge U.S. authority, and its decisions will have a major impact not only on whether $1 + 4$ or $0 + x$ wins out, but whether the operation of either structure will tend toward the benign or the malign. That, in turn, gives key elements of choice to Japan, Russia, and India. The nature of U.S. superpowerdom in a $1 + 4$ structure, and its strategy for maintaining a $1 + x$ structure, hinge crucially on how it relates both to great powers and to regions. In this section I will look more closely at these relationships. The first thing to notice is how crucial these relationships are to the superpower status of the United States. More than mere material factors, they define much of what makes the United States's position unique. The basic pattern might be called a *swing power* strategy, and is likely to remain the dominant one so long as the United States does not abandon, or lose, its superpower status. This strategy depends not only on U.S. power, but also on a specific framework of institutionalization.

What is remarkable about the U.S. position in Europe, East Asia, and South America (though not the Middle East) is the degree to which its position has become institutionalized through the construction of superregional projects: Atlanticism, Asia-Pacific (or Pacific-Rim), and Pan-Americanism (Buzan, 1997). These projects usually contain a strong mixture of superregional economic integration (or aspirations thereto), and mutual defense and security arrangements—the particular mix varying according to the local circumstances and history. Their attendant labels and rhetorics enable the United States to appear to be an actual member of these regions, rather than just an intervening outside power, and thus help to desecuritize its role. Interestingly, the United States is not commonly thought of as a *member* of the Middle East, and this correlates with the lack of superregional institutions. But where superregional projects exist, it is quite common for the United States to be thought of, and perhaps to think of itself as, a member of those security regions. In this view, the United States is part of the Americas, part of the Atlantic community, and an Asia-Pacific power. By seeming to put the United States inside these regions, superregional projects blur the crucial distinction between regional and global-level security dynamics, and make them difficult to see from within the United States. This blurring becomes an important tool for the management of the United States's sole superpower position, not least in preventing the emergence of more independent regional integrations that might threaten its influence. This is not to deny that these projects have substantial and sometimes positive political effects. But they can also hide the distinction between being a superpower and being a great or regional power, as well as the fact that the U.S. role in East Asia, South America, and Europe is comparable to its role in the Middle East—an outside global power penetrating into the affairs of a region. The key point supporting this argument is that there can be debates about a global-level power withdrawing, or being expelled, from the region concerned. Germany cannot withdraw from Europe, nor Japan from East Asia, nor Brazil from South America. But the United States can remove itself (or be removed from) Europe, East Asia, and South America, and there are regular debates both in the United States and in those regions about the desirability of such moves. The superpowerdom of the United States is expressed in its ability to act as a swing power, engaged in several regions but not permanently wedded to any of them, and in principle able to vary the degree and character of its engagement according to its own choice.

Because it has the option to delink from, or reduce the priority of its engagement in, any region, the United States can use threats and inducements of increasing or decreasing its levels of engagement as a means of playing off one region against another. The United States is able to move its attention and favor among East Asia, Europe, and South America. This pattern of behavior was visible during the Cold War, but constrained by the overriding need to hold together a common front against the Soviet Union. Now that there is no superpower rival, the U.S. swing strategy is the dominant pattern. Since East Asia and Europe contain all four great powers, the swing option between them is the key to U.S. post–Cold War strategy. These superregions are designed to prevent the consolidation of East Asian and European regions that might shut the United States out, or even develop as global power rivals to it. As Wyatt-Walter (1995: 83–97) notes, this has been perhaps easiest to observe in the GATT/WTO negotiations, in which the tactical quality of the U.S. shift from globalism to regionalism was an attempt to gain more leverage over the EU and East Asia by playing them off against each other. The object of the swing strategy is not for the United States to choose one of these regions over the others, but to use the possibility of such choice to maintain its leverage in all of them. Since each of these regions is dependent on the United States in important ways, it is not impossible to imagine a kind of bidding war among Europe, Latin America, and East Asia to engage U.S. attention and commitment. Mahbubani's (1995) polemic in favor of a new and rising "Pacific impulse," as against an old and declining Atlantic one, might be seen as an example of just this kind of wooing. Seen in this light, Simon's (1994: 1063) argument that the United States is becoming a "normal state" in the Asia-Pacific community, "neither its hegemon nor its guarantor," is almost wholly wrong. While the United States may be becoming more normal in playing traditional foreign policy games of balance, its overall position is highly exceptional. It is the key partner for many other states both economically and military-politically, and it is the only successful purveyor of universal values.

The U.S. engagements in other regions do not have this core quality and reflect more instrumental concerns. Although the United States is at the moment heavily engaged in the Middle East, that region is peripheral to the swing strategy. The U.S. interest there hinges on its special relationship with Israel, and its concerns about oil, and is unlikely to outlast them should those ties weaken. The United States has never been heavily engaged in South Asia, and were it not for the issue of nuclear proliferation, and after September 11, terrorism, would have little interest there. That, however, could change should China come to be seen in the United States as a global challenger. In that case the United States might well look to India as a major ally and fellow democracy.

In thinking about the security dynamics of a 1 + 4 world, it is of course not only the superpower that is important. What the great powers do—how they interact both with each other and with their surrounding regions—makes a difference to the political, economic, and strategic operation of the 1 + 4 system, and even to its sustainability. While superpower(s) may be more important than great powers, they do not determine the whole system as a unipolar designation suggests. For some regions, neighboring great powers play leading outside roles. South Asia, for example, is heavily affected by the '4' element of 1 + 4. China penetrated South Asia during the Cold War, but with the withdrawal of Soviet power from the region, and continued US indifference to it during the 1990s, the material position of China has been strengthened. Africa is unique in having not much of either superpower or great power intervention. South America has only superpower intervention. In Europe and Asia, the great powers are both embedded in their own regions and to varying degrees neighbors to each other. This means that regional and global level security dynamics are closely intertwined, and are among the key shapers of both the character and sustainability of a 1 + 4 system.

In Europe, the standing of both the EU and Russia as great powers hinges crucially on regional factors. Europe was the region most fully overlaid during the Cold War and therefore the end of the Cold War had most immediate and dramatic effects here. Despite the maintenance of the primary Cold War institutions linking the United States and Europe (NATO, OSCE), and the continued key U.S. role in politico-military developments in Europe (Bosnia, Serbia, Kosovo), the relationship is no longer one of overlay. Europe once again has its own distinctive regional security dynamics. For a part of the 1990s, Europe had open questions about the number, boundaries, and structure of regional security complexes. Originally after the end of bipolarity, Russia seemed to be becoming part of a large all-European regional security complex. Not that the visions for OSCE as all-European collective security system were realistic, but a more informal concert held together a large region of mutual accommodation and partly overlapping organizations. However, from around 1993, a Russia-centered CIS complex and an EU-centered one parted ways while the Balkans for a while held the potential of drifting off as a third regional security complex but were eventually drawn into the EU European one. In Europe, the end of overlay revealed both the centrality of the EU as the main security institution, and the raising of the stakes in the global great power status, or not, of the EU. It also showed the difference between the security community dynamics of Western Europe as compared with conflict formation dynamics in the former Soviet Union and its former empire. In both West-Central Europe and the post-Soviet region, the regional and the global levels play strongly into each other because the regional dynamic is responsible for the emergence/reproduction (or not) of a great power. The EU-dominated part of Europe is a uniquely interesting instance of a centered regional security complex being formed without a power at the center (much as North America was from the late eighteenth to late nineteenth century). In the West, regional institutions have to work if the EU is to count as a great power. The formal construction of the EU is therefore a large part of the story; its ability to structure (dominate) the rest of the region (in a friendly way) as well as to some extent emerge as a global actor is another part. Now that the United States has no need of the EU as a bulwark against the Soviet Union, it is not clear that it is any longer in its interest to support the EU project. This explains the ambivalence in U.S. (de)securitizations toward the EU (and, for similar reasons, Japan).

The post-Soviet space (CIS) is a centered regional security complex, too, but of a partly imposed nature, with Russia acting as a more traditional great power, not (as the EU) a postsovereign formation gaining legitimacy for its central role from nonmembers. In the East, Russia has to be able to create a centered complex, for, if it fails to do so, it ends up with the same problem as India (i.e., sharing its region with other regional powers), and risks sinking to regional power status. The main question in the post-Soviet region is whether a countercoalition will form against Russia within the current regional boundaries, or countries drift off one by one, or Russia manages to integrate the region as a centred regional security complex. This will crucially influence the role Russia can play outside the region. In CIS Europe, the success or failure of Russia in imposing itself on the successor states to the Soviet Union is crucial to sustaining or losing its standing as a great power. Central and Southeast Europe, and probably the Baltic states, have escaped Russia's grip, but for the states in the Caucasus and Central Asia, not to mention Belarus and Ukraine, Russia is and will remain the dominant fact of life in security affairs.

In EU Europe, the question is about the internal and external consequences of integration, in CIS Europe about the internal and external consequences of disintegration. But neither Russia (because it is too weak), nor the EU (because it is too incoherent politically, and too tied to the United States in many ways) are likely to mount major challenges either within or to the 1 + 4 order.

In Asia, the situation at first looks quite different, with China and Japan seemingly holding their great power status, with many fewer questionmarks about how they relate to their region. But at least for China, its long-term possibilities also depend crucially on how it relates to its region. The interesting questions in Asia for a 1 + 4 world are not just how China and Japan relate to the United States, discussed earlier, but how they relate to each other and their neighbors. In East Asia, as in South Asia, the demise of the Soviet Union contributed strongly to the relative empowerment of China, and its move toward the center of the U.S. debate about possible peer competitors. It is commonplace to think that if a challenge is going to come to the United States as sole superpower, it will almost certainly come from Asia (Friedberg, 1993–1994). China is the most obviously placed great power to affect both its own region and U.S. choices. What China will do depends heavily on how it evolves internally, and there are too many variables in play to allow any certainty of prediction. China could falter economically and politically, succumbing for a time to the many internal contradictions building up from its rapid development, and fail to fulfill the material aspirations to power. Just as plausibly, it could continue to gather strength. In the latter case, it could become more nationalistic, authoritarian, and assertive, or more liberal, democratic, and cooperative. A scenario of weakening, or one of strength accompanied by more compatibility with the dominant values of international society, would make the management and continuation of a 1 + 4 system easier, and relieve the neighboring powers (Russia, Japan, and India) of some extremely difficult choices. A scenario of malign strengthening could disrupt the stability of the 1 + 4 structure. It would pose acute problems for Japan, which could hardly avoid either kowtowing to the new Chinese power, or becoming the frontline against it. Japan has been capable in the past of making rapid and spectacular internal changes in response to serious outside pressures (mid-nineteenth century, post-1945), and this talent makes it a more interesting and important variable among the '4' than turn-of-the-century gloom about its prospects might suggest.

The continuation of the strong U.S. link to Japan muted what would otherwise have been the impact of a more regionally defined great power dynamic between Japan and China. The U.S. position in the region worked to increase securitization between it and China, while apparently dampening down securitizations of China elsewhere in the region. China is central, but probably not in the near future strong enough to create a centered Asian complex. Rather, it is the main power in a regional balance-of-power system whose operation is strongly affected by the historical and present penetration of an external power, the United States, and by the question of how the U.S. role will unfold in the future. China's centrality primarily works through the widespread expectation that its position within Asia could become unipolar, in which case its claim for superpower status would become strong.

## CONCLUSIONS

In order to understand the security dynamics of the post–Cold War world, it is necessary to abandon the traditional understanding of polarity and introduce a tripartite distinction among superpowers, great powers, and regional powers. As demonstrated earlier, the interplay among the superpower and the great powers offers many structural insights into how the system works and what its potentialities are. The cost is that one loses the simplicity of a single classification that was one of polarity theory's attractions. But since it never delivered all that much, the loss is not great.

As these arguments show, the operation of a 1 + 4 global security order cannot only be understood at the global level. It also depends in crucial ways on how great powers and superpowers relate to their regions. The superpower status of the United States hinges crucially not only on its domestic politics, but also on its swing power role. For three of the four great powers (the EU, Russia, and China), their long-run standing hinges on what happens in their regions. For the EU, the success or failure of its integration projects determines its standing as a great power. For Russia, the success or failure of its imperial project determines in considerable part whether it sustains its great power claim or drops to regional power status. China's possibility for superpower status depends on achieving some kind of hegemony in Asia.

## NOTES

1. This chapter builds on work done jointly with Ole Wæver (2003). Some of the research for this chapter was funded by the ESRC.

# 11

# Prospects For a New World Order

David Goldfischer

> Just as within the state every government, though it needs power as a basis
> of its authority, also needs the moral basis of the consent of the governed,
> so an international order cannot be based on power alone, for the simple
> reason that mankind will in the long run always revolt against naked power.
> —Carr, *Twenty Years' Crisis*

The conclusion of E. H. Carr's (1961) *Twenty Years' Crisis*, entitled "The Prospects of a New International Order," comprises an inquiry into how power and morality could be combined in the design of a peaceful world. This chapter draws on Carr's approach to consider the same question. There are several reasons for looking back to Carr's contribution at this particular juncture. First, despite the passage of more than six decades and the vast differences between the war started by Hitler and the one launched by Bin Laden, there are also some striking parallels. More important, the theoretical tools that Carr applied to an understanding of that world may turn out to be more useful, and more timely, than the instruments crafted by Cold War-era realists. Finally, his substantive prescription for a postwar peace has considerable resonance, and may even have greater practical appeal than proved the case in the 1940s, when a Cold War shredded Carr's hope for an enlightened realism, leaving him marginalized as the "Red professor" (Jones, 1998).

As a realist, Carr believed that any moral vision of international relations had first to recognize the realities of the balance of power. For Carr, however, considering the capabilities and geography of states provided only part of the picture of that balance. At least equally important were the material interests both of privileged elites who sought to use the state to advance their objectives both domestically and internationally and the masses who were liable to "revolt against naked power." Finally, Carr's (1961) analysis of power, in a method he called historical realism, embedded power relations in the evolving history of the capitalist world economy. This chapter begins by looking at the limits of state-centric structural realism, which came in vogue during the Cold War, for examining the events of 9/11 and their aftermath. I then propose that, rather than look at current world politics primarily in terms of efforts by major powers to pursue their security and other interests, we consider the war on terrorism in terms of the shifting concerns of what might be called the "capitalist security community" (CSC).[1]

The CSC refers to that group of capitalists, along with their intellectual and political supporters, who equate their own safety and well-being with the effective management of a global market system, which they are confident can generate economic growth, widespread prosperity, and peace. Despite (or in pursuit of) those benign objectives, the CSC has proven willing to use violence to protect its interests, and it is implicated in much of the warfare of the past century. The CSC's membership includes businesspeople who seek to profit from transnational commercial enterprises, shareholders in their companies, workers who believe they are getting a fair share of the profits, the leaders—at least since the end of the Cold War—of most of the world's states, and a host of scholars and strategists to whom those leaders may turn for advice. Yet even at the post–Cold War height of its power, the CSC has had many opponents, including owners and workers of commercial enterprises threatened by imports, leftist antiglobalization protesters, right-wing nationalists, and violent extremists like Osama Bin Laden.

Because states have long been the most important instruments of power, the CSC (like anyone who seeks real power) has sought to gain and to preserve control over the instruments of the state (and, ultimately, over all states). In those domestic struggles, the CSC has proven to be more than just another interest group. It not only has enormous wealth, it can plausibly argue that the long-term welfare and security of the state and its citizens require its leadership. Put another way, for the CSC, whose members have benefited most from capitalism's historical conquests over rival social orders, the pursuit of national security and further globalization have long been indistinguishable objectives.

After providing a brief historical overview of the challenges faced by the CSC as it has evolved since the nineteenth century, I consider the relative merits of looking at the current security environment in terms of great power politics or CSC politics, and at the relationship between them. Finally, I draw on Carr's (1961) analysis of the connection between the decline of British hegemony and the two world wars, in order to examine the prospects for the emergence of a new world order after September 11.

## TWENTY-FIRST CENTURY REALISM:
## THE TRAGEDY OF GREAT POWER CONFLICT
## OR AN EMERGENT HARMONY OF INTERESTS?

When the Cold War ended, much of mainstream scholarship on international security divided into two schools of thought regarding the future of conflict.

Some Cold War-era realists predicted that the world was headed "back to the future," that is, toward the sorts of great power rivalries that preceded 1945 (see Mearsheimer, 1990). A second camp, the liberals, tended to embrace the oft-cited "end of history" thesis advanced by Francis Fukuyama, in which the most notable development was the global triumph of universal liberal norms rooted in the Enlightenment. As a result, interstate conflict would generally be supplanted by the virtuous synergy of the "democratic peace" and the market-driven "commercial peace."

Realists predictably, and with some justification, dismissed such liberal assessments as naive. "We should not forget," maintained Robert Kagan (1998) in the midst of post–Cold War liberal euphoria, "that utopian fancies about the obsolescence of military power and national governments in a transnational, 'economic' era have blossomed before, only to be crushed by the next 'war to end all wars'" (pp. 24–35). Given such dark (albeit vague) prophesies, it was not surprising that the events of 9/11 provoked some commentaries that smacked a bit of realist "triumphalism." As Fareed Zakaria proclaimed in the aftermath of 9/11: "This is surely the End of the End of History—the notion that after the Cold War, ideological or political tussles were dead and life would be spent managing the economy and worrying about consumerism. . . . The state is back, and for the oldest Hobbesian reason in the book: the provision of national security."

Ever since Alexander Hamilton's sharp rebuttal of the argument for the "commercial peace," which had originally been presented by Montesquieu in 1750,[2] realists have had the upper hand in this "either/or" debate with the liberals. Yet there were several elements in the events surrounding 9/11 that should have prompted more realist self-doubt than we have seen so far. First, not only does the current war on terrorism lack a component of major power rivalry; it is in fact the first major world conflict in which all the major powers are aligned on the same side.

The notion that al Qaeda can have such a potent structural effect defies realist logic (since it is the number and rank of major powers that drive alignment patterns), and realists can simply assert that 9/11 will appear retrospectively as a minor historical event (Jervis, 2002). However, in light of expert consensus that there is a high likelihood of future and far more devastating attacks (i.e., with true mass destruction weapons), rational world leaders seem to have quickly recognized that the prospect of catastrophic terrorism is substantially affecting the dynamics of world power. Realists from time to time, in their effort to demonstrate the absurdity of states ever overcoming anarchy, have suggested that nothing short of an attack from outer space could unite the governments on earth. It is now more plausible that a purely terrestrial event—the specter of al Qaeda armed with nuclear weapons or anthrax—may, at least for the major powers, be sufficient to achieve that result (perhaps in conjunction with other material interests unrecognized by realists).

A second, related problem for the realists is that the critical axis for this conflict is North–South. Perceiving conflict as North–South garnered barely any interest from realists during the Cold War (except during a brief moment of panic following the oil price shocks of 1973). After all, the South couldn't threaten the North militarily, and southern grievances could consequently be brushed off with the realist aphorism: "The strong take what they can; the weak grant what they must." But what happens to the theory when the "weak," having already mastered today's global communications and transportation networks, proceed to acquire mass destruction weapons?

A final problem with efforts by Cold War era realism to come to grips with 9/11 is that it seems to have so little to do with the balance of interstate power, that is, with the analytical framework they contend is decisive for understanding world politics. Hatred of the United States, and an effort to break its hold on the Middle East, are certainly consistent with the notion of a power struggle. Yet the Islamist bid for power isn't rooted in the cynical realpolitik of some modern Bismarck, who stirs up nationalism to enhance the power of his state. When one looks to the sources of the challenge, its cause seems to be embraced most fervently by a combination of some of the world's poorest inhabitants, and, as Fouad Ajami (2002) put it, by elements within "an Arab world unsettled and teased by exposure to a modern civilization it can neither master nor reject" (p. 10). In those senses, 9/11 can be characterized as a blow against globalization. In short, the sense of shared threat among the major powers, the blurring of power disparities between the strong and the weak, and the transnational, revolutionary nature of the threat, all undercut the relevance of the state-centric realism that dominated Cold War security studies.

The Cold War literature that did focus both on North–South conflict and on transnational forces, known as dependency theory, gained scarce attention in the literature on international security, and was considered part of the separate body of scholarship known as political economy. One reason for that lack of interest on the part of security scholars is that dependency theory drew on the intellectual tradition of Marxism, and implied that the U.S. government was on the wrong side of various wars in the South, where it opposed movements whose avowed purpose was "national liberation" from exploitation by greedy capitalists. Virtually all security experts in the United States, after all, whether or not they supported particular military interventions in the Third World, simply accepted capitalism as one of the core values subsumed under the overall umbrella of U.S. national security. To the extent one considered the spread of markets in the South (no one was yet calling this process globalization), it was regarded as a mechanism for economic and political development. Thus, liberal ideology, the economic interests of multinational corporations, and the geopolitical requirements of waging the Cold War, all had the same implications for U.S. policy in the South: those respectful of property rights were to be protected; national leaders or mass movements that challenged property rights were to be crushed wherever possible.

As the Cold War recedes, the arguments offered by dependency theorists seem less removed than they once appeared from the realist tradition. Indeed, realism's Waltzian phase, which tended to regard security as distinct from, and taking precedence over, economics, may increasingly appear as an anomaly rooted in the particular features of the Cold War.[3] Dependency theory is traceable not only to the Marxist tradition, but also to realist scholarship on the economic dimension of power that was being produced before that line of research was largely bypassed as the result of the Cold War.[4] In general, pre-Cold War realism, though concerned in part with anarchy-driven interstate competition, was also more broadly concerned with the material interests of powerful actors, for whom control over the instruments of state power is a necessary prerequisite for defeating both domestic and foreign challengers.[5] For E. H. Carr, whose 1939 *Twenty Years' Crisis* holds up as one of the foremost contributions to realist thought, the very concept of national security was no more than an effort by privileged groups to equate their own position with the good of the nation, just as international security represents an effort to equate the position of the most privileged nation (or nations) with that of the entire world (1961, p. 82).

The essence of realism, according to Carr (1961), was the belief that politics is driven by "some material force" (p. 66). One branch of realism was geopolitics; the other branch, originated by Karl Marx, inquired into how historically changing economic forces redistributed power. All realists, Carr included, agree that the state, for several centuries, has been the most important instrument of power. But to determine the purpose for which that instrument was used, Carr was drawn to inquire into who was benefiting most from the spread of the market economy, and to consider the influence of market forces on the interests of important actors.

For the period marking the emergence of a global market economy—the middle of the nineteenth century—Carr provided a direct answer to that line of inquiry: British industrial capitalists had achieved hegemonic power, both domestically and internationally. Beyond mere power, they were also convinced that the system of free markets, from which they were the leading beneficiaries, represented the basis for a global "harmony of interest" that would provide the basis for world prosperity and peace. Carr brilliantly illuminated the economic and political forces that, by the end of the nineteenth century, were revealing this liberal conceit by British international bankers, industrialists, and their intellectual defenders as both utopian and self-serving. Nevertheless, that privileged group in England represented, in a sense, the birth of a community of capitalists—whom I have labeled the capitalist security community—who equated their own interests with the effective management of a global system based on economic growth, and peace.

The CSC was thus the first group whose actual material interests directly coincided with the global liberal agenda fashioned by thinkers like Montesquieu, James Mill, and Richard Cobden. Though the CSC lacks a specific founding document or moment of origin, one could associate its onset with the publication of Adam Smith's *Wealth of Nations* in 1776, conveniently giving it the same birthdate as the United States.[6] Those disposed to regard history since that point in terms of the ascendancy of the United States often refer to the worldwide phenomenon of "Americanization." Those who interpret the same time span in terms of the ascent of the CSC are apt to favor the term "globalization."

The CSC was making three specific errors when they claimed (and, Carr maintains, believed in) a universal harmony of interests. First, they were badly mistaken in perceiving a harmony of interests between themselves and the new class of industrial workers, whose organization and radicalization would ultimately threaten the very survival of capitalism. Second, they were guilty of a mistaken premise regarding the interests of their own class, whose commercial rivalries were driving great power conflicts across the colonial world, and whose "economic warfare" helped set the stage for World War I. Finally, imagining that they were generously bearing the "white man's burden" of uplifting other races under their rule, they overlooked the fact that colonized peoples bitterly resented their subjugation, even though their profound relative weakness would keep them largely docile well into the twentieth century.

Despite those enormous initial blinders, and the resulting series of subsequent disasters and near disasters, the CSC would ultimately demonstrate a remarkable capacity to learn from its mistakes, and consequently not only to survive but to expand, to include a widening collection both of old capitalist rivals from other states as well as large portions of the laboring class throughout the industrialized world. More specifically, the CSC has confronted, and mastered, five successive (though sometimes overlapping) challenges, though with the events of 9/11 it now faces a sixth. If durably successful once again, the CSC will arguably have achieved what Carr (1961) aptly described as a delusion just a century ago: its own ascension as the designer of a global harmony of interests in support of the peaceful pursuit of the system from which it profits. In a sense, liberalism and realism would then no longer be opposed doctrines, as liberal realists would have conquered the earth.

## THE HISTORICAL EXPANSION OF THE CAPITALIST SECURITY COMMUNITY

To shed light on how the CSC is likely to cope with its latest challenge—a movement based on theocratic fascism originating from the South—it is worth briefly considering past historical challenges that have shaped the worldview and strategic approach of the CSC. The five prior challenges that have confronted the CSC during the more than two centuries of its existence are: wresting control of the state from precapitalist authority, warding off a revolutionary working-class challenge, transcending great power war (the problem of nationalism and fascism in the West), transforming the Soviet Union, and warding off socialist-inspired movements in the South. The arrival of the new, fascist challenge from the South, I will argue, poses an equally potent threat to those thus far faced by the CSC.

Marxist historians have characterized the ascent of capitalism in eighteenth-century England as "a world-historical struggle between a rising middle class and a declining aristocracy" (Gallagher, 1998, p. 6), while a more recent post-Marxist approach characterizes the struggle more in terms of a division within the aristocracy between those who embraced and those who resisted the new opportunities offered by the commercialization of agriculture, industrialization, and the emergence of the stock market.[7] Either interpretation leads to the same basic conclusion: the revolutionary ascent of a new capitalist class. As markets broadened and deepened, a host of economists (mainly in England and France) began to make the case for establishing a global order based on free trade, including the idea of the commercial peace.[8]

The second challenge, which confronted capitalists wherever their increasing share of the national wealth had already conferred power within the state, was the challenge from within, as working-class movements divided between reformers calling for better working conditions and participation in government, and radicals who prepared for war against the capitalist class. As in subsequent challenges, members of the CSC divided into hawks and doves. In this case, the hawks set about using the military, the police, and private security companies to subdue the workers. For CSC doves, for whom the "harmony of interests" is both a self-serving rationalization of power and a genuine aspiration, facing this challenge dictated appeasing the workers through a substantial sharing of wealth and political power. Their ultimate success in wresting the reins of policy from those who were trying simply to crush the workers' movements would ultimately save—even as it altered and broadened—the CSC. The CSC's failure, however, in the midst of the First World War, either to suppress or appease the revolutionary movement in Russia, would ultimately lead to five decades of warfare on a global scale between the CSC and its class enemies.

The third challenge to the CSC occurred as the search for raw materials and markets spilled beyond national boundaries to give renewed impetus to the search for colonies (as well as control over disputed European territory). During this period, a number of distinct capitalist groups identified their own wealth and power with that of their states (over which they had achieved varying measures of control), leading to a fateful overlap between commercial and national rivalries. Indeed, the realpolitik rationale for addressing the domestic grievances of workers was the need to mobilize the entire state for the more pressing struggle against foreign enemies.[9] This synergy between the Darwinian struggle characterizing capitalism and the structural conflict inherent in an anarchic state system contributed greatly to the outbreak of the First World War. In 1914, the CSC failed the challenge of transcending great power war, which, thanks to the advent of the Fordist stage of industrial production and other technological advances, was approaching the potential to destroy human civilization.[10]

It failed that challenge again at Versailles in 1918, where a fundamental choice needed to be confronted. Would it actually take concrete steps to construct a world in which free markets would prevail, regardless of the consequences for national power—as John Maynard Keynes (1920) recommended in his role as advisor to the British delegation. Or would it pursue the union of capitalism and state power, in which economic and military competition among the industrialized powers would persist, and in which the most one could hope for was that those who had come out on top in 1918 could use their advantage to ward off future challenges? Keynes, in *The Economic Consequences of the Peace*, showed in 1920 why the economic exclusion of Germany (from what I am calling the CSC) would lead inevitably to renewed world war; Carr (1961) would later describe Nazism as a symptom of the instability resulting from that British and French-led effort to preserve their economic advantage at the cost of German recovery. The resulting "Carthaginian Peace" (as Keynes described it) set the stage for World War II.

Only at Bretton Woods, as a conflict that would take fifty million lives drew to a close, did the CSC succeed in regaining the reins of global economic policy that had been dropped when British hegemony had declined. This time it successfully met the challenge of integrating the industrialized world within a liberal economic system. Just as the CSC's inclusion of workers domestically had required a substantial redistribution of wealth and power, the "wise men" charged with promoting the CSC from America now presided over a "New Deal" for all the capitalist states that had only recently been fighting each other to the death, exemplified by the Marshall Plan and preferential trading rules designed to promote European and Japanese recovery, even including encouragement for a European Common Market that could lead to the emergence of a competing economic superpower.[11]

Just as the inclusion of workers domestically had once furthered the realpolitik objective of maximizing strength against other capitalist powers, the post–World War II inclusion of all of the rival capitalist powers within a single CSC was seen as a realpolitik necessity for waging global war for capitalism's very survival. On one hand, defeating the Soviet Union should have proved quite easy; as Willhelm Ropke had noted in 1942: "The situation of an isolated country engaged in a war against the powers standing for world economy is next to hopeless" (p. 105). Even Marx and Engels, one could argue, might have perceived the death sentence hovering over the Soviet Union, having prophesized as early as 1848 that capitalist-driven advances in production and communication would "compel all nations, on pain of extinction, to adopt the bourgeois mode of production" (1978: 477).

Making matters worse, from the Soviet perspective, an enlightened CSC had by now headed off the only two possible paths to salvation. First, the institutionalization of the welfare state, followed by the postwar economic boom, had destroyed any chances of recruiting the "fifth columns" of Communists that Churchill had warned could destroy the West from within. Moreover, the institutionalization of the CSC throughout the industrialized world (via implementation of the Bretton Woods economic regime along with the military alliances represented by NATO and the Japanese-American Security Treaty) quashed any remaining Leninist fantasies about renewed warfare among the capitalist powers. Despite these overwhelming obstacles, the Soviet Union was able to capitalize on two separate developments. The first was the arrival of the nuclear age, which enabled the Soviets by the late 1960s to achieve an apparent balance in the correlation of forces, and for a time seemed to refute the rule that military power must rest on the strength of a state's economy. The second was the spread of revolts in much of the South. There, the familiar story of the poor taking up arms against the rich took the form first of anticolonialism, and then anticapitalism. For a time, these struggles gave apparent moral substance to the case against "neocolonialism," and the reflected glory gained from assisting popular socialist-inspired mass uprisings distracted attention from the horrors of Soviet internal policies, helping to buttress the legitimacy of the Soviet state.

In retrospect, the preoccupation of scholarship and statecraft with the nuclear balance of terror proved a huge distraction, in the sense that beneath the military stalemate was a progressive widening, starting in the 1970s, of the already enormous Western economic advantage. What the Soviet realization of an "assured destruction" capability did achieve, by ending the prospect of nuclear coercion by the United States, was to shift the terms of the hawk versus dove debate within the CSC in favor (though never decisively) of the doves. Thus, serious calls within the U.S. defense establishment for preventative nuclear war in the 1950s gave way to the search, beginning in the 1960s, for a détente accompanied by the granting of MFN status to the Soviets (a plan frustrated by hawks in the U.S. Senate). Whatever the twists and turns of Western political and military strategy, economic integration within the West was now engendering new technologies, production methods, and economies of scale that were leaving the Soviet economic system in the dust. In short, the CSC's achievement of the welfare state compromise with labor and the disadvantaged, coupled to the inclusion of all the advanced capitalist states within the community, galvanized the productive capacity of the market system, and allowed time for "globalization" to win the Cold War.[12] Once the war was over, the CSC mobilized to do for Eastern Europe and the Soviet Union (followed by the CIS) what it would have been prepared to do in 1945 for a capitalist East: to help rebuild devastated economies and facilitate their economic integration within an expanded CSC.

If CSC hawks and doves wrestled over policy toward the Soviet enemy, the idea of accommodation was never extended to antifree market forces in the South. Long before serious bonds were forged between leftist movements in the Third World and the Soviet Union, U.S. forces (often covertly) were dispatching leaders inclined to nationalize foreign property (e.g., Mossadegh in Iran, Arbenz in Guatemala), and the détente of the 1970s never meaningfully reduced that pattern. (Allende was deposed, with CIA and MNC help, not long after the 1972 onset of détente.) Even during the last phase of the Cold War, when the West and Soviet leader Gorbachev were pursuing rapprochement, the United States pressed its successful military campaigns against leftist regimes in Nicaragua and Afghanistan.

It is true that following the OPEC price shocks, more steps were taken to address southern grievances (in terms of increased foreign aid by some European states, and the granting of greater trade preferences to the poorest states), but these gestures fell orders of magnitude short of the southern demand for a "New International Economic Order (NIEO)." This was the period when southern voices on the left began making apocalyptic prophesies about the nuclear destruction of the North, forecasts that were given credence by a few sympathetic Western leaders. Said Francois Mitterand in 1981: "I am convinced that the balance between the two parts of the world, the industrialized nations and the others, will be one of the causes of the most serious tragedies at the end of the century, to be explicit, of world war" (Reston, 1981).

But the fundamental reality, as the realist Robert Tucker (1977) persuasively argued in *The Inequality of Nations* (written at the apparent height of southern bargaining leverage), was that calls for an NIEO were doomed by the South's lack of power. As in the case of workers before they formed militant unions, or of Germany before it produced the nightmare represented by Nazism, or of the Soviets before they built thousands of nuclear weapons, the CSC was calculating that a major change in policy—that is, a far-reaching expansion to actually include the South in a "harmony of interests"—was unnecessary. By the early 1990s, the realists had apparently been proved correct, as, except for the lonely holdout of Castro's Cuba, southern opposition to capitalism had collapsed, even though many of the southern states within the capitalist market system were floundering, and that the gap in wealth between North and South was steadily growing wider. The CSC had defeated the challenge of socialism in the South.

What can one learn from how the CSC coped with the challenges it has faced since its formation? For one thing, while it has proved highly adaptable, it has made major changes only at times of profound danger. In such cases, however, it has shown the capacity to learn. Moreover, learning has taken the form of the same basic lesson applied to different circumstances: evolution in a direction designed to enhance its legitimacy. Put another way, the CSC has repeatedly, at times of deep crisis, taken far-reaching measures that have enhanced the credibility of its central claim: that there is indeed a global harmony of economic interests. In doing so, it has proved willing to abandon the laissez-faire credo (which its hawks regard as a nonnegotiable point of honor) that forms the heart of classical liberal theory, and to embrace the idea that the outcome of unrestricted economic competition is unfair and intolerable. The result has been the inclusion of new groups, including a measure of economic redistribution and power sharing that tends to reinforce the CSC's "doves" during future challenges. Put another way, the CSC has been willing to dilute its capitalism with overtures that smack of a "progressive" perspective on domestic and international politics.

## WHO IS THE HEGEMON? THE CSC OR THE UNITED STATES?

The foregoing analysis implies that, as we look at the world's response to 9/11, it may make more sense to envision the primary actor as the CSC rather than the United States. This view is admittedly problematic, in ways that need to be made explicit. First, it is the United States, not some nebulous CSC, that has the guns in the current war on terror. Second, the U.S. government is evidently not, as Marx and Engels famously described the governments of all capitalist states, "the executive committee of the ruling class." Even if there is an identifiable group of people in business, the government, and the academy who share the outlook I attribute to the CSC, the CSC is engaged in constant struggle over the instruments of state power. Part of that struggle is with capitalists who reject various alliances the CSC has made (with labor, with foreign capitalists in the WTO, etc.), or whose particular material interests do not coincide with policies designed to advance the general interests of the CSC. (Russian President Vladimir Putin, for example, may wish to advance the current CSC interest in suppressing international terrorism, while powerful domestic capitalists, who profit from business interests in Iraq and Iran, may resist his efforts.) Part of the struggle is always with organized labor, which habitually insists on more of a share of wealth and power than the CSC wishes to grant. Finally, even among the hypothetical "card-carrying members" of the CSC, there are inevitably profound debates over strategy, despite basic agreement on the peaceful, prosperous liberal world order to which all members aspire.

Nevertheless, there is good reason to regard the key unit of power in the world today as the CSC rather than the United States (and other major powers). That is because motives attributable to the CSC seem to explain important features of world politics better than competing expectations that structural realist scholars derive from the interstate balance of power. Here are a few suggestive examples. After the Cold War, state-centric realists predicted the demise of NATO, based on the sound premise that alliances form for defense against threats, and dissolve when the threat has passed. Thus, if NATO were primarily an alliance among states, it should have long since dissolved. As a CSC alliance, however, marshaling most of the power of the capitalist world, it faces continuing threats on a global scale (as the war against al Qaeda threatens continuing globalization), in addition to the ongoing prospect of internal challenges (i.e., political nationalism or even fascism, economic protectionism, etc.), against which an overarching military regime can help reinforce the credibility of more benign institutions.

That is particularly the case when it comes to Western policy toward Russia. NATO is only remotely comprehensible from a state-centric realist perspective to the extent that it excludes Russia (whose nuclear weapons and economic potential might be stretched by some into the dimensions of a future threat). How can a military alliance take steps, as NATO may well be doing, toward including Russia—in other words, toward existing without even a hypothetical enemy?

The case of NATO suggests another test case: why didn't the United States "come home" after the end of the Cold War? Put another way, why, in the absence of even a remote threat by another major power or combination of powers, didn't the United States retreat to the role of "offshore balancer," as some realists prescribed with powerful logic? The fact that this perfectly reasonable realist idea had about as much appeal to U.S. decision makers as calls for unilateral nuclear disarmament did during the Cold War, suggests that state-centric realist assumptions regarding U.S. strategic interests have become far-fetched. Finally, if America wasn't coming home (as defensive realists suggested), why isn't it assertively accumulating power at a moment of unprecedented opportunity to dominate all possible rivals, as offensive realists—who have called, for example, for a U.S. effort to slow Chinese growth—suggest? (Mearsheimer, 2001: 402). While realists trying to divine U.S. interests from the structure of interstate power flounder among the widest possible assortment of grand strategies, the main thrust of U.S. statecraft since the end of the Cold War seems to follow very directly from the core interests of the CSC.

The point of analyzing world politics in terms of CSC dominance, however, is ultimately to supplement, rather than supplant, structural theory based on the interstate balance of power. After all, since states remain the essential instruments of power, the CSC's ability to direct global politics is dependent on its control over pivotal states. It follows that the transnational power of the CSC relies on its achievement of domestic hegemony within the major states (and, ideally, all states). The optimal situation for the CSC is the presence of a hegemonic superpower in which the CSC dominates domestic politics. That, of course, is not far from the situation today, despite disconnected efforts by labor and business in import-threatened industries, politically influential "realists," right-wing anti-immigration demagogues, left-wing antiglobalization protesters, and so forth, to topple the CSC's grip on power in the United States. Current CSC hegemony within a hegemonic state is somewhat analogous to the international context in which the CSC first assumed a global role: that of nineteenth-century British hegemony. It is worth recalling Carr's characterization of the "harmony of interests" that then prevailed:

> The predominance of the manufacturer and the merchant was so overwhelming that there was a sense in which an identity between their prosperity and British prosperity as a whole could be correctly asserted. . . . Nevertheless, the doctrine of the harmony of interests and of solidarity between the classes must have seemed a bitter mockery to the under-privileged worker, whose inferior status and insignificant stake in 'British prosperity' were consecrated by it; and presently he was strong enough to force the abandonment of laissez-faire and the substitution for it of the 'social service state,' which implicitly denies the natural harmony of interests and sets out to create a new harmony by artificial means.
>
> The same analysis may be applied to international relations. British . . . statesmen, having discovered that free trade promoted British prosperity, were sincerely convinced that . . . it also promoted the prosperity of the world as a whole. British predominance in world trade was at that time so overwhelming that there was a certain undeniable harmony between British interest and the interest of the world. British prosperity flowed over into other countries, a British economic collapse would have meant world-wide ruin. . . . Nevertheless, this alleged international harmony of interests seemed a mockery to those under-privileged nations whose inferior status and insignificant stake in international trade were consecrated by it. The revolt against it destroyed that overwhelming British preponderance which had provided a plausible basis for the theory (Carr, 1961: 81).

The relative decline of Britain was one step in a calamitous sequence that culminated in two world wars. It is worth considering whether recent events, by also signifying a "revolt" against American preponderance, have posed choices similar to the ones faced by the CSC during the first decades of the twentieth century. The purpose of the following, final section is to consider whether past errors are repeating themselves, and what CSC strategy offers the best hope of forging a path toward a new world order.

## THE END OF THE OLD ORDER, AND THE FUTURE OF THE CSC

The mirage of the 1990s was, as we now know, the reflection of a century past beyond recall—the golden age of continuously expanding markets, of a world policed by the self-assured and not too onerous American hegemony, of a coherent "Western" civilization whose conflicts could be harmonized by a progressive extension of the area of common development, of the easy assumptions that what was good for one was good for all and that what was economically right could not be morally wrong. The reality that had once given content to this utopia was already in decay before the twentieth century had reached its end, though it took the events of September 11, 2001, to finally puncture liberal hopes about "the end of history."

Remove the final clause, change the "1990s" to the "1920s," and substitute "British" for "American hegemony," and the above is a direct quotation from the beginning of E. H Carr's 1939 commentary on "the end of the old order" (1961: 224). Carr, who believed in historical progress, would no doubt have repudiated anyone's claim that history repeats itself (and so would disdain Kenneth Waltz's (1979) premise that a fixed international structure reduces history to a dismal repetitiveness).[13] It is nevertheless of interest to note that, in both cases, the leaders of a hegemonic power had ended the previous century confident that their promotion of free markets and Western values represented an irresistible fusion of power and morality, destined for adoption as the indispensable standards for peaceful global governance. And, in both cases, the new century appeared to mock their hopes with a plunge into shocking violence.

For Carr, the descent from the heyday of British power to the darkness of the mid-1930s represented two distinct phases. The first phase was marked by the collapse of the liberal order, which had been based on British power rather than a genuine commercial peace. The second phase was the supplanting of a liberal illusion by a realist one (corresponding to the views now held by so-called defensive realists), that there was a universal interest in preserving peace based on the status quo. (It is often forgotten that Carr's critique of realism in *The Twenty Years' Crisis* is as lengthy, and as sharp, as his critique of liberalism). It is in terms of that succession of errors: the failure of liberalism, followed by the failure of realism, that leads Carr to what he regards as both a practical and moral solution to the problem of world order.

## THE FAILURE OF LIBERALISM

The appeal by proponents of laissez-faire economics to the long-term maximization of wealth, argued Carr (1961), ignored the fact that this ultimate common good "was preceded by a struggle for life . . . in which not only the good, but the very existence, of the loser were eliminated altogether from the picture" (p. 49). That realization had been postponed, Carr maintained, by the huge expansion in production, population, and prosperity that had occurred during the century following publication of Adam Smith's *Wealth of Nations*, developments that limited the intensity of commercial competition, forestalled the outbreak of class warfare, and infused humankind with a general sense of optimism that there was a rational plan in place that harmonized humanity's aspirations (Carr, 1961: 44–46). Yet markets could not expand continuously, a problem first dramatized as the wave of nineteenth-century colonization culminated in clashes over the few remaining sites of value. As the nineteenth century ended, Carr notes that mounting pessimism over continued economic expansion led to growing agitation in Western Europe against alien immigration, and a rise in European anti-Semitism (characterized by Carr as "the recurrent symptom of economic stress"). The "apparent harmony" of interests was now yielding to the "transparent clash of interests" (1961: 60–62).

While realists are fond of invoking or restating Carr's conclusions regarding the implications of 1914 for international economic liberalism, some seem to have forgotten his equally severe critiques of the policies enacted between 1918 and the 1930s; that is, the failure to construct a world order that might have prevented the rise of fascism and the renewal of world war. These dimensions of Carr's depiction of the "end of the old order" deserve at least equal current attention, since they provide plausible accounts of disasters that can result when a doctrine of national security supplants the search for a just world order. In fact, the passages that actually analyze the twenty years' crisis between 1919 and 1939 are wholly unconcerned with the illusions of economic liberals (whose doctrine, as Carr notes, had been rejected in the aftermath of World War I). Instead, Carr's wrath is directed at policies driven by beliefs that today come under the umbrella of realist thought.

In recent years, realists have divided themselves into two categories: "defensive" and "offensive" (Mearsheimer, 2001: 19–22). Although those labels did not exist during Carr's lifetime, he depicted the essence of each view, and offered critiques of both (in the context of events between 1919 and 1939) that have gone unanswered during the six decades since he wrote his most famous work. The first error, that states are compelled to maximize their power over potential rivals, today forms the central axiom of "offensive realism." The second error that he attributed to the statesmen of that period, that is, the presumption that defense of the status quo is the key to a peaceful world order, is today embraced by self-described defensive realists. Carr decried what is now called defensive realism as a particularly pernicious variant of utopianism, and he characterized offensive realism as a "sterile" misunderstanding of the fundamental nature of power. Since it is the "defensive realist" strand that most corresponds to current policy dilemmas, the following looks at defensive realism's role in the failure of diplomacy during the interwar years, then applies Carr's analysis to the search for a stable order in the world after 9/11.

## The Failure of Defensive Realism

There is an overlap in the beliefs of liberal proponents of the commercial peace and defensive realists: each believes that wars between major powers are unprofitable, and each believes that realization of that material reality is the key to peace. There is an important difference, of course, in the material basis identified by each theory for providing a rational incentive to preserve peace: liberals focus on war's role in severing the economic links that are crucial to private profit and general economic growth, defensive realists focus on the wartime military advantages of the defense. Yet both perspectives start with an empirical claim that bids for conquest do not pay, adds a presumption that leaders, once aware of that demonstrable fact, will refrain from aggression, and insists that the result of this awareness (i.e., peace) is an objective that reasonable people agree should be a central goal of international relations theory and practice.

For Carr, both the liberal and the defensive realist's case for the status quo are flawed for the same reason: each conflates a self-interested objective with a universal good, and each consequently overlooks the sense of grievance that can lead to war regardless of the calculation of costs and benefits. If World War I proved a major setback to proponents of a natural harmony of economic interests, it reinforced (at least in the minds of the victors) the idea of an essential political harmony of interests based on the assumption that everyone at least shares an interest in peace. After 1918, the liberals' error of ignoring the prospective dangers of unconstrained market competition was now compounded by sheer hypocrisy, as the victors used their power to keep the vanquished weak, then defended the status quo as the moral basis for permanent international peace and security. At that point, the doctrine of the harmony of interests lost any foundation in reality and became merely a "cloak for the vested interests of the privileged," who proceeded to invoke such time-honored slogans of privileged groups as "security" and "law and order," slogans that were promoted as equivalent to "international morality." Carr concludes: "Just as the ruling class in a community prays for domestic peace, which guarantees its own security and predominance . . . so international peace becomes a special vested interest of predominant Powers" (1961: 82).

For Carr, however, this conception of peace represented the mark of foredoomed utopianism, for it ignored the inevitability of German resentment against the status quo, which, once compounded by economic depression, would culminate in fascist totalitarianism. What was the connection, in Carr's view, between grievance and increasingly virulent nationalism? "Countries which are struggling to force their way into the dominant group naturally tend to invoke nationalism against the internationalism of the controlling Powers" (1961: 86). These are the forces that undermine the capacity of a defensive advantage to prevent war. Indeed, in a sense, when wealth and power seem to make a defender impregnable, the resulting temptation to refuse to appease even the legitimate demands of the weak may be precisely what sets in motion the process of resistance that culminates in war. Invoking Carr to attack the central premise of Stephan Van Evera's case for defensive realism, Richard Betts (1999) concludes: "If the aim of avoiding war is subordinate to some other normative value . . . it is a leap of faith to accept that the uniform answer is . . . securing stability through recognition that defense is easier than attack" (1961: 170). Put another way, defense can be reliably dominant over offense only when the status quo is normatively acceptable.

## Prospects for a New World Order

As the CSC faces yet another challenge, it is worth recalling E. H. Carr's depiction of the fundamental prerequisite for maintaining power: "Those who profit most" from a peaceful international order "can in the long run only hope to maintain it by making sufficient concessions to make it tolerable to those who profit by it least; and the responsibility for seeing that these changes take place as far as possible in an orderly way rests as much on the defenders as on the challengers" (1961: 169). While the CSC applied that lesson to the working class in the industrialized world, and again to the rival capitalist powers (which today means all the world's important states), the lessons were learned only in the context of terrific struggle, and at the price of communist revolution and world war. Moreover, the lessons are not written in stone, and are subject to endless challenge by neoliberal purists, who, one might say, apply the following formulation of Adam Smith (1976) to both domestic and international politics: "Civil government, so far as it is instituted for the security of property, is in reality instituted for the defence of the rich against the poor, or of those who have some property against those who have none at all" (v. 2, 236).

Against that view, which can equally be interpreted as a liberal defense of laissez-faire economics and as a realist vision of national or international security, Carr offered an alternative vision: "If . . . it is utopian to ignore the element of power, it is an unreal kind of realism which ignores the element of morality in any world order" (1961: 238–239). As to the substance of Carr's own 1939 effort to reconcile realism and utopianism: "We cannot return to the pre-1939 world. . . . Frank acceptance of the subordination of economic advantage to social ends, and the recognition that what is economically good is not always morally good, must be extended from the national to the international sphere" 1961: 238–239).

Is this lesson applicable to the war against Bin Laden and al Qaeda? In at least two ways, it may initially appear irrelevant to the war that must now be fought. One obvious point of comparison between 1939 and 9/11 is that once a fascist movement begins a war on a global scale, there is no alternative but to mobilize every available military and intelligence resource to defeat it. And just as the participants in the Manhattan Project recognized that the world was in a race to defeat Hitler before he acquired nuclear weapons (which could require acquiring them first), there is a similar sense of the essential need to stop al Qaeda before it manages a true mass destruction attack.

Another reason for questioning the applicability of Carr's prescription is that neither the al Qaeda leadership, nor the suicide hijackers of 9/11, seem to represent the world's most disadvantaged masses. Nevertheless, the sense of grievance into which they have tapped, as illustrated by the celebrations of 9/11 among throngs of the poor in Pakistan, Palestine, Indonesia, the Middle East, and much of Africa, suggests that the social base on which the long-term viability of the movement rests is ultimately rooted in global poverty. If that is the case, then even the effective suppression of the most dangerous current terrorist organization is unlikely to durably prevent the rise of new movements. In a sense, the defeat of socialism in the South may have increased the threat, since the abandonment of aspirations to a universalist vision of social justice may have opened the door to far more apocalyptic visions of the ends of politics. This has been exacerbated by the problem of timing, in which intensified rage has been accompanied by a new stage in mastery of techniques associated with globalization to enhance their striking power. The adept use of modern communications and acquisition of sophisticated technical skills have been coupled with establishing bases in those countries most glaringly left out of the presumably universal benefits of a global market system.[14]

Thus, there should be vastly increased alarm over what have long become familiar statistics—for example, the fact that half the world's six billion people earn less than $2 a day. As Strobe Talbot (2001) wrote soon after 9/11, in referring to poverty as "the other evil": "that fifty-fifty ratio is unstable. . . . The numbers of poor are growing faster than the numbers of rich, and the gap between rich and poor is widening. When self-perceived losers outnumber self-perceived winners, it's lose–lose for everyone" (2001: 75).[15] The income gap between the fifth of the world's population in the richest countries and the fifth in the poorest grew from 30 to 1 in 1960, to 60 to 1 in 1990, and to 74 to 1 in 1995. In citing those statistics more than a year before 9/11, Fouad Ajami (2000) offered the following assessment: "A world of this magnitude of inequality is inherently unstable. Its peace must rest, as the Arabic expression would have it, on the palm of a devil" (2000: 34).

There is no natural harmony of interests between the impoverished of the South and those who inhabit the Capitalist Security Community.[16] The greatest permanent problem for that community is that, despite its accurate claim to be custodian of the first system of wealth generation that can end the problem of scarcity for humankind, it will always be highly vulnerable. Indeed, the higher the level of global integration, the greater the likelihood that even local disasters can ripple through the system. If the need for security after 9/11 indeed means, as Zakaria would have it, that "the state is back," there will be little cause for celebration. As the world witnessed in 1914 and particularly after 1929, the breakdown of economic integration can unleash a vicious cycle of poverty, extremist ideology, and, ultimately, world war.

At the same time, the CSC has never been in a better position to make the final essential step toward reformation and inclusion. In contrast to British hegemony at the end of the nineteenth century, America's relative power, and thus its capacity for leadership, is holding steady. Moreover, if, in 1900, the beginning of a new naval arms race represented the synergy of Darwinian economics and Darwinian realpolitik, the fact that the CSC now embraces all the major powers has drained the system of the most potent source of major war. The missing ingredient, thus far, particularly under the U.S. leadership of the Bush administration, has been clear awareness of the need to combine the war on terror with the beginning of a search for a more equitable basis for world order. Even here, the movement from unilateralism toward a concert of great powers, the movement from repudiation of nation-building toward attempting it in Afghanistan, and the progress from contempt for foreign aid toward a proposed 50% increase, all suggest a response to two sets of structural pressures: the unprecedented global inclusiveness of the CSC and the global nature of the threat the CSC now faces. It remains to be seen whether these responses represent the first stirrings of a deliberate global project, in which the problem of unjust and unsustainable economic inequality, one of the most prominent among the many follies that lead humans into violence, will be decisively addressed. If the CSC is quick enough to recognize and confront that challenge, it will likely discover that the cost and complexity of such an enterprise, while daunting, are of no greater magnitude than the wars it has already waged, or the concessions it has already made, and that those costs pale before the profits to be reaped should it succeed in the next stage of its search for a global harmony of interests.

## NOTES

1. While I have taken this phrase from Buzan (1995: 198–199), my conception of the CSC differs substantially from Buzan's.

2. Wrote Montesquieu (1989: 338): "The natural effect of commerce is to lead to peace. Two nations that trade with each other become reciprocally dependent; if one has an interest in buying, the other has an interest in selling, and all unions are founded on mutual needs."

3. Five factors may account for that temporary separation of political economy from security studies in international relations scholarship. First, the principle U.S. security threat was a military but not an economic rival. Second, the only U.S. economic competitors (Western Europe and Japan) were military allies. Third, the nuclear balance of terror seemed to challenge the importance of economic power, since it enabled a small economic power to destroy a large one. Fourth, classical liberalism, which formed the ideological foundation for the defense of the West, includes a normative appeal for the separation of politics and markets. By contrast, an analytical approach emphasizing the ineradicable interconnectedness of economics and politics (i.e., Marxism) was shunned by Western security experts. For a useful discussion of reasons 1–3, see Mastanduno (1998). For a discussion of reasons 4 and 5, see Goldfischer (2002).

4. Thus, in the 1980 expanded version of his classic realist treatise (written during World War II) *National Power and the Structure of Foreign Trade*, Albert O. Hirschman noted that he could claim to have originated dependency theory, through his analysis (applied to Europe) of how apparently "harmless" trade relations can result in the dependency of a relatively poor country on a relatively rich one.

5. To reduce "realism" to the few writers who are interested only in the consequences of anarchy for state behavior would exclude nearly the entire realist pantheon of theorists and practitioners (Machiavelli, Richelieu, Disraeli, Bismarck, Stalin, Kennan, Kissinger, etc.) for whom the manipulation of domestic politics was deemed as fundamental to exerting power as international behavior.

6. Though his contribution to economic liberalism is unrivaled, Smith of course was not completely willing to subordinate national security to free trade. See Earle (1944: 121–123).

7. For a description of this debate (including the quotation) and references to historical research, see Gallagher (1998).

8. For a review of British and French arguments connecting economic liberalism and peace, see Silberner (1946).

9. For Carr's description of the connection between Bismarck's and Disraeli's establishment of welfare states as preparation for imperialist ventures, see Carr (1961). For a general tracing of the relationship between war and the expansion of the welfare state, see Porter (1994).

10. In a sense, World War I represented the culmination of the CSC's loss of control over foreign policy in the major capitalist states. In that intraclass struggle among capitalists, the CSC (which then included international bankers, allied with merchants and agricultural interests involved in trade) lost out to large-scale, Fordist industrial capital. As that occurred, the CSC's liberal internationalist vision based on free trade and peace gave way to militarism and colonialism. For an instructive historical analysis of how this changing balance of power within capitalism reshaped American foreign policy in the 1890s, see Trubowitz (1998: 31–95). For a general overview of this phase of intracapitalist conflict, see Rupert (2000: 44) and van der Pijl (1998). All these works illuminate how what I call the CSC achieves political representation in domestic politics, a subject beyond the scope of this chapter.

11. For a combined biography of six men, whose careers straddled Wall Street and Washington and exemplified the "establishment" crafting U.S. security and economic policy in the early postwar years, see Isaacson and Thomas (1966).

12. For a well-documented argument that the Soviet Union was defeated by globalization, see Brooks and Wohlforth (2000/1).

13. Writes Waltz: "The texture of international politics remains highly constant ... and events repeat themselves endlessly. The relations that prevail internationally ... are marked ... by dismaying persistence" (1979: 66).

14. For a cogent realist analysis connecting the disintegrative consequences of globalization for some of the world's poorest states to growing prospects for war (and the growing appeal of the "equalizing" potential of mass destruction weapons and terror), see the chapter in this volume by Mohammed Ayoob.

15. Ken Booth's chapter in this volume offers more grim statistics regarding the gap between haves and have-nots. His discussion of Mark Twain's commentary on Europe of the 1790s in terms of two "Reigns of Terror" eloquently illustrates our tendency to ignore the "daily terror" of the masses of suffering poor, while becoming riveted by the "'horror of swift death'" inflicted on a relatively tiny number in events such as 9/11.

16. For a discussion of ways in which policies associated with globalization have harmed the South (with particular documentation concerning the countries of the Arab Middle East and North Africa), see Bahgat Korany's chapter in this volume.

# 12

# Turbulence and Terrorism

## Reframing or Readjusting the Model?

James N. Rosenau

Widespread is the understanding that the terrorism of September 11, 2001, constituted a system perturbation (SP) so profound as to initiate transformations of local, domestic, and international life wherein long-standing structures everywhere have given way to new patterns, orientations, and practices. As one analyst put it, "few veteran foreign policy watchers can remember when a single event has had so instant and so profound an effect on the entire dynamic of world politics" (Schmemann, 2001: B3). Such observations are pervaded with assumptions and insights that may or may not be accurate, but their accuracy must await the passage of time to determine whether in fact the SP surfaced new patterns that will be enduring configurations rather than momentary blips in the thrust of long-run tendencies at every level of community. Patience in this regard is not easily achieved. Even distinguished historians who are professionally committed to being wary of immediate events as signifiers of historical breakpoints have not hesitated to presume that the terrorist attack gave rise to irreversible changes.[1] Still others acknowledge that the 9/11 attacks posed enormous challenges while at the same time stress that they did not change anything (Halliday, 2002).

Yet there are good reasons to be impatient. Whether the 9/11 attacks were system transforming or merely part of a historic pattern,[2] an initial effort to comprehend their larger meanings and potential cannot be justifiably postponed. At the very least there is a need to explore whether the way in which officials and publics in various parts of the world think about security, military and otherwise, as an aspect of world affairs is now substantially different from what it was prior to September 11. Such foci seem especially compelling because of the United States's insistence that the world has been caught up in a war on terrorism rather than being faced with horrendous crimes best met through police actions.

A qualification is in order here: while alterations in the ways officials and publics think about change is a form of change, such assessments may not give rise to the changes they presume to be necessary. Analysts may perceive 9/11 as having created new circumstances that call for corresponding policy shifts—as one observer put it, "Security . . . has a new meaning, for which little in our history and even less in our planning has prepared us" (Gaddis, 2001: 10)—but some officials who make policy may not share such understandings. Indeed, certain kinds of change, especially those that require altered conduct on the part of large, bureaucratic organizations, may encounter habitual responses that are of long duration and thus resistant to transformation irrespective of the perceived need for change. Bureaucratic practices, for example, can be so rooted in inertia that the need for change never moves beyond perception to implementation. There is already persuasive evidence that deeply entrenched patterns are hindering the adaptation of needed alterations in American military structures, strategies, and tactics (Keller, 2002).

In short, the concepts of change and transformation are elusive. No single formulation of them has ever enjoyed widespread usage. Analysts tend to take for granted that change is readily distinguishable from continuity, even though they may differ greatly on whether new patterns have surfaced and how long they must endure to qualify as fundamental and permanent change. The phrase "new patterns" is the key to a meaningful understanding of any potential transformation. Systemic patterns are empirical; they can be observed, and whether they occur abruptly or slowly evolve, observers can reasonably conclude that differences between the patterns at times 1 and 2 constitute change. Viewed in this way, the aftermath of 9/11 offers a quintessential opportunity to perfect techniques for assessing the nature of systemic patterns and their vulnerability to alteration. It compels us to clarify what we mean by transformation and how we know change when we see it.

For analysts wedded to an underlying theory of world politics, as I am, the possibility of a new, post-9/11 world poses another troublesome and elusive conceptual challenge, that of whether their theories need to be abandoned or whether they need to be modified to remain viable. It is not an easy question to ponder. Whatever their conception of systemic coherence and transformation, analysts are rarely so persuaded by new developments that they abandon their long-standing theoretical perspectives. The inclination to see what one wants to see, to interpret new data in such a way that they appear to conform to the main outlines of one's theory, is a powerful impulse. Such an attitude certainly prevails in my case. To speculate that 9/11 led to fundamental systemic change is not to conclude that my turbulence model has been negated.[3] Indeed, not only am I disinclined to reframe the model, but my analytic antennae also tell me that such a reframing is not needed, that the model only needs to be readjusted to highlight how it accommodates the new forms of terrorism. Admittedly, such a conclusion may stem as much from major flaws in the model as from a tendency to see what I want to see. Conceivably, the model is so broad that it can absorb any development that may arise on the world scene, a characteristic that must be avoided if a model is to have any viability at all. I will return to this question shortly after outlining the original formulation of the model.

## THE TURBULENCE MODEL PRIOR TO 9/11

The core of the model involves the transformation of three basic parameters as a consequence of a number of dynamics that accelerated following the end of World War II to the point where they no longer serve as constant boundary conditions. The three parameters, now variables, are distinguished by the levels of aggregation at which they are operative—the micro, macro, and micro-macro levels. These three dynamics of change, of course, impact importantly on each other, thus further accelerating the turbulence at work in world politics.

The transformation of the micro parameter involves change unfolding among ordinary people, activists, and elites who are not public officials. The theory asserts that people in every part of the world have undergone and are still undergoing a three-part skill revolution. One part pertains to their analytic skills, by which is meant a growing capacity to trace distant events back into their homes and pocketbooks. The second part consists of their emotional skills, which refers to an increasing ability to know what they are for and what they are against. The third dimension focuses on their imaginative skills, which are conceived to be founded on an expanding imagination about the nature of other cultures and societies. These greater analytic, emotional, and imaginative skills are posited as deriving from a variety of sources, from exposure to more education, travel, technological innovations such as global television, the Internet, and fiber-optic cable, and the rigors of life in large urban communities. But the theory does not posit people as converging around common values. Rather it hypothesizes that their skills expand in the context of their own culture, so that the Paris sophisticate, the Asian peasant, and the Islamic fundamentalist, for example, are each likely to be differently skilled in these ways relative to, say, their grandparents.[4]

The transformation of the macro variable consists of a major change in the basic structures through which world politics unfold. Where the dominant structure for centuries prior to the present era was an anarchic state-centric system in which states, their organizations (IGOs), and their interactions shaped the course of events, today another system, the multicentric system consisting of diverse nongovernmental collectivities (NGOs), has evolved as a competing structure that often conflicts, sometimes cooperates, and endlessly interacts with the state-centric system. As a consequence, the global system has undergone and continues to undergo a profound bifurcation. The presence of this bifurcated structure is readily apparent whenever IGOs such as the IMF, the World Bank, the WTO, or the United Nations convene to ponder major issues, numerous and diverse NGOs will also assemble to deliberate the same issues and press their conclusions on the state-centric institutions. The events surrounding the 1995 gathering of states to assess women's rights in Beijing and the clashes that accompanied the 1999 WTO meeting that came to be known as the Battle of Seattle are but the more pronounced incidents of the recurring patterns of global bifurcation.

The micro-macro variable refers to the links and interactions between people at the micro level and their collectivities at the macro level. Its transformation involves a proliferation and intensification of authority crises throughout the world. Many, if not most, national governments as well as numerous other types of organizations ranging from churches to corporations to the mafia have experienced and continue to experience a diminution in the degree to which their leaderships can evoke the compliance of their followers. In their most spectacular form, authority crises take the form of protest marches, but even more pervasive are the crises that result from an inability to frame and implement goals, thereby fomenting paralysis and stalemate. Viewed in this way, for example, present-day China is and has long been mired in an authority crisis, hesitant to move toward its goal of breaking up its large and inefficient state-owned enterprises (SOEs) out of fear of swelling further the ranks of unemployed persons in the cities even as its vast rural areas are also marked by extensive discontent and restlessness.

The turbulence model also stresses the many ways in which change is sustained through the interaction of the three prime variables. The tendencies toward noncompliance on the part of publics, for instance, are fostered by the skill revolution that, in turn, generates a proliferation of organizations and a further disaggregation of authority on a worldwide scale that deepens the degree of global bifurcation. A major result of the complex interactions among the three parameters-turned-variables is that world affairs have been and continue to be increasingly vulnerable to individuals having consequence for how issues play out at every level of community. Another consequence is the weakening of states and territoriality as the skill revolution and organization explosion sustain the dynamics of bifurcation.

Does the turbulent model's presumption of continuing change facilitate the prediction of future events and tendencies? Or does it only allow for retrospective interpretation? Yes and no. Yes in the sense that it points to a range of possible outcomes under specifiable circumstances, and no in the sense that it does not pretend to anticipate particular developments at particular times. The range of possible outcomes precludes quiescent citizens and publics, a preponderance of stable governments, and the absence of a superpower or great power coalition that can effectively command the direction in which issues unfold. In effect, the model is one that presumes unexpected events and locates where such developments are likely to originate.

The previous paragraph is relevant to the aforementioned question of whether the turbulence model is so broad that it can accommodate any changes or constancies that may become salient on the world stage. The answer lies in the further question of whether that stage can be marked by any developments that would negate the model. An affirmative response comes immediately to mind: if all the world's major governments should simultaneously become majority governments capable of taking decisive actions and thereby meeting the needs of their people, cooperating with other governments, and coping readily with challenges from the multicentric world, then clearly the turbulence model will have been falsified. The likelihood of such an eventuality in the foreseeable future strikes me as very slim indeed.

## THE TURBULENCE MODEL SINCE 9/11

Although the events of that horrendous Tuesday in New York and Washington generated such huge commotion as to conform to the metaphoric conception of turbulence,[5] their consequences were largely consistent with my analytic (and nonmetaphoric) formulation of the concept. Indeed, more than a few of the turbulence model's main features were evident on 9/11 and in its aftermath. Most notable, perhaps, were the terrorists themselves. Besides the remarkable organizational skills reflected in their actions, what they did was another instance of the long-term process whereby authority is undergoing disaggregation, with new actors who clamber onto the world stage and exercise authority through horizontal networks rather than hierarchical chains of command and, in so doing, have the capacity to challenge states and generate widespread consequences. The arrival of Osama Bin Laden and al Queda on the stage has not been welcomed by the civilized world, but few would question that terrorists have become major actors who may shape the course of events in the decades to come. The war between the world's hegemon and a diffuse, nongovernmental organization is a classic instance of the disaggregated and bifurcated global structures posited by the turbulence model.

Likewise, the various skills that enabled the terrorists to successfully implement the plans they carried out on 9/11 are illustrative of the micro transformations anticipated by the model. The skill revolution does not presume that people will necessarily employ their newly acquired competencies in morally desirable ways. It simply asserts that they are likely to be increasingly competent. And that is what the terrorists demonstrated with their takeover of commercial planes and their use of them as bombs.

Hardly less conspicuous are the ways in which developments subsequent to 9/11 demonstrated the centrality of new technologies as a source of the skill revolution underlying the conduct of people at the micro level. Word of the tragedy spread quickly through global television and the Internet. The reactions of governments and of people in American and Islamic streets flowed in torrents across fiber-optic cable and through orbiting satellites; as the news surged around the world, numerous persons experienced intense patriotism and others expressed intense joy, but few were so far out of the loop as to be unaware that a SP was unfolding. The intensity of the awareness was expanded further by the violent turn of the Israeli–Palestine conflict, a turn that was also in part fostered by the 9/11 attacks and the subsequent war on terrorism. The increased awareness of terrorism and violence induced by these events led people at the micro level to converge in protest marches or otherwise ponder the meaning of the SP for their lives and conduct. And the readiness of suicide bombers to destroy themselves on behalf of their cause brought home to many people the immediacy, randomness, and pervasiveness of terrorism, thereby heightening their sensitivities to their links with the larger world.[6] If it can happen anywhere, people seem to feel, it can happen here. In short, the experiential underpinnings of the skill revolution underwent a huge leap forward in the fall of 2001 and spring of 2002.

At the macro level, too, the impact of the terrorist attacks is consistent with the turbulence model. While the coalition against terrorism pushed by the United States consisted mainly of governments, they interacted with a number of organizations in the multicentric world in the effort to address Afghanistan's military, security, and welfare problems. And while these interactions revealed the constructive side of the bifurcation of global structures, so did the factional infighting among diverse groups of Afghans and the difficulties their rivalries posed for the fledgling government demonstrate its deleterious aspects.

Only with respect to one dimension of the micro-macro level could the aftermath of 9/11 be interpreted, at this writing, as somewhat counter to the turbulence model. The response to the terrorist attacks in the United States involved a coming together, a rallying around, on the part of publics. Most specifically, where the U.S. government had been the focus of considerable cynicism and alienation, subsequent to 9/11 broad segments of the citizenry looked to Washington for guidance as poll after poll revealed unprecedented levels of continuing support for the president. If American society lacked coherence and bordered on one or another form of authority crisis prior to the terrorist attack, such characteristics were less clear-cut in the early months after 9/11. They were not entirely absent, however. The turbulent model conceives of authority crises to include stalemated governments that cannot frame or implement policies, and in this respect the United States is not as free of crisis as the war-induced unity seems to suggest. More than a few domestic policies languish as a consequence of the close division within both houses of the Congress. Viewed in this way, the extraordinary closeness of the 2000 presidential election is as much a measure of the country's authority crisis as the rally-around-the-president phenomenon that followed the terrorist attacks. Furthermore, as the moment for an invasion of Iraq drew closer, public support for the president began to wane, thereby reaffirming the premises of the turbulence model.

## THE TRANSFORMATION OF SECURITY

Perhaps the most conspicuous and least ambiguous change since the 9/11 attacks is to be found in the realm of security. Most notably, a readjustment of military strategy and tactics has been necessitated by the unmistakable evidence that the long-term trend anticipated by the turbulence model toward a proliferation of organizations and a continuing bifurcation of global structures has accelerated the disaggregation of authority and led to an ever greater density of actors on the global stage. With terrorist organizations being among the actors that can now act on a global scale, historic military doctrines based on states as potential enemies are no longer sufficient to the needs of national security. Today it is no longer clear who the enemies are and where they are located, obscurities for which long-established military strategies and tactics offer no guidelines. Combating terrorist organizations is, as the United States discovered in Afghanistan, a vastly different enterprise than warring against a state and its military organization. As one observer put it, "today's threats may be much more difficult to handle precisely because force and power and threat have become much more diffuse. . . . Creating an American strategy to deal with this different form of enemy throws into doubt many of our existing assumptions and structures" (Kennedy, 2001: 60–61).

Indeed, the new circumstances generated by the advent of worldwide terrorist organizations have not only altered the meaning of security, but they have also given rise to new conceptions of combat. With "the geographical position and the military power of the U.S. . . . no longer sufficient to ensure security" (Gaddis, 2001: 6), understandings of security and combat have had to be broadened insofar as the United States is concerned. Most notably perhaps, increasingly military strategy will be founded on information technologies and the ways in which the technologies have altered the balance between networks and hierarchies as organizational mechanisms for waging wars (Arquilla & Ronfeldt, 2001). In addition, and no less important, now "[t]he concept of 'homeland security' . . . has become synonymous with national security. Such is the revolution in our thinking forced upon us by the events of that day [in September 2001]. It means that Americans have entered a new stage in their history in which they can no longer take security for granted: it is no longer free—anywhere, or at any time" (Gaddis, 2001: 6). Furthermore, the repercussions of this broadened conception of security involve far more than a rethinking of military strategy, tactics, and organization. They have also necessitated "a reexamination of many aspects of the American way of life, of America's attitude toward other countries and of the well springs of American power. In so many ways, the U.S. will have to think and act differently, and this transformation will have to be orchestrated from the top—president and Congress—testing our policy-making process to a degree not since 1941" (Kennedy, 2001: 57–58).

How well the U.S. government can cope with the test posed by the new forms of turbulence is far from clear. More precisely, whether it can cope without compromising its core principles and institutions remains an open question. The war on terrorism is not likely to end, thus rendering the threat to long-standing institutions an enduring as well as a new one. The years since 9/11 have not been entirely reassuring in this respect. The rule of law along with the rules of warfare have been subjected to enough tampering to justify questioning whether key dimensions of the long-standing institutions—such as the hasty adoption of the antiterrorism bill by Congress and the president's even more hasty creation of the Office of Homeland Security with sweeping but vague powers—have undergone erosion. In the words of one analyst, "To secure genuine victory, we must make sure that [the terrorists] fail, not just in their assault on our safety but also in their challenge to our most fundamental values" (Koh, 2001: 169).

## CONCLUSION

The central conclusion to be derived from this analysis is that while the 9/11 attacks may have initiated new and enduring patterns at every level of aggregation, their vast repercussions are neither surprising nor inexplicable. Rather, they are quite consistent when assessed from the perspective of the turbulence model. In that context, they can be viewed as more of the same rather than as entirely new patterns. The model tells us that as the skill revolution and the organizational explosion continue to expand, that security concerns continue to remain high on political agendas, and that therefore so will incidents of terrorism.

## NOTES

1. For example, see Gaddis (2001: 1–21) and Kennedy (2001: 53–79).

2. For a cogent discussion that posits the 9/11 attacks as more of an instance of one of "four deep trends shaping the early twenty-first century" than as a system-transforming event, see Ferguson (2001: 79).

3. The model is most elaborately set forth in Rosenau (1990).

4. For an elaboration of the skill revolution, see Rosenau (2003: ch. 10). For data in support of the revolution, see Rosenau and Fagen (1997: 655–686); Neisser (1997: 440–447; 1998); Flynn (1999: 5–20); and Dickens and Flynn (2001: 346–369).

5. In the words of one observer, "the waters" through which ships of state must pass "in the twenty-first century [may be] even more tricky to navigate, and even more turbulent, than those of the century just gone" (Kennedy, 2001: 79).

6. I am indebted to Yale Ferguson for noting that while suicide bombers are evidence of the salience of action at the micro level, they rely on organizations at the macro level for the equipment to carry out their awful missions.

# Conclusion

## Seeking Conceptual Links for Changing Paradigms

Ersel Aydinli

### Understanding Globalization

Scholars of globalization studies have suffered from what could be called an uneasy preoccupation with definitional issues. Naturally so, perhaps, when we consider that it is still nearly impossible to attend a conference on globalization without hearing globalization critics' cries of "Haven't you defined it yet?" Books on the topic of globalization often carry a tone of apology for not being able to offer a precise and generally agreed-on definition. Efforts to respond to the need for definition may have, to some extent, delayed scholarly inquiry from moving in what could be a more fruitful direction, namely, looking at globalization's interaction with other forces and subsequent impacts. For those still preoccupied with definitions, an approach that looks at these interactions might well serve as a more effective way of clarifying the essential nature of globalizing phenomena.

Approaching globalization in an interaction context highlights the large extent to which it is a dynamic and contingent process. It has been often pointed out that globalization is not so much a prevailing condition as it is a process (Cerny, 1996; Clark, 1997; Giddens, 2000; Held, McGrew, Goldblatt, & Perraton, 1999; Rosenau, 1997). It is, moreover, a process that shifts, surges, and feeds on dynamic relationships. It is not, in other words, a constant process with unvarying sources. When history encourages liberation from conceptual jails (such as existing paradigms that we cling to as identities) or policy jails (such as certain polarity structures), a booming of interactions between global actors—including individuals—becomes salient. These periods of increased interaction can be considered as surges in the long history of globalization. Moreover, when individual and collective actors experience globalization, they not only go through transformations themselves, but they also reshape the globalization processes with which they interact. For example, the reactions of major states to globalization are likely to foster new dynamics that, in turn, may serve as inputs for altered relationships and interactions between actors and situations.

Observing and analyzing globalization are most feasible when done in conjunction with probes of major issues and factors in world politics. Thus, you have not read many attempts to define globalization in this volume. Rather its chapters sought to go beyond definition, to explore the interaction of globalization with other major dimensions of international affairs—most notably, with security and the nation-state.

## WHY GLOBALIZATION AND SECURITY SHOULD BE STUDIED TOGETHER

Studying globalization and security separately can first be seen as unproductive in the sense that separate agendas do not contribute to the comprehensive accumulation and integration of knowledge. Such an agenda is also impractical in light of the realities of world politics. Most people would agree that processes of accelerated global interactions are bringing countries and regions closer together and creating a growing web of ties both geographically and functionally. These ties lead to new and transformed types of security issues. For example, factors such as the skill revolution, authority crises, and an organizational explosion, feed into so-called "fragmegrative" sources of instability, such as technological, transportation, organizational and economic revolutions, and foster pressure for the diffusion of authority (Rosenau, 1997).

Even traditional security establishments, which for a long time ignored globalizing processes as a major consideration in their planning, now recognize that globalization is indeed having a profound impact on current and future security affairs (Kugler & Frost, 2001). While in some cases the processes of globalization may lessen security dangers, they may also magnify others. The 9/11 attacks are an obvious example in this regard. These attacks revealed the globalization of terror, and showed how globalization may give rise to new military missions, purposes, and priorities in a more global context.

Additionally, the concepts of globalization and security are related at theoretical levels of analysis. There cannot be a preferred level of analysis for globalization studies, since such phenomena unfold at virtually every level and in nonlinear formats. When considering interactions between globalization and security, therefore, it is possible to go beyond the traditional distinction between external and internal—a natural outcome of the state-centric paradigm—which has had a limiting effect on the study of International Relations (IR). While traditional security issues have been largely occupied with external threats, with the advance of globalization, security issues and challenges have become increasingly transnational and multilevel. Security studies must speed up its efforts to find ways of further conceptualization of multilevel and nonlinear understandings.

## GLOBALIZATION AND SECURITY STUDIES

The concepts of globalization and security have, directly or indirectly, been considered together in various studies. Many works have argued, for example, that globalization produces further complications for security agendas, thus placing a heavy emphasis on the negative consequences of globalization (e.g., Cha, 2000; Clark, 1999; Guehenno, 1998; Rodrik, 1997; Scholte, 2000; and Zangl & Zurn, 1999). One could also include in this list most of the contributions to the three-volume work edited by Kugler and Frost (2001). Even Friedman's *The Lexus and the Olive Tree* (2000), generally a pro-globalization book, admits that globalization does not necessarily foster integration or stability.

Studies that have in some way discussed the concepts of globalization and security together can generally be grouped into three main types: policy-oriented studies, socioeconomic studies, and IR studies. Policy-oriented studies (e.g., Kugler & Frost, 2001; Mackinlay, 2002) have been largely produced in response to the 'new' security/insecurity challenges of the present era. These studies, often commissioned by state-supported institutions, seem to assume that the new security challenges are the result of advancing globalization. As such, they attempt to provide policy answers or state strategies to meet these challenges. Also within this strand of research, it is possible to find studies examining the role that technology has played in the development of the current international system (e.g., O'Hanlon, 2000; Skolnikoff, 1993). A general theme of this type of inquiry focuses on how scientific research was at the service of the state in the twentieth century and how this cooperation may now be changing with the advance of globalization and the global spread of technology as a resource of actors other than states.

A second strand of studies that indirectly brings together the concepts of globalization and security are those that pursue a socioeconomic approach. These studies (e.g., Beck, 2000; Giddens, 2000) view globalization as leading to major socioeconomic transformations that generally produce insecurities for domestic/societal and international actors of world politics. This strand has operationalized the relationship between globalization and security in two primary ways. The first of these is that uneven development will create conflict. Particularly at the national level, globalization critics find a direct correlation between globalization-fed corporate profits and global poverty. Poverty is seen as a major source of conflict since national security has increasingly been equated with economic security (Flanagan, 2001). At the national level, globalization produces rising elites and a middle class, both of which demand bigger shares of the pie than other segments of society. When the gap between these groups grows, the result may be antigovernment movements (e.g., China and Iran) and even violent conflicts (e.g., Indonesia). The second major perspective is that unchecked economic globalization leads to global economic crises that can be devastating for developing state economies. For example, the speed, volatility, and sudden withdrawals of financial flows led some countries into serious recession during the 1997–1998 Asian crisis (Rothkopf, 2001; Stiglitz, 2002).

Yet another example that could be considered in this second group, one that emphasizes the social dimensions of economic factors, is that of Huntington's clash of civilizations (1993). He predicted that violence resulting from international anarchy and the absence of common values and institutions would erupt among and between civilizations rather than among and between states. His argument raises the additional question of whether statehood is losing its primacy with respect to the future of international conflict. The general perspective is that more interaction means more conflict, and more interaction stems from more globalization. For a similar argument based on a clear connection between globalization and conflict on the one hand and religious and cultural identity on the other, see Johnston (2001).

The third strand of studies on globalization and security involves conceptualizations of IR. Some of these works are interested in understanding how traditional security dilemmas have been affected by the dynamics of globalization. Others focus on how the international system and its primary actors—traditionally considered to be states—are affected when attempting to cope with globalizing dynamics. Examples of this type of work include those by Clark (1997); Held, McGrew, Goldblatt, & Perraton (1999); Rosenau (1997); Scholte (2000); and Sorensen (2001).

Yet another cluster of IR studies is focused on economic globalization and security. Although such works may seem more closely tied with the socioeconomic strand, the types of research questions they ask (e.g., what is the relationship between economic interdependence and conflict?) help keep them in line with an IR perspective. Two general types of methodological directions are taken in these works. The first are those historical studies, many of which have been highly influenced by world systems theory and Lenin's imperialism theory. The second group is of a largely comparative and quantitative nature (e.g., Barbieri & Schneider, 1999; Dorussen, 1999; Gowa, 1994; Mansfield, 1994; Mansfield & Pollins, 2001).

Within all types of globalization and security studies, in fact, those with economic dimensions seem to be the most numerous. This is perhaps to be expected since, even before globalization studies began to accelerate in the 1990s, there was already an IR research agenda on interdependence and conflict. Often interdependence then came to be equated with globalization. Since economic dimensions were generally seen as the first factors to expand as a result of interdependence and globalization, both of these concepts were first identified and presented in terms of their economic aspects.

The works in this volume can be considered as fitting within the third, or IR, strand of studies incorporating concepts of globalization and security. While an extensive literature has often linked these two concepts, it has been pointed out that work still needs to be done to more fully develop the conceptual connections between globalization and security (Cha, 2000). The diverse literature on these matters could well be strengthened by the development of a taxonomy consisting of key variables that sustain the relationship between these dynamics. Primary causalities could be hypothesized and explored in more depth, and all of this is best done without paying heed to disciplinary boundaries or limiting levels of analysis.

A major aim of the chapters in this volume, therefore, was to contribute to further conceptualizing and operationalizing of the relationship between security and globalization. In consideration of the preceeding chapters and in conjunction with the broader literature outlined earlier, it becomes possible to distinguish certain emergent conceptual links, which may serve as starting guidelines for a much needed focusing of research inquiries.

## CONCEPTUAL LINKS BETWEEN GLOBALIZATION AND SECURITY

### Change

Three initial issues seem to provide an appropriate framework within which to link the phenomena embraced by globalization and security. The first of these issues is "change." One of the greatest challenges now addressed in security studies involves the processes of change and the uncertainty they can generate in global affairs. With security often understood as an aspect of control, maintaining the status quo, mastering it, or adapting to it thus becomes one of the primary aims of actors in the international system. Changing environments and the resulting insecurities have become a primary research inquiry for security studies.

At the same time, change can be seen as very much a factor associated with globalization. However one may choose to define globalization (e.g., acceleration and constriction of historical trends, universalization/diffusion of world values and traditions, or rapidly growing and uneven cross-border flows of goods, services, people, money, technology, information, ideas, culture, crime, and weapons), change is likely to be treated as a central feature of the processes that unfold. Globalization has thus been a constant source of the change and uncertainty that have inspired security studies in the post–Cold War era. By studying the changes in security wrought by globalization, research can benefit and help generate an accumulation of generalizable knowledge on world affairs.

## Power

Security studies have also long been preoccupied with the concept of power, which provides a second useful issue on which to base a conceptualization of the links between globalization and security. Since reconfigurations of power distribution and their implications in the international arena often lead to conflict, they have always been a primary research focus of security. Power reconfigurations present a conceptual linkage between globalization and security in the sense that globalization tends to generate new contexts both at the national and international level for power reconfigurations, or what might be called shifting spheres of authority. Examples of how authority is shifting can be seen in the conduct of international terrorist groups or organized-crime units, which have been moving their activities increasingly from the national level into the transnational arena. Other examples include some national level entities such as NGOs and business corporations, which were previously treated as trivial in terms of their capacities but are now enjoying a greater degree of deference at the expense of formerly unquestioned power centers such as state security establishments.

## Duality

A third reason why the links between globalization and security should be studied is related to the ways in which globalization has generated a bifurcation of global structures. Along with the advance of globalization studies, IR scholarship has observed a duality between a traditional state-centric system and an emerging multicentric one (Rosenau, 1990). While security and security studies represent clear reflections of a state-centric world, globalization has fostered and sustained a multicentric one. Perhaps most important to this formulation is the idea that globalization and the emerging multicentric world have not replaced the traditional foundations of the state-centric world. In fact, a large scholarship—including several of the authors in this volume—now implicitly or explicitly suggests that both worlds coexist, sometimes cooperatively, often conflictually, and always interactively. As Mittleman notes, international studies have entered an "interregnum between the old and the new" (2002: 12).

In terms of security, globalization and the emerging multicentric world have not eliminated traditional geopolitical concerns and conceptualizations.

The images and understandings of the state-centric world are still very much preoccupied with traditional security considerations such as the primacy of state interests, state-to-state alliances, balancing against threat as well as many lingering geopolitical conflicts over geography, military competition, and ethnic issues. On the other hand, the advent of globalization and the multicentric world have created several alterations of the traditional security concepts at various levels.

Both conceptually and as policy issues, in short, stability and security emerge as significant research challenges within this dualistic epoch—an epoch that has been characterized by innovative terminology such as "fragmegration" (Rosenau, 1997) (fragmentation and integration), "glocalization" (Robertson, 1995) (globalization and localization), or "chaord" (Hock, 1995) (chaos and order). Hoffman (2002) draws on one of these characterizations: he views the 1990s as a period dominated by the tension between the fragmentation of states that border on or slip into failure and the progress of economic, cultural, and political integration fostered by globalization. He refers to 9/11 as the "bloody link" between the two worlds of interstate relations and global society.

## WHY THE STATE SHOULD BE INCORPORATED INTO GLOBALIZATION AND SECURITY STUDIES

The foregoing discussion suggests possible links between the processes of globalization and the processes of change, power reconfiguration, and systemic duality. Likewise, the state itself can be relocated and reframed in terms of its interaction with these three processes.

### Duality and the State

In terms of duality, the emergence of a multicentric world has brought new actors into the global arena alongside the states of the traditional state-centric world. The globalization literature tends to talk about transnational nongovernmental actors (e.g., NGOs, corporations, and global civil society), global governance structures (e.g., the United Nations, the IMF, and the World Bank) and their roles in terms of controlling, taming, and managing globalization. Whether as the controllers of 'chaos' in the globalization era, or as fine-tuners to meet changing global norms, states are still recognized widely as actors that can and will continue to play important management roles. Taming both the geopolitics and globalization of the current duality has been described as a "key challenge of statecraft" (Flanagan, 2001: 10).

If we accept that the state's role remains important, we also need to ask which states should be the focus of inquiry. The answer is that a research agenda incorporating states, security, and globalization must be a truly global one. Particularly after the events of 9/11, the lines between core and periphery (in terms of security) have disappeared, weakening arguments of an insulated duality between zones of conflict and zones of peace (Singer & Wildavsky, 1993). Insecurities in the periphery have the ultimate potential to threaten and even hurt the core. Globalization, security, and the state studies cannot follow the mistakes of IR in ignoring the periphery and arguing that small states do not matter (Ayoob, 1998; David, 1997).

Globalization and the state literature has also questioned whether the state itself is likely to remain the same, be transformed, or has already lost its primary mission as a result of globalization. Though this debate is far from concluded, a transformationalist strand, arguing that the state neither remains the same nor has lost its strength but is transforming in response to globalization, seems to be the most widely accepted interpretation. If this is so, such a transformation would have significant consequences for security studies. Depending on the way that the role of the state is conceived, security studies may have to redefine its treatment of this 'primary' reference object.

## Power, Change, and the State

Within a duality as previously described, competing actors will emerge and, subsequently, various shifts of power configurations are likely to follow. Studies should identify, for example, how the state will deal with such power reconfigurations and also how it will manage to project its remaining capacities on behalf of its international and regional missions (e.g., building up regional economic organizations as well as security ones, such as ASEAN and MERCOSUR, are among the mechanisms states employ for this purpose). In general, such reconfigurations affect the states themselves as well as their abilities and choices in managing the changes they face in the new epoch.

While traditionally states could respond to many international phenomena as unitary actors, globalization makes such responses less and less likely (an inadequacy that itself presents a security challenge worthy of study). Rather it is very likely that a variety of responses will emanate from the different agencies of states and governments. In other words, the globalizing processes of different segments of a nation-state might evoke different reactions from its various parts that result in domestic power shifts and reconfigurations. For example, a state's business sector might take advantage of globalization and thereby gain power vis-à-vis other state branches such as the bureaucracy or the political elite.

Even in the most developed countries, which are supposed to be managing and adapting best to globalization, one can observe this variation. In the case of the U.S. government, for example, security, economic, science and technology, and law enforcement policies essential to coping with the challenges of the global era are still developed largely in isolation from one another (though the recent construction of the Homeland Security Department implies that there is awareness of the need for change).

The situation is even more problematic when it comes to less developed countries. Here one can see even clearer fault lines between various state segments. It is not surprising, therefore, that foreign service bureaucracies or business elite of some governments in the developing world, such as Russia, China, Turkey, and Iran, have been involved with different dimensions of globalization than have these countries' armed forces. The number of varying categories of relationships with globalization can rise exponentially when you look at the individual level (see, e.g., the "12-worlds" in Rosenau, 2003).

If the state is not ready institutionally to transform itself and adapt in order to accommodate globalization, political and economic stability could suffer, leading to a growth in corruption and bribery, or even criminal networks. The Russian case may be seen as an example here. Its more aggressive units, such as clandestine networks, have taken advantage of globalization and manipulated the "opening up" unchecked by the political authority. The attention-grabbing ability of these groups helps to give the impression that globalization may benefit these groups more than less violent ones. Ultimately, these developments could confuse public opinion about whether globalization is positive or negative. In turn, the state may become distracted from a necessary focus on the management of globalization.

All of this seems to imply that states may be increasingly insecure in this new globalizing world that requires at least a modicum of transformation some states are often not prepared to make. Thus, there can be a pervasive sense of losing control (for a compelling account of this phenomenon, see Del Rosso, 1995). Moreover, it is increasingly evident that the costs of the negative consequences are high if states are not well prepared to directly confront and manage the negative challenges. For example, 9/11 and the global insurgence of terrorism revealed how states and the state system were not ready for such challenges, both conceptually (not expecting the attack from a multicentric actor) and also practically (see T.V. Paul, this volume). Perhaps the best example of this dualistic structure in world politics with respect to security can be seen in the war on terrorism. If individuals without clear state support or involvement can pose a security challenge to which the state system is having difficulty responding with traditional state tools, it clearly indicates the coexistence of dual worlds. It then follows that we must find a way of studying the globalization/security relationship within this dualistic worldview.

## CONCLUSION

I have argued here for the need to study globalization and security in conjunction, and have offered three conceptual tools as a step toward an operationalization in future studies. I have also proposed that globalization and security studies could benefit from a concentration on the state as a useful platform for reflecting what happens when globalizing dynamics meet with traditional and new security issues. The state is thus a litmus test for exploring what happens when globalization and security converge.

The works in this volume sought to draw links between the concepts of globalization, security, and the nation-state. In doing so, the various chapters explored the connections between security and global transformations and the changes in state structures in response to the emergent connections. As such, the combined results of this volume represent starting points in a conceptual linking of security and globalization, in identifying how the state concept provides a common ground for studying the interaction of globalization and security, and in projecting the possible effects of this conceptual convergence on the international system.

Attempts to consider large concepts such as globalization, security, and the state in conjunction with one other but without guiding tools will run the obvious risk of becoming lost—an unfortunate result reflected in the often dispersed literature on these issues. Such a lack of coordination is especially likely when these concepts are undergoing rapid change—both within themselves and in their interactions with each other. Thus, we need to introduce guiding conceptual tools to provide a focus to globalization and security studies. Duality, power, and change may offer a starting point for future research.

# Bibliography

Abdel Mo'ati, A-B. (ed.) (1998). *Globalization and social transformation in the Arab world.* Cairo: Center for Arab Research and Arab Sociological Society. Madbouli Publishers (in Arabic).

Acharya, Amitav. (1998). Beyond anarchy: Third world instability and international order after the Cold War. In S. G. Neumann (Ed.), *International relations theory and the third world* (pp. 159–211). New York: St. Martin's Press.

Afontsev, Sergey. (2001). *Problema Globalnogo Upravleniya Mirokhozyastvennoi Sistemoi: Teoreticheskie Aspecty* [The Problem of Global Governance of the World Economy System: Theoretical Aspects] Mirovaya Ekonomika i Mezhdunarodnye Otnosheniya, 5.

Ajami, Fouad. (2000). The new faith. *Foreign Policy,* 119, 30–34.

Ajami, Fouad. (2002). Iraq and the thief of Baghdad. *The New York Times Book Review,* May 19.

Albrow, Martin. (1997). *The global age.* Cambridge: Polity Press.

Allison, Graham. (2000).The impact of globalization on national and international security. In Joseph S. Nye & J. D. Donahue (Eds.), *Governance in a globalizing world* (pp. 70–85). Washington, DC: Brookings Institution Press.

Amin, G. (2002). *Globalizing suppression: The United States, Arabs and Muslims before and after the events of September, 2001.* Cairo: Dar Al-Shorooq (in Arabic).

Aristotle. 1985. *Nichomachean Ethics,* translated by T. Irwin. Indianapolis: Hackett.

Arquilla, John, & Ronfeldt, David. (2001). *Networks and netwars: The future of terror, crime, and militancy.* Santa Monica, CA: Rand Corporation.

Arquilla, John, & Ronfeldt, David. (2001). The advent of netwar revisited. In J. Arquilla & D. Ronfeldt (Eds.), *Networks and netwars* (pp. 1–25). Santa Monica, CA: Rand Corporation.

241

Art, Robert J. (1980). To what ends military power? *International Security, 4*(4), 3–35.

Ayoob, Mohammed. (1991). The security problematic of the third world. *World Politics, 43*(2): 257–283.

Ayoob, Mohammed. (1993). Unraveling the concept: 'National security' in the third world. In Bahgat Korany, Paul Noble, & Rex Brynen (Eds.). *The many faces of national security in the Arab world* (pp. 31–55). New York: St. Martin's Press.

Ayoob, Mohammed. (1995). *The third world security predicament: State making, regional conflicts, and the international system.* Boulder, CO: Lynne Rienner.

Ayoob, Mohammed. (1998). Subaltern realism: International relations theory meets the Third World. In Stephanie G. Neumann (Ed.), *International relations theory and the third world* (pp. 31–54). New York: St. Martin's Press.

Ayoob, Mohammed. (2002a). Humanitarian intervention and state sovereignty. *International Journal of Human Rights, 6*(1), 81–102.

Ayoob, Mohammed. (2002b). Inequality and theorizing in international relations: The case for subaltern realism. *International Studies Review, 4*(3), 27–48.

Barber, Benjamin R. (1996). *Jihad vs. McWorld.* New York: Ballentine Books.

Barbieri, Katherine, & Schneider, Geri. (1999). Globalization and peace: Assessing new directions in the study of trade and conflict. *Journal of Peace Research, 36*(4), 387–404.

Bartkus, V. O. (1999), *The dynamic of secession.* Cambridge: Cambridge University Press.

Bazhanov, Yevgeny. (2002). Globalizatsiya kak Objectivny Protsess [Globalization as an objective process]. *Nezavisimaya Gazeta,* March 13.

Beck, Ulrich. (1992). *Risk society: Towards a new modernity.* London: Sage.

Beck, Ulrich. (2000). *What is globalization?* Cambridge: Polity Press.

Bell, Daniel A 1971: Ten theories in search of reality: The prediction of Soviet behaviour. In Vernon V. Aspaturian, *Process and Power in Soviet Foreign Policy* (pp. 289–323). Boston: Little, Brown.

Bell, Daniel A. (2000). *East meets west: Human rights and democracy in East Asia.* Princeton, NJ: Princeton University Press.

Bergsten, Fred. (2000) East Asian regionalism: Towards a tripartite world. *The Economist,* July 15, pp. 23–26.

Berki, R.N. (1986). *Security and society: Reflections on law, order, and politics.* London: J. M. Dent.

Betts, Richard. (1999). Must war find a way? *International Security, 24*(2), 166–198.

Bigo, Didier (1996): *Polices en Réseaux—l'expérience européenne.* Paris: Presses de Sciences Po.

Blair, Tony. (2000). Speech by Prime Minister Tony Blair (Warsaw: Polish Stock Exchange).

Blair, Tony (2000). Speech by Prime Minister Tony Blair (Zagreb: EU/Balkan Summit).

Blair, Tony (2001). Labour Party Conference Speech. http: //politics.guardian.co.uk/labour2001/story/0,1414,562006.html

Bobrow, Davis B. (2001) Visions of (in)security and American strategic style. *International Studies Perspectives, 2*(1), 1–12.

Booth, Ken. (1979). *Strategy and ethnocentrism.* London: Croom Helm.

Booth, Ken. (1987). New challenges and old mind-sets: Ten rules for empirical realists. In Carl G. Jacobsen, (Ed.), *The uncertain course: New weapons, strategies and mindsets.* Oxford: Oxford University Press for SIPRI.

Booth, Ken. (1995). Human wrongs and international relations. *International Affairs, 71*(1), 103–126.

Booth, Ken. (1999). Three tyrannies. In Tim Dunne and Nicholas J. Wheeler, (Eds.), *Human rights in global politics.* Cambridge: Cambridge University Press.

Booth, Ken. (2000a), Where are we now? World politics between helplessness and hope. Millennium Public Lecture Series: University of Wales, Aberystwyth. Unpublished paper.

Booth, Ken. (2000b), The Kosovo tragedy: Epilogue to another 'low and dishonest decade.' *Politikon, 27*(1), 5–18.

Booth, Ken. (2003). *Security, community and emancipation in world politics.* Boulder CO: Lynne Rienner.

Booth, Ken. (Ed.). (1991). *New thinking about strategy and international security.* London: Harper Collins.

Booth, Ken. (Ed.). (1998). *Statecraft and security: The Cold War and after.* Cambridge: Cambridge University Press.

Booth, Ken, & Dunne, Tim. (Eds.). (2002). *Worlds in collision: Terror and the future of global order.* Basingstoke: Palgrave Macmillan.

Bordo, Michael, Eichengreen, Barry, & Irwin, Douglas. (1999). Is globalization today really different than globalization a hundred years ago? NBER Working Paper #W1795.

Bordo, Michael, Eichengreen, Barry, & Ki, J. (1998). Was there really an earlier period of international financial integration comparable to today? NBER Working Paper #W6738.

Brandt Commission. (1985). *Common crisis: North-south cooperation for world recovery.* Cambridge, MA: MIT Press.

Brawley, Mark R. (2002). *The politics of globalization.* Peterborough, ON: Broadview Press.

Brodie, Bernard. (Ed.). (1946). *The absolute weapon: Atomic power and world order.* New York: Harcourt Brace.

Brooks, Stephen G, & Wohlforth, William C. (2000/1). Power, globalization and the end of the Cold War: Reevaluating a landmark case for ideas. *International Security, 25*(3), 5–53.

Brooks, Stephen G, & Wohlforth, William C. (2002). American primacy in perspective. *Foreign Affairs, 18*(4), 20–33.

Brown, Chris L. (1984). *International politics and the Middle East: Old rules, dangerous game.* Princeton: Princeton University Press.

Bull, Hedley. (1977). *The anarchical society.* New York: Columbia University Press.

Burlak, V. (1992). Humankind needs a program for survival. *International Affairs* (Moscow), *38*(1), 16–24.

Buruma, Ian. (2002). The cult of ultimate sacrifice, *The Guardian,* June 4.

Butterfield, Herbert. (1951). *History and Human Relations.* London: Collins.

Buzan, Barry. (1983). *People, states and fear.* Brighton: Wheatsheaf.

Buzan, Barry. (1991). *People, states and fear: An agenda for international security studies in the post Cold-War era,* 2nd ed. London: Harvester Wheatsheaf.

Buzan, Barry. (1995). Security, the state, the 'new world order,' and beyond. In R. D. Lipshutz (Ed.), *On security* (pp. 187–211). New York: Columbia University Press.

Buzan, Barry. (1997). The Asia Pacific: What sort of region in what sort of world? In A. McGrew & C. Brook (Eds.), *A Pacific community? Perspectives on the Pacific Rim in the contemporary world order* (pp. 68–87) Milton Keynes: Open University.

Buzan, Barry. (1998). Conclusions: System versus units in theorizing about the third world. In S. Neumann (Ed.), *International relations theory and the third world* (pp. 213–234). New York: St. Martin's Press.

Buzan, Barry. (forthcoming). *After bipolarity what?* London: International Institute of Strategic Studies, Adelphi Paper.

Buzan, Barry, & Segal, Gerald. (1996). The rise of the 'lite' powers: A strategy for postmodern states. *World Policy Journal, 13*(3), 1–10.

Buzan, Barry, & Segal, Gerald. (1998). *Anticipating the future.* London: Simon & Schuster.

Buzan, Barry, & Wæver, Ole. (2003). *Regions and powers: The structure of international security.* Cambridge: Cambridge University Press.

Buzan, Barry, Little, Richard, & Jones, Charles. (1993). *The logic of anarchy: Neorealism to structural realism.* New York: Columbia University Press.

Buzan, Barry, & Little, Richard. (2000). *International systems in world history.* Oxford: Oxford University Press.

Buzan, Barry, Waever, Ole, & de Wilde, Jaap. (1998). *Security: A new framework for analysis.* Boulder, CO: Lynne Rienner.

Calleo, David. (1999). The United States and the great powers. *World Policy Journal, 16*(3), 11–19.

Callinicos, Alex. (2000). *Equality*. Cambridge: Polity.

Cammilleri, Joseph A., & Falk, Jim. (1992). *The end of sovereignty? The politics of a shrinking and fragmented world*. Aldershot: Edward Elgar.

Campbell, Kurt M., & Flournoy, Michele A. (2001). *To prevail: An American strategy for the campaign against terrorism*. Washington DC: CSIS Press.

Carpenter, Ted G. (1991). The new world disorder. *Foreign Policy, 84*, 24–39.

Carr, Edward H. [1939] (1961). *The twenty years' crisis 1919–1930: An introduction to the study of international relations*. London: Macmillan & Co.

Carriere, Jean-Claude. (1999).'Answering the sphinx,' In Umberto Eco et al. (Eds.), *Conversations about the end of time* (pp. 95–107). London: Allen Lane.

Cerny, Philip. (2000). The new security dilemma: Divisibility, defection and disorder in the global arena. *Review of International Studies, 26*(4), 623–646.

Cerny, Philip G. (1996). International finance and the erosion of state policy capacity. In P. Gummett (Ed.), *Globalization and public policy* (pp. 83–104). Cheltenham, Glos., and Brookfield, VT: Edward Elgar.

Cha, Victor D. (2000). Globalization and the study of international security. *Journal of Peace Research, 17*(3), 391–403.

Chaudhry, K. (1997). *The price of wealth: Economies and institutions in the Middle East*. Ithaca: Cornell University Press.

Chiraq, Jacques (2000). Our Europe (Berlin: Speech to the German Bundestag, 2000).

Christensen, Thomas. (2002). *Russian security policy according to a Hegelianised Copenhagen School*, unpublished MA Thesis: Institute of political science, University of Copenhagen.

Clapham, Christopher. (1996). *Africa and the international system*. Cambridge: Cambridge University Press.

Clark, Ian. (1997). *Globalization and fragmentation: International relations in the twentieth century*. Oxford: Oxford University Press.

Clark, Ian. (1999). *Globalization and international relations theory*. Oxford: Oxford University Press.

Clausewitz, C. Von, (1976). *On war*, trans. M. Howard and P. Paret. Princeton: Princeton University Press.

Cohen, Eliot A., Eisenstadt, J. Michael, & Bacevich, A. (1998). *Knives, tanks & missiles: Israel's security revolution*. Washington: The Washington Institute for Near East Policy.

Cohen, Eliot A. (1996). A revolution in warfare. *Foreign Affairs, 75*(2), 37–54.

Cook, Robin. (1999). "It is Fascism that we are fighting 'Ours is the Modern Europe of the Human Rights Convention'." *The Guardian*, May 5.

Copson, Raymond W. (1994). *Africa's wars and prospects for peace*. Armonk, NY: M. E. Sharpe.

Cortright, David, Lopez, George, & Stephanides, J. (Eds.) (2002). *Smart sanctions: Targeting economic statecraft.* Lanham, MD: Rowman & Littlefield.

Cover Story (1991). "Communism's collapse poses a challenge to America's military. *U.S. News and World Report, 3*:16, October 14: 28.

Cox, Michael, Booth, Ken, & Dunne, Tim. (Eds.) (1999). *The interregnum: Controversies in world politics 1989–1999.* Cambridge: Cambridge University Press.

Cox, Robert. (1997). Economic globalization and limits to liberal democracy. In A. G. McGrew (Ed.), *The transformation of democracy? Globalization and territorial democracy* (pp. 49–72). Cambridge: Polity Press.

Cox, Robert W. (1999). Social forces, states and world orders: Beyond international relations theory. *Millennium: Journal of International Studies, 10*(2), 126–155.

Cox, Robert W., & Sinclair, Timothy. (1996). *Approaches to world order.* Cambridge: Cambridge University Press.

Crenshaw, Martha (2001). Why America? The globalization of civil war. *Current History, 100,* 425–432.

Croft, Stuart, Redmond, John, Rees, G. Wyn, & Webber, Mark. (1999). *The enlargement of Europe.* Manchester & New York: Manchester University Press.

Cronin, Bruce. (1999). *Community under anarchy: Transnational identity and the evolution of cooperation.* New York: Columbia University Press.

Crothers, Lane, & Lockhart, Charles. (Eds.) (2000). *Culture and politics.* New York: St. Martin's Press.

Daalder, Ivo H. (1999). *NATO, the UN, and the use of force.* Paper presented for UNA-USA. Available at http://www.unausa.org/issues/sc/daalder

Dahl, Robert A. (1999). Can international organizations be democratic? A skeptic's view. In I. Sharpiro & C. Hacker-Cordón (Eds.), *Democracy's edges* (pp. 19–37). Cambridge: Cambridge University Press.

David, Steven. R. (2002). The primacy of internal war. In S. G. Neumann (Ed.), *International relations theory and the third world* (pp. 77–101). New York: St. Martin's Press.

Davis, Lance, & Huttenback, Robert. (1986). *Mammon and the pursuit of empire.* New York: Cambridge University Press.

Del Rosso, Stephen J. Jr. (1995). The insecure state: Reflections on 'the state' and 'security' in a changing world. *Daedalus, 124*(2).

Deudney, Daniel, & Ikenberry, G. John. (1999). The nature and sources of liberal international order. *Review of International Studies, 25,* 179–196.

Deutsch, Karl et al. (1957). *Political community: North-Atlantic area.* New York: Greenwood Press.

Diamond, Jared. (1997). *Guns, germs and steel.* New York: W. W. Norton.

Dickens, William T., & Flynn, James R. (2001). Heritability estimates versus large environmental effects: The IQ paradox resolved. *Psychological Review, 108,* 346–369.

Diez, Thomas (2002). "Last Exit to paradise? The European Union, the Cyprus conflict and the problematic 'catalytic effect'," In Thomas Diez (Ed.), *The European Union and the Cyprus conflict: Modern conflict, postmodern union* (pp. 139–162). Manchester: Manchester University Press.

Dorussen, Han. (1999). Balance of power revisited: A multi-country model of trade and conflict. *Journal of Peace Research, 36*(4), 443–462.

Dunne, Tim, & Booth, Ken. (2002). Where will this war end? *The Western Mail,* September 12.

Earle, Edward M. (1944). Adam Smith, Alexander Hamilton, Friedrich List: The economic foundations of military power. In E. M. Earle (Ed.), *Makers of modern strategy* (pp. 117–154). Princeton, NJ: Princeton University Press.

Economist Intelligence Unit, May 2002.

*Economist, The.* When trade and security clash. April 6, 2002.

Ekins, Paul. (1992). *A new world order: Grassroots movements for global change.* London: Routledge.

Ellsberg, Daniel. (1961). The crude analysis of strategic choices. *American Economic Review, 51,* 472–478.

Ellwood, Wayne (2002). We all have AIDS. *New Internationalist, 346* (June), 9–12.

Evans, Peter (1997). The eclipse of the state? Reflections on stateness in an era of globalization. *World Politics, 50*(1), 62–87.

Fandy, Mamoun. (1999). *Saudi Arabia and the politics of dissent.* New York: St. Martin's Press.

Faraj, Ayman Sabri. (2002). *Memoirs of an Afghan Arab.* Cairo: Dar El-Sherouk (in Arabic).

Federation of American Scientists. (2002). *Smart weapons.* Available at [http://www.fas.org/man/dod-101].

Ferguson, Niall. (2001). Ten years from now, historians will look back and see the events of Sept. 11 as mere ripples in a tidal wave of terrorism and political fragmentation. *New York Times Magazine,* December 2.

Fischer, Joschka. (2000). From confederacy to federation: Thoughts on the finality of European integration. Speech given at University of Humboldt, Berlin.

Flanagan, Stephen. J. (2001). Meeting the challenges of the global century. In R. L. Kugler, & E. L. Frost (Eds.), *The global century: Globalization and national security* (pp. 7–32). Retrieved December 28, 2002, from National Defense University Online Books Web site: http://www.ndu.edu/inss/books/books%20-%202001/Global%20Century%20-%20June%202001/globcencont.html

Flynn, John R. (1999). Searching for justice: The discovery of IQ gains over time, *American Psychologist, 54,* 5–20.

Freedman, Lawrence. (2000). Revolutions in military affairs. In G. Prins & H. Tromp (Eds.), *The future of war.* Boston: Kluwer Law International.

Friedberg, Aanon L. (1993). Ripe for rivalry: Prospects for peace in a multipolar Asia. *International Security, 18*(3), 5–33.

Friedman, Thomas. (2000). *The Lexus and the Olive Tree.* New York: Farrar, Straus & Giroux.

Friis, Lykke. (1999). *An ever larger union? EU enlargement and the European integration. An anthology.* Copenhagen: DUPI.

Friis, Lykke, & Murphy, Anna. (1998). 'Turbo-charged negotiations': The EU and the stability pact for South Eastern Europe. *Journal of European Public Policy, 7*(5: Special Issue), 95–114.

Fukuyama, Francis. (1993). *The end of history and the last man.* London: Penguin.

Gaddis, John Lewis. (2001). And now this: Lessons from the old era for the new one. In Strobe Talbott & Nayan Chanda (Eds.), *The age of terror: America and the world after September 11* (pp. 1–21). New York: Basic Books.

Galbraith, John K. (1992). *The culture of contentment.* London: Sinclair-Stevenson.

Gallagher, Susan E. (1998). *The rule of the rich? Adam Smith's argument against political power.* University Park: Pennsylvania State University Press.

George, Alexander L. (1991). *Foreceful persuasion.* Washington DC: United States Institute of Peace Press.

George, Susan. (1999). *The Lugano Report: On preserving capitalism in the twenty-first century.* London: Pluto Press.

Giddens, Anthony. (1998). Affluence, poverty and the idea of a post-scarcity society. In K. Booth (Ed.), *Statecraft and security: The Cold War and after* (pp. 308–322). Cambridge: Cambridge University Press.

Giddens, Anthony. (1990). *The consequences of modernity.* Cambridge: Polity Press.

Giddens, Anthony. (2000). *Runaway world: How globalization is reshaping our lives.* New York: Routledge.

Gill, K. S. (2001). Terrorism: Utilitarian versus millenarian, www.thenewspaper-today.com, October 18.

Gilpin, Robert. (1981). *War and change in world politics.* Cambridge: Cambridge University Press.

Gilpin, Robert. (1987). *The political economy of international relations.* Princeton, NJ: Princeton University Press.

"Globalizatsiya—eto kolonizatsitya?" (2002). [Is Globalization a Colonization?] *Russkiy Zhurnal* ttp: www.russ.ru/politics/20020212 (in Russian).

Goldfischer, David. (2002). E. H. Carr: A historical realist approach for the globalization era. *Review of International Studies, 28*(4), 697–717.

Goldgeier, James M., & McFaul, Michael. (1992). A tale of two worlds: Core and periphery in the post-Cold War era. *International Organization, 46*(2), 467–491.

Goldmann, Kjell. (1997). Miljöhet, migration och terrorister i Tokyo—om begreppet säkerhetspolitik. In Leif Leifland (Ed.), *Brobyggare: En vänbok till Nils Andrén* (pp. 3–19). Stockholm: Nerenius & Santérus Förlag.

Gordimer, Nadine. (1999). *Living in hope and history: Notes from our century.* London: Bloomsbury.

Gowa, Joanne S. (1994). *Allies, adversaries, and international trade.* Princeton: Princeton University Press.

Gray, Colin S. (1999a). *Modern strategy.* Oxford: Oxford University Press.

Gray, Colin S. (1999b). Clausewitz Rules. OK? The future is the past—with GPS. In Michael Cox, Ken Booth, & Tim Dunne (Eds.), *The interregnum: Controversies in world politics 1989–1999* (pp. 161–182). Cambridge: Cambridge University Press.

Gray, Colin S. (2002). World politics as usual after September 11: Realism vindicated'. In Ken Booth & Tim Dunne (Eds.), *Worlds in collision: Terror and the future of global order* (pp. 226–234). Basingstoke: Palgrave Macmillan.

Gray, John. (2002). Why terrorism is unbeatable. *New Statesman,* February 25.

*Guardian* (2002). Marvellous . . . isn't it? Football has become a global experience. Editorial, May 31.

Guéhenno, Jean-Marie. (1998–1999). The impact of globalization on strategy. *Survival, 40*(4), 5–19.

Guéhenno, Jean-Marie. (1995). *The end of the nation state.* Minneapolis: University of Minnesota Press.

Hall, John A. (1996). *International orders: A historical sociology of state, regime, class, and nation.* Cambridge: Polity Press.

Hall, John A. (2001) The return of the state. Retrieved December 28, 2002, from SSRC Web site on September 11, 2001: http://www.ssrc.org/sept11/essays/hall.htm

Halliday, Fred. (2002). New world, but the same old disorder. *The Observer,* March 10.

Hansen, Birthe. (2000). *Unipolarity and the Middle East.* Richmond: Curzon Press.

Hansen, Lene. (1995). NATO's new discourse. In Birthe Hansen (Ed.), *European security—2000* (pp. 117–135). Copenhagen: Copenhagen Political Studies Press.

Harding, Luke. (2002). Pakistan switches troops from Afghan duty to Indian border. *The Guardian,* May 31.

Harmon, Christopher C. (2000). *Terrorism today.* London: Frank Cass.

Harold, H. K. (2001). Preserving American values: The challenge at home and abroad. In Strobe Talbott & Nayan Chanda (Eds.), The age of terror: America and the world after September 11 (pp. 145–169). New York: Basic Books.

Harrison, Lawrence, & Huntington, Samuel. (2000). *Culture matters.* New York: Basic Books.

Hassner, Pierre. (1993). Beyond nationalism and internationalism: Ethnicity and world order, *Survival, 35*(2), 49–65.

Heilbronner, Robert. (1995). *Visions of the future.* New York: Oxford University Press.

Held, David, & McGrew, Anthony G. (1993). Globalization and the liberal democratic state. *Government and Opposition, 28,* 261–285.

Held, David, McGrew, Anthony, Goldblatt, David, & Perraton, Jonathan. (1999). *Global transformations: Politics, economics and culture*. Stanford, CA: Stanford University Press.

Henry, Clement, & Springborg, Robert. (2001). *Globalization and the politics of development in the Middle East*. Cambridge: Cambridge University Press.

Herz, John. (1950). Idealist internationalism and the security dilemma, *World Politics, 2*(2), 157–181.

Herz, John. (1951). *Political realism and political idealism. A study in theories and realities.* Chicago: The University of Chicago Press.

Herz, John. (1959). *International politics in the atomic age.* New York: Columbia University Press.

Heydemann, Stephen. (Ed.) (2000). *War, institutions and social change in the Middle East.* Berkeley: University of California Press.

Hirschman, Albert O. (1980). *National power and the structure of foreign trade.* Berkeley: University of California Press.

Hirst, Paul. (1997). The global economy: Myths and realities. *International Affairs, 73*(3), 409–426.

Hirst, Paul. (2001). *War and power in the 21st century.* London: Polity.

Hirst, Paul, & Thompson, Grahame. (1996). *Globalization in question: The international economy and the possibilities of government.* Cambridge: Polity Press.

Hirst, Paul, & Thompson, Grahame. (1999). *Globalization in question.* 2nd ed. Cambridge: Polity.

Hobbes, Thomas. (1946). *Leviathan.* Oxford: Blackwell.

Hock, Dee W. (1995). Institutions in the age of mindcrafting. In Mike Featherstone, Scot Lash, & Roland Robertson (Eds.), *Global modernities* (pp. 1–2). Thousand Oaks, CA: Sage.

Hoffman, Bruce. (1998). *Inside terrorism.* New York: Columbia University Press.

Hoffman, Bruce. (1999). Terrorism: Trends and prospects. In I. O. Lesser et al. (Eds.), *Countering the new terrorism* (pp. 7–38). Santa Monica, CA: Rand Corporation.

Hoffman, Mark. (1987). Critical theory and the inter-paradigm debate. *Millennium: Journal of International Studies, 16*(2), 232–249.

Hoffmann, Stanley. (1981). *Duties beyond borders: On the limits and possibilities of ethical international politics.* Syracuse, NY: Syracuse University Press.

Hoffmann, Stanley. (2002). Clash of globalizations: A new paradigm. *Foreign Affairs, 81*(4), 104–115.

Hollis, Rosemary. (1999). Barcelona's first pillar: An appropriate concept for security relations? In Sven Behrendt and Christian-Peter Hanelt (Eds.), *Security in the Middle East*, Munich, Guetersloh: Bertelsman Foundation, unpublished working papers, Center for Applied Policy Research.

Holm, Hans-Henrik, & Sorensen, Georg. (Eds.). (1995). *Whose world order? Uneven globalization and the end of the Cold War.* Boulder: Westview Press.

Holsti, Kalevi J. (1996). *The state, war, and the state of war.* Cambridge: Cambridge University Press.

Homer-Dixon, Thomas. (2002). The rise of complex terrorism. *Foreign Policy, 128,* January–February, 52–62.

Huntington, Samuel P. (1993). The clash of civilizations. *Foreign Affairs, 72*(3), 22–49.

Huntington, Samuel P. (1996). *The clash of civilizations and the remaking of world order.* New York: Simon and Schuster

Huntington, Samuel P. (1999). The lonely superpower. *Foreign Affairs, 78*(2), 35–49.

Hutton, Will, & Giddens, Anthony. (Eds.). (2001). *On the edge: Living with global capitalism.* London: Vintage.

Isaacson, Walter, & Thomas, Evan. (1986). *The wise men: Six friends and the world they made (Acheson, Bohlen, Harriman, Kennan, Lovett, McCloy).* London: Faber & Faber.

Ishay, Micheline R. (1997) *The human rights reader.* New York: Routledge.

Jachtenfuchs, Markus. (1994). *International policy-making as a learning process: The European Community and the greenhouse effect.* Unpublished PhD Thesis, European University Institute, Florence, Italy.

Jachtenfuchs, Markus, & Huber, Michael. (1993). Institutional learning in the European Community: The response to the greenhouse effect. In J. D. Lifferink, P. D. Lowe, & A. P. J. Mold (Eds.), *European integration and environmental policy* (pp. 36–58). London: Belhaven.

Jackman, Robert W. (1996). *Power without force: The political capacity of nation-states.* Ann Arbor: University of Michigan Press.

Jackson, Robert. (2000). *The global covenant: Human conduct in a world of states.* New York: Oxford University Press.

Jacques, Martin. (2002). The new barbarism. *The Guardian,* May 9.

James, Alan. (1999). The practice of sovereign statehood in contemporary international society. In Robert Jackson (Ed.), *Sovereignty at the millennium* (pp. 35–51). Madden, MA: Blackwell.

Jervis, Robert. (2002). Theories of war in an era of leading-power peace. *American Political Science Review, 96,* 1–14.

Jindy Pettman, Jan (2003). Questions of identity: Australia and Asia. In K. Booth (Ed), *Security, community and emancipation in world politics.* Boulder, CO: Lynne Rienner.

Job, Brian L. (1999). *Managing rising and declining powers.* Paper presented at the workshop on Security Order in the Asia-Pacific, East-West Center, Honolulu, October 1999.

Johnston, Douglas. M. (2001). Religion and Culture: Human Dimensions of Globalization. In Kugler, Richard L. & Frost, Ellen L. (Eds.), *The global century: Globalization and national security* (pp. 665–681). Retrieved December 28, 2002, from

National Defense University Online Books Web Site: http: //www.ndu.edu/
inss/books/books%20–%202001/Global%20Century%20–%20June%202001/glob-
cencont.html

Johnston, Douglas, & Sampson, Cynthia. (Eds.). (1994). *Religion, the missing dimension
of statecraft.* Oxford: Oxford University Press.

Joenniemi, Pertti, & Wæver, Ole. (1997). Balternes "kolde krig" mod Rusland er ved at
være slut. *Mandag Morgen, 12,* 25–29.

Juergensmeyer, Mark. (2000). *Terror in the mind of god.* Berkeley: University of California Press.

Jurgaitienè, Kornelija. (1993). Romantic nationalism and the challenge of Europeanization: A case of Lithuania. In Pertti Joenniemi and Peter Vares (Eds.), *New
actors on the international arena: The foreign policies of the Baltic countries* (pp. 89–112).
Tampere: TAPRI.

Jurgaitienè, Kornelija, & Wæver, Ole. (1996). Lithuania. In Hans Mouritzen, Ole
Wæver, Haakan Wiberg, with Anjo Harrayvan et al., *European integration and
national adaptations: A theoretical inquiry* (pp. 185–225). Commack: Nova Science
Publishers.

Kagan, Robert. (1998). The benevolent empire. *Foreign Policy, 111,* 24–35.

Kagan, Robert. (2002). Power and Weakness. *Policy Review, 113,* 3–28.

Kaldor, Mary. (2001).[1999] *New & old wars: Organized violence in a global era.* Stanford, CA: Stanford University Press.

Kapstein, Ethan B. (1999a). *Sharing the wealth.* New York: Norton.

Kapstein, Ethan B. (1999b). Does unipolarity have a future? In E. B. Kapstein & M.
Mastanduno (Eds.), *Unipolar politics: Realism and state strategies after the Cold War*
(pp. 464–490). New York: Columbia University Press.

Kazan, Işıl (2003). *Regionalisation of security and securitisation of a region: Turkish security policy after the Cold War.* unpublished Ph.D. dissertation, University of Copenhagen.

Keck, Margaret E., & Sikkink, Kathryn. (1998). *Activists beyond borders: Advocacy networks in international politics.* Ithaca: Cornell University Press.

Keen, David. (1998). *The economic functions of violence in civil wars.* Adelphi Paper 320.
London: Oxford University Press.

Keller, Bill. (2002). The fighting next time. *New York Times Magazine,* March 10.

Kelly, Sean. (1993). *America's tyrant. The CIA and Mobutu of Zaire.* Washington, DC:
The American University Press.

Kennedy, Paul. (1989). *The rise and fall of the great powers: Economic change and military
conflict from 1500–2000.* London: Fontana.

Kennedy, Paul. (2001). Maintaining American power: From injury to recovery. In
Strobe Talbott & Nayan Chanda (Eds.), *The age of terror: America and the world after
September 11* (pp. 53–79). New York: Basic Books.

Keohane, Robert O. (1990). Le Istituzioni internazionali del mondo nuovo, *Relazioni Internazionali*, December: 3–17.

Keynes, John M. (1920). *The economic consequences of the peace.* New York: Harcourt, Brace and Howe.

Khalizad, Zalmay & Byman, Daniel L. (2000). *Afghanistan: The consolidation of a rogue state.* RAND publication 978.

Khlopetski, Anatoly. (Ed.). (2000). *Strategiya razvitiya Kaliningrtadskoi Oblasti kak 'pilotnogo regiona' sotrudnichestva Rossiyskoi Federatsii i Evropeskogo Soyuza: Mezhdunarodnye aspekty regionalnoi strategii* [A strategy of development of the Kaliningrad region as a "pilot region" in the context of co-operation between the Russian Federation and the European Union: International aspects of a regional strategy]. Kaliningrad: The Kaliningrad Branch of the All-Russian Co-ordination Council of Russian Industrialists (in Russian).

Khrustalev, Mark. (1992). *After the disintegration of the Soviet Union: Russia in a new world.* Moscow: MGIMO.

Klare, Michael T. (2001). Waging postindustrial warfare on the global battlefield. *Current History, 100,* 433–437.

Klein, Naomi. (2000). *No logo: Taking aim at the brand bullies.* London: Flamingo.

Klyuchnik, F. (2002). Rossiya v globalnoi derevne [Russia in the Global Village] *Russkiy Zhurnal* http: www.russ.ru/journal/odna_8/98–02–25/kluch.htm (in Russian).

Korany, Bahgat. (1976). *Social change, charisma and international behavior.* Leiden & Geneva: Sijthoff & The Graduate Institute of International Studies.

Korany, Bahgat. (1986). Strategic studies and the third world: A critical evaluation *International Social Science Journal, 38*(4), 547–652.

Korany, Bahgat. (1989). Les etudes stratégiques critiques. In C. David (Ed.), *Les etudes stratégiques: Approches et méthodes.* Montreal & Paris: G. Marin.

Korany, Bahgat. (1997). The old/new Middle East. In L. Guazzone (Ed.), *The Middle East in global change* (pp. 135–152). New York: St. Martin's Press.

Korany, Bahgat. (2002). The accumulation of Arab strategic vulnerability: The importance of the neglected cultural dimension. *El-Moustaqbal El-Arabi, 172,* 55–70 (in Arabic).

Korany, Bahgat et al. (1986). *How foreign policy decisions are made in the third world: A comparative analysis.* Boulder, CO: Westview Press.

Korany, Bahgat, Brynen, Rex, & Noble, Paul. (Eds.). (1998). *Political liberalization and democratization in the Arab world. Vol. 2: Comparative experiences.* Boulder, CO: Lynne Rienner.

Korany, Bahgat, Dessouki, Ali et al. (1991). *The foreign policies of Arab states.* Boulder, CO: Westview Press, 2nd ed.

Korten, David C. (1995). *When corporations rule the world.* London: Earthscan.

Kozhinov, Vadim. (2001). *XXI vek.: Rossiya i globalizatsiya* [21st Century: Russia and "Globalization"] http: //ekg.method.ru/pub/inoe-2001–koginov-prn.html (in Russian).

Krasner, Stephen. (1985). *Structural conflict*. Berkeley: University of California Press.

Krasner, Stephen. (1993). Economic interdependence and independent statehood. In R. H. Jackson and A. James (Eds.), *States in a changing world* (pp. 301–321). Oxford: Oxford University Press.

Krasner, Stephen. (1995). Compromising Westphalia. *International Security, 20*(3), 115–151.

Krausse, Keith. (1998). Critical theory and security studies. *Cooperation and Conflict, 33*(3), 298–333.

Kugler, Richard L. & Frost, Ellen L. (Eds.). (2001). *The global century: Globalization and national security*. Retrieved December 28, 2002, from National Defense University Online Books Web Site: http: //www.ndu.edu/inss/books/books%20–%202001/Global%20Century%20–%20June%202001/globcencont.html

Kupchan, Charles A. (1998). After Pax Americana: Benign power, regional integration, and the sources of stable multipolarity. *International Security, 23*(2), 40–79.

Kurtz, Howard. (2002). Interview sheds light on Bin Laden's views. *Washington Post,* February 7, A12.

Kuzminov, Y., & Yakovlev, A. (2000). *Modernizatsiya ekonomiki: Globalnye tendentsii, bazovye ogranicheniya i varianty strategii* [Modernization of Economy: Global Trends, Basic Limitations and Variants of Strategy] OPEC.RU http: //www.opec.ru/library/article.asp?tmpl=def_article_print&d_no=289&c_no= 26 (in Russian)

*La Premiere Guerre du XXI Siecle.* (2001). Paris: L'Express Editions.

Lake, David A. (1999). Ulysses's triumph: American power and the new world order. *Security Studies, 8*(4), 44–78.

Lake, David A., & Morgan, Patrick M. (1997). *Regional orders: Building security in a new world,* University Park: Pennsylvania State University Press

Laqueur, Walter. (1999). *The new terrorism*. Oxford: Oxford University Press.

Larsen, Henrik. (2000). The discourse on the EU's role in the world. In Birthe Hansen & Bertel Heurlin (Eds.), *The new world order: Contrasting theories* (pp. 217–244). Houndsmills, Basingstoke & London: MacMillan Press.

Lash, Scott. (1993). Reflexive modernization: The aesthetic dimension. *Theory, Culture, and Society, 10*(1), 1–25.

Layne, Christopher. (1993). The unipolar illusion: Why new great powers will rise. *International Security, 17*(4), 5–51.

Layne, Christopher. (1997). From preponderance to offshore balancing: America's future grand strategy. *International Security, 22*(1), 86–124.

Leadbeater, Charles. (2002). *Up the down escalator: Why the global pessimists are wrong.* London: Viking Penguin.

Linden, Eugene. (1998). *The future in plain sight: Nine clues to the coming instability.* New York: Simon & Schuster.

Luard, Evan. (1990). *The globalization of politics.* London: Macmillan.

Lyons, Gene M., & Mastanduno, Michael. (1995). Introduction: International intervention, state sovereignty, and the future of international society. In G. M. Lyons & M. Mastanduno (Eds.), *Beyond Westphalia? State sovereignty and international intervention* (pp. 1–18). Baltimore, MD: Johns Hopkins University Press.

Mabrouk, M. (1999). *Islam and globalization.* Cairo: El-Dar El-Qawmiyya El-Arabiyya (in Arabic).

MacFarlane, Alan. (1989). The cradle of capitalism: The case of England. In J. Baechler, J. A. Hall, & M. Mann (Eds.), *The cradle of capitalism: The case of England, in Europe and the rise of capitalism* (pp. 185–203). Oxford: Basil Blackwell.

Mackinlay, John. (2002). *Globalization and insurgency.* Adelphi Paper 352.

Madeley, John. (1999). *Big business: Poor peoples. The impact of transnational corporations on the world's poor.* London: Zed Books.

Mahbubani, Kishore. (1995). The Pacific impulse. *Survival, 37*(1), 105–120.

Makarychev, Andrei. (2002). *Liberal and conservative perceptions of globalization: Russian élites' discourses.* Nizhny Novgorod: University of Nizhny Novgorod Press.

Makarychev, Andrei, & Sergounin, Alexander. (2000). Globalization. In K. Segbers & K. Imbusch (Eds.), *The globalization of Eastern Europe* (pp. 397–424). Hamburg: Lit.

Malik, Kenan. (1995). *The meaning of race. Race, history and culture in western society.* Basingstoke: Macmillan.

Mann, Michael. (1997). Has globalization ended the rise and rise of the nation-state? *Review of International Political Economy, 4*(3), 472–496.

Mansfield, Edward D., & Pollins, B. M. (2001). The study of interdependence and conflict: Recent advances, open questions, and directions for future research. *Journal of Conflict Resolution, 45*(6), 834–859.

Mansfield, Edward D. (1994). *Power, trade and war.* Princeton: Princeton University Press.

Marx, Karl, & Engels, Friedrich [1848] (1978). Manifesto of the Communist Party. In R. C. Tucker (Ed.), *The Marx–Engels reader,* 2nd ed. New York: W. W. Norton.

Mastanduno, Michael. (1997). Preserving the unipolar moment: Realist theories and U.S. grand strategy after the Cold War. *International Security, 21*(4), 49–88.

Mastanduno, Michael. (1998). Economics and security in statecraft and scholarship. *International Organization, 52*(4), 825–854.

Mastanduno, Michael, & Kapstein, Ethan B. (1999). Realism and state strategies after the Cold War. In E. B. Kapstein & M. Mastanduno (Eds.), *Unipolar politics: Realism and state strategies after the Cold War* (pp. 1–27). New York: Columbia University Press.

Matveyeva, Y. (1994). Russia's far east: Tired, cold and ready for independence. *Moscow News,* September 30-October 6, p. 13.

Matvienko, Valentina. (1996). The center and the regions in foreign policy. *International Affairs* (Moscow), *4*, 88–97.

McGrew, Anthony. (1998). Realism vs. cosmopolitanism: A debate between Barry Buzan and David Held. *Review of International Studies, 24,* 387–398.

McSweeney, Bill. (1999). *Security, identity and interests.* Cambridge: Cambridge University Press.

Mearsheimer, John J. (1990). Back to the future: Instability in Europe after the Cold War. *International Security, 15,* 5–56.

Mearsheimer, John J. (2001). *The tragedy of great power politics.* New York: W.W. Norton.

Miniotaite, Grazina. (2000). *The Security Policy of Lithuania and the 'integration dilemma.* Copenhagen: COPRI Working Paper no. 5

Ministry of Defense of the Russian Federation. (1992). Osnovy voennoy doktriny Rossii [Basic Provisions of the Military Doctrine of Russia], *Voennaya Mysl,* Special Issue, May 3–9 (in Russian).

Mittleman, James H. (2002). Globalization: An ascendant paradigm? *International Studies Perspectives, 3*(1), 1–14.

Mohan, Giles et al. (2000). *Structural adjustment: Theory, practice and impacts.* New York: Routledge.

Mokkadam, M. (2002). *The Afghan Algerians: From the Gama'a to al-Qai'da.* Algiers: Publications of the National Institution for Communication and Publication (Report, on Terrorist Files) (in Arabic).

Molchanov, Mikhail (1999). Istoki Rossiyskogo krizisa: Globalizatsiya ili vnutrennie problemy? [The Sources of the Russian Crisis: Globalization or Domestic Problems?] *Polis* http: //www.politstudies.ru/fulltext/1999/5/9.htm (in Russian).

Montesquieu. [1750] (1989). *The spirit of the laws.* Cambridge: Cambridge University Press.

Moran, Daniel. (2002). Strategic theory and the history of war. In John Baylis, James Wirtz, Eliot Cohen, & Colin S. Gray (Eds.), *Strategy in the contemporary world* (pp. 17–44). Oxford: Oxford University Press.

Morgan, Patrick. (1977). *Deterrence: A conceptual analysis.* Beverly Hills: Sage.

Morgenthau, Hans J. (1948). *Politics among nations.* New York: Alfred A. Knopf.

Mueller, John. (1990). *Retreat from doomsday: The obsolescence of major war.* New York: Basic Books.

Neisser, Ulric. (1997). Rising scores on intelligence tests. *American Scientist, 85,* 440–447.

Neisser, Ulric. (Ed.). (1998). *The rising curve: Long-Term gains in IQ and related measures.* Washington, DC: American Psychological Association.

Neklessa, Alexander (1998). Globalnye sdvigi i ikh vozdeistvie na Rossiyskoe obshestvo [Global Shifts and their Implications for the Russian Society] *Russkiy Arkhipelag,* http: //www.archipelag.ru/text/016.htm (in Russian).

Neumann, Stephanie G. (Ed.). (1998). *International relations theory and the third world.* New York: St. Martin's Press.

*New Internationalist.* (1997). Sound bites. Oxford: New Internationalist Publications.

*New Internationalist.* (1999). no.3. Oxford: New Internationalist Publications.

*New Statesman.* (2001). Never forget the other Terror (editorial), November 5.

Newman, Edward. (2001). Human security and constructivism. *International Studies Perspectives, 2*(3), 239–251.

*North-South: A Program for Survival.* (1980). Report of the Independent Commission on International Development Issues. Cambridge, MA: MIT University Press.

Nye, Joseph S. (1987). The long-term future of deterrence. In Roman Kolkowicz (Ed.), *The logic of nuclear terror* (pp. 233–250). Boston: Allen and Unwin.

Nye, Joseph S. (1992). What new world order? *Foreign Affairs, 71*(2), 94–96.

O'Brien, R., Goetz, A-M., Scholte, J., & Willliams, M. (2000). *Contending global governance.* Cambridge: Cambridge University Press.

O'Hanlon, Michael. (2000). *Technological change and the future of warfare.* Washington, DC: Brookings Institution Press.

Ohmae, Kenichi. (1995). *The end of the nation state.* New York: Free Press.

Palmer, Robert R. (1971). Frederich the Great, Guibert, Bulow: From dynastic to national war. In E. M. Earle (Ed.), *Makers of modern strategy: Military thought from Machiavelli to Hitler.* Princeton: Princeton University Press.

Paul, Thazha V. (1994). *Asymmetric conflicts: War initiation by weaker powers,* Cambridge: Cambridge University Press.

Pavlovaite, Inga. (2000). *Paradise regained: The conceptualisation of Europe in the Lithuanian debate.* Copenhagen: COPRI, Working Paper 24.

Peres, Shimon. (1993). *The new Middle East.* New York: Henry Holt.

Petersen, Philip A. (1996). Russia's Volga region: Bridgehead for Islamic revolution or source for an indigenous alternative political paradigm? *European Security, 1,* 113–140.

Pillar, Paul R. (2001). *Terrorism and U.S. foreign policy.* Washington DC: Brookings Institution Press.

Plimak, Y. (1996). Glavnye alternativy sovremennosti [Main Alternatives of Our Time] *Svobodnaya Mysl, 8,* 42–52 (in Russian).

Podberezkin, Alexei. (1996). Geostrategicheskoe polozhenie i bezopasnost Rossii [Russia's Geostrategic Position and Security] *Svobodnaya Mysl, 7,* 86–90 (in Russian).

Porch, Douglas. (2000). *Wars of empire.* London: Cassell.

Porter, Bruce. (1994). *War and the rise of the state: The military foundations of modern politics.* New York: The Free Press.

Portyakov, Vladimir. (1996). Kitaytzy idut? Migratzionnaya situatziya na dalnem vostoke Rossii [The Chinese Are Coming? The Migration Processes in the Russia's Far East], *Mezhdunarodnaya Zhizn* (Moscow), 2, 80–84 (in Russian).

Putin, Vladimir. (2000). Kontseptsiya natsionalnoy bezopasnosti Rossiyskoi Federatsii [The National Security Concept of the Russian Federation] *Nezavisimaya Gazeta*, January 14, 4–5 (Russian).

Putnam, Robert. (2001). *Bowling alone: The collapse and revival of American community.* New York: Simon & Schuster.

Quester, George. (1977). *Offense and defense in the international system.* New York: Wiley.

Reich, Robert. (1991). What is a nation? *Political Science Quarterly, 106*(2), 193–209.

Reston, James. (1981). Interview with Francois Mitterand. *New York Times,* June 1981.

Richards, Alan, & Waterbury, John. (1998). *A political economy of the Middle East.* Boulder, CO: Westview Press, 2nd ed.

Richards, Glyn. (1995). *The philosophy of Gandhi.* Richmond: Curzon Press.

Richardson, James L. (1993). The end of geopolitics? In R. Leaver & J. L. Richardson (Eds.), *Charting the post-Cold War order* (pp. 39–50). Boulder, CO: Westview Press.

Risse-Kappen, Thomas. (1996). Collective identity in a democratic community: The case of NATO. In Peter Katzenstein (Ed.), *The culture of national security* (pp. 357–399). New York: Columbia University Press.

Robertson, Roland. (1995). Glocalization: Time—space and homogeneity—heterogeneity. In Mike Featherstone, Scott Lash, & Roland Robertson (Eds.), *Global modernities* (pp. 25–44). Thousand Oaks, CA: Sage Publications.

Rodrik, Dani. (1997). *Has globalization gone too far?* Washington, DC: Institute for International Economics.

Rogowski, Ronald. (1989). *Commerce and coalitions.* Princeton: Princeton University Press.

Ropke, Wilhelm. (1942). *International economic disintegration.* New York: Macmillian.

Rosecrance, Richard. (1986). *The rise of the trading state.* New York: Basic Books.

Rosecrance, Richard. (1992). A new concert of powers. *Foreign Affairs, 71*(2), 64–82.

Rosecrance, Richard. (1995). The end of war among trading states. *New Perspectives Quarterly, 21*(1), 44–51.

Rosenau, James N. (1982). Order and disorder in the study of world politics. In R. Maghroori & B. Ramberg (Eds.), *Globalism versus realism: International relations' third debate* (pp. 1–7). Boulder, CO: Westview Press.

Rosenau, James N. (1990). Turbulence in world politics: A theory of change and continuity. Princeton: Princeton University Press.

Rosenau, James N. (1997). *Along the domestic-foreign frontier: Exploring governance in a turbulent world.* Cambridge: Cambridge University Press.

Rosenau, James N. (2001). Stability, stasis, and change: A fragmegrating world. In Richard L. Kugler & Ellen L. Frost (Eds.), *The global century: Globalization and national security* (pp. 127–153). Retrieved December 28, 2002, from National Defense University Online Books Web site: http: //www.ndu.edu/inss/books/books%20–%202001/Global%20Century%20–%20June%202001/globcencont.html

Rosenau, James N. (2003). *Distant proximities: Dynamics beyond globalization.* Princeton: Princeton University Press.

Rosenau, James N., & Fagen, Michael W. (1997). Increasingly skillful citizens: A new dynamism in world politics? *International Studies Quarterly, 41,* 655–686.

Rosset, Clement. (1993). *Joyful cruelty: Toward a philosophy of the real.* New York: Oxford University Press.

Rothkopf, David J. (2001). Foreign policy in the information age. In Richard L.Kugler & Ellen L. Frost (Eds.), *The global century: Globalization and national security* (pp. 215–239). Retrieved December 28, 2002, from National Defense University Online Books Web site: http: //www.ndu.edu/inss/books/books%20–%202001/Global%20Century%20–%20June%202001/globcencont.html

Ruggie, John G. (1993). Territoriality and beyond: Problematizing modernity in international relations. *International Organization, 47,* 139–174.

Rupert, Mark. (2000). *Ideologies of globalization: Contending visions of a new world order.* London: Routledge.

Sas, Ivan. (2002). VTO v tumane [WTO in the fog] *Nezavisimaya Gazeta,* October 22, p. 3 (in Russian).

Sassen, Saskia. (1996). *Losing control? Sovereignty in an age of globalization.* New York: Columbia University Press.

Schelling, Thomas C. (1966). *Arms and influence.* New Haven, CT: Yale University Press.

Schmemann, Serge. (2001). A growing list of foes now suddenly friends. *New York Times,* October 5.

Scholte, Jan Aart. (2000). *Globalization: A critical introduction.* New York: St. Martin's Press.

Sekatskiy, Alexander. (2002). Khimery globalizatsii [Chimeras of Globalization] *Russkiy Zhurnal,* http: www.russ.ru/politics/20020131–sek-pr.html (in Russian).

Sergounin, Alexander. (1996). *Regional security system in Russia: Challenges and opportunities.* Nizhny Novgorod: University of Nizhny Novgorod Press.

Sergounin, Alexander. (1999). *The process of regionalization and the future of the Russian Federation Copenhagen.* Copenhagen Peace Research Institute (COPRI Working Papers; No. 9, 1999).

Sergounin, Alexander. (2001). *External determinants of Russia's regionalization*. Zurich: Center for Security Studies and Conflict Research.

Sergounin, Alexander. (2002). The Russian post-Communist discourse on Northern Europe: A chance for region-building? In Gunna Lassinantti (Ed.), *Focal point North-West Russia—The future of the Barents Euro-Arctic Region and the Northern Dimension* (pp. 11–30). Sweden: Lulea.

Shapinov, Victor. (n.d.). *Mify globalizatsii* [Myths of Globalization] http://www.communist.ru/cgi-bin/article.cgi?id=0300shap0106.

Shapland, G. (1997). *Rivers of discord: International water disputes in the Middle East*. New York: St. Martin's Press.

Shaw, Martin. (1994). *Global society and international relations: Sociological concepts and political perspectives*. Cambridge: Polity Press.

Shishkov, Y. (2001). O geterogennosti globalistiki i stadiyakh ee razvitiya [On Heterogeneity of Global Studies and the Phases of its Development] *Mirovaya Ekonomika i Mezhdunarodnye Otnosheniya*, 2 (in Russian).

Sick, Gary, & Potter, Lawrence (Eds.). (1997). *The Persian Gulf at the millenium: Essays in politics, economy, security & religion*. New York: St. Martin's Press.

Silberner, Edmund. (1946). *The problem of war in nineteenth century economic thought*. Princeton, NJ: Princeton University Press.

Simon, Sheldon W. (1994). East Asian security: The playing field has changed. *Asian Survey, 34*(12), 1047–1063.

Singer, Max, & Wildavsky, Aaron. (1993). *The real world order: Zones of peace / zones of turmoil*. Chatham, NJ: Chatham House Publishers.

Skolnikoff, Eugene B. (1993). *The elusive transformation: Science, technology and the evolution of international politics*. Princeton, NJ: Princeton University Press.

Sloan, Elinor. (2002). *The revolution in military affairs*. Montreal: McGill-Queen's University Press.

Smith, Adam. (1976). *The wealth of nations*. Chicago: University of Chicago Press.

Smith, Stephen. (2002). Copenhagen flirts with fascism. *The Guardian*, June 5.

Sokolov, Viktor. (2001). Kontury budushego mira: Natsii, regiony, transnatsionalnye obshnosti [The Contours of the Future World: Nations, Regions, Transnational Communities] *Mirovaya Ekonomika i Mezhdunarodnye Otnosheniya*, 3 (in Russian).

Sørensen, Georg. (1998a). *Democracy and democratization: Processes and prospects in a changing world*. Boulder: Westview Press.

Sørensen, Georg (1998b). States are not "like units": Types of state and forms of anarchy in the present international system. *The Journal of Political Philosophy, 6*(1), 79–98.

Sørensen, Georg. (2001). *Changes in statehood: The transformation of international relations*. London & New York: Palgrave.

Soros, George. (2002). *George Soros on globalization*. New York: Public Affairs.

Special Issue on Globalization, Cooperation and Conflict. (2002). *Cooperation and Conflict, 37*(3), 243–362.

Spiro, Peter J. (2000). The new sovereigntists: American exceptionalism and its false prophets. *Foreign Affairs, 79*(6), 9–15.

Stern, Jessica. (1999). *The ultimate terrorists.* Cambridge: Harvard University Press.

Stiglitz, Joseph E. (2002). *Globalization and its discontents.* New York: W.W. Norton.

Strange, Susan. (1996). *The retreat of the state: The diffusion of power in the world economy.* Cambridge: Cambridge University Press.

Strange, Susan. (1999). The Westfailure system. *Review of International Studies, 25*(3), 345–355.

Stratfor.Com, (2001). *Ground war strategy Part I: Grand strategy,* November 6.

Talbott, Strobe. (2001). The other evil. *Foreign Policy, 127,* 75–76.

Teitelbaum, Joshua. (2000). *Holier than thou: Saudi Arabia's Islamic opposition.* Washington DC: The Washington Institute for Near East Policy.

The World Bank (1994). *A strategy for managing water in the Middle East and North Africa.* Washington, DC: The World Bank.

Thomas, Caroline. (1999). Where is the third world now? In Michael Cox, Ken Booth, and Tim Dunne (Eds.), *The interregnum: Controversies in world politics 1989–1999* (pp. 225–243). Cambridge: Cambridge University Press.

Tilly, Charles. (1985). War making and state making as organized crime. In Peter B. Evans, Dietrich Rueschemeyer, & Theda Skocpol (Eds.), *Bringing the state back in* (pp. 169–191). New York: Cambridge University Press.

Tilly, Charles. (1990). *Coercion, capital, and European states, AD 990–1990.* Cambridge: Blackwell.

Tilly, Charles. (Ed.). (1975). *The formation of national states in western Europe.* Princeton, NJ: Princeton University Press.

Timofeev, T. (1992). A transformed Russia in a new world. *International Affairs* (Moscow), *38*(4–5), 81–104 (in Russian).

Timofeev, T. (1999). Vyzovy XXI veka i debaty ob alternativakh [Challenges of the 21st Century and the Debate on Alternatives] *Polis,* http: //www.politstudies.ru/full-text/1999/6/3.htm (in Russian).

Tostensen, Arne, & Bull, Beate. (2002). Are smart sanctions feasible? *World Politics, 54*(3), 373–403.

Trubowitz, Peter. (1998). *Defining the national interest.* Chicago: University of Chicago Press.

Tucker, Robert W. (1977). *The inequality of nations.* New York: Basic Books.

Tunander, Ola. (1989). *Cold water politics: The maritime strategy and geopolitics of the northern front.* London: Sage.

UNDP. (1999). *Globalization with a human face.* Oxford: Oxford University Press.

UNDP. (1994). *Human development report*. New York: Oxford University Press. Some sections reprinted, Redefining Security: the Human Dimension in *Current History*, May 1995, 229–236.

UNDP. (1998). *Human development report*. Oxford: Oxford University Press.

United States Air Force. (2002). U.S. Air Force Fact Sheets. Available at www.af.mil/news/factsheets.

United States Secretary of Defense (2002). Press conference in Warsaw, Poland, on September 25, 2002. Available at http://www.defenselink.mil/news/Sep2002/to9252002_t925warsaw.html.

Utgoff, Victor. (Ed.). (2000). *The coming crisis: Nuclear proliferation, U.S. interests & world order*. Cambridge: MIT Press.

Vale, Peter (2003). New ways to remember . . . Community in Southern Africa. In Ken Booth (Ed.), *Security, community and emancipation in world politics*. Boulder CO: Lynne Rienner.

Van der Pijl, Kees. (1998). *Transnational classes and international relations*. London: Routledge.

Van Evera, Stephen. (1984). The cult of the offensive and the origins of the First World War. *International Security, 9*(1), Summer 1984, 58–107.

Vayrynen, Raimo. (Ed.). (Forthcoming). *The waning of major war*. London: Frank Cass.

Veber, Aleksandr. (2001). Antiglobalistskie dvizheniya—Nachalo velikoi smuty XXI veka? [Anti-globalist Movements: The Beginning of a Great Turmoil of the 21st Century?] *Mirovaya Economika i Mezhdunarodnye Otnosheniya*, 12, 50–56 (in Russian).

Videman, V. (2002). *Istoricheskiy vyzov globalizatsii* [Historical challenge of globalization], http: //www.imperativ.net/imp7/5.html (in Russian).

Vincent, John R. (1974). *Non-intervention*. Princeton, NJ: Princeton University Press.

Wæver, Ole. (1989). Conflicts of vision—visions of conflict. In Ole Wæver, Pierre Lemaitre, and Elzbieta Tromer (Eds.), *European polyphony: Beyond East–West confrontation* (pp. 283–325). London: Macmillan.

Wæver, Ole. (1990). Three competing Europes: German, French, Russian. *International Affairs, 66*(3), 477–493.

Wæver, Ole. (1994). Resisting the temptation of post foreign policy analysis, in Walter Carlsnaes and Steve Smith (Eds.), *European foreign policy analysis: The EC and changing perspectives in Europe*. London: Sage.

Wæver, Ole. (1995). Securitization and desecuritization. In Ronnie D. Lipschutz (Ed.), *On security* (pp. 46–86). New York: Columbia University Press.

Wæver, Ole. (1996a). Europe's three empires: A Watsonian interpretation of post-wall European security. In Rick Fawn and Jeremy Larkins (Eds.), *International society after the Cold War: Anarchy and order reconsidered* (pp. 220–260). London: Macmillan and Millennium.

Wæver, Ole. (1996b). European security identities. *Journal of Common Market Studies, 34*(1 March), 103–132.

Wæver, Ole. (1998). Security, insecurity, and asecurity in the West European non-war community. In Emmanuel Adler and Michael Barnett (Eds.), *Security communities* (ch. 3), Cambridge: Cambridge University Press.

Wæver, Ole. (2000). The EU as a security actor: Reflections from a pessimistic constructivist on post-sovereign security orders. In Morten Kelstrup and Michael C. Williams (Eds.), *International relations theory and the politics of European integration: Power, security and community.* London: Routledge,

Wæver, Ole. (2002). *Security: A conceptual history for international relations.* Unpublished paper presented at the meeting of ISA in New Orleans.

Wæver, Ole, & Buzan, Barry. (1999). Europe and the Middle East—an inter-regional analysis: NATO's new strategic concept and the theory of security complexes. In Sven Behrendt and Christian-Peter Hanelt (Eds.), *Security in the Middle East* (pp. 73–110). Munich: Guetersloh, unpublished working papers, Center for Applied Policy Research, Bertelsmann Foundation.

Wæver, Ole, and Buzan, Barry. (2000). An inter-regional analysis: NATO's new strategic concept and the theory of security complexes. In Sven Behrendt and Christian-Peter Hanelt (Eds.), *Bound to cooperate: Europe and the Middle East* (pp. 55–106). Gütersloh: Bertelsmann Foundation Publishers.

Waever, Ole, Buzan, Barry, Kelsrup, Morten, & Lemaitre, Pierre. (1993). *Identity, migration and the new security order in Europe.* London: Pinter.

Wagnsson, C. (2000). *Russian political language and public opinion on the west, NATO, and Chechnya: Securitization theory reconsidered.* Unpublished Ph.D. dissertation. University of Stockholm.

Wallander, Celeste A. (2000). Institutional assets and adaptability: NATO after the Cold War. *International Organizations, 54*(4), 705–735.

Waltz, Kenneth N. (1993a). The emerging structure of international politics. *International Security, 18*(2), 44–79.

Waltz, Kenneth N. (1993b). The new world order. *Millennium, 22*(2), 187–195.

Waltz, Kenneth N. (2000). Structural realism after the Cold War. *International Security, 25*(1), 5–41.

Waltz, Kenneth N. (1979). *Theory of international politics.* New York: Random House.

Waltz, Kenneth N. (2002). The Continuity of international politics. In Ken Booth & Tim Dunne (Eds.), *Worlds in collision: Terror and the future of global order* (pp. 348–353). Basingstoke: Palgrave Macmillan.

Walzer, Michael. (1977). *Just and unjust wars: A moral argument with historical illustrations.* Harmondsworth: Penguin Books.

Watson, Adam. (1992). *The evolution of international society.* London: Routledge.

Weiss, Linda. (1998). *The myth of the powerless state: Governing the economy in a global era.* Cambridge: Polity Press.

Wendt, Alexander. (1992) Anarchy is what states make of it. *International Organization, 46,* 394–419.

Wendt, Alexander. (1999). *Social theory of international politics.* Cambridge: Cambridge University Press.

Wheeler, Nicholas J. (2000). *Saving strangers: Humanitarian intervention in international society.* New York: Oxford University Press.

Wheeler, Nicholas J., & Booth, Ken. (1992). The security dilemma. In John Baylis & N.J. Rennger (Eds.), *Dilemmas of world politics.* Oxford: Clarendon Press.

William, Michael C. (1996). Hobbes and international relations: A reconsideration. *International Organization, 50*(2), 213–236.

Wohlforth, William C. (1999). The stability of a unipolar world, *International Security, 24*(1), 5–41.

Woodward, Susan. (1995). *Balkan tragedy: Chaos and dissolution after the Cold War.* Washington DC: Brookings Institution.

Wriston, Walter B. (1992). *The twilight of sovereignty.* New York: Charles Scribners Sons.

Wyatt-Walter, Andrew. (1995). Regionalism, globalism, and world economic order. In Louise Fawcett & Andrew Hurrell (Eds.), *Regionalism in world politics* (pp. 74–121). Oxford: Oxford University Press.

Wyn Jones, Richard. (1999). *Security, strategy and critical theory.* Boulder, CO: Lynne Rienner.

Yablakov, Alexei. (1992). *A transformed Russia in a new world.* Unpublished paper from the conference on Russia's Security Doctrine, Moscow.

Yeltsin, Boris. (1992). Zakon Rossiyskoi Federatsii o bezopasnosti [The Law on Security of the Russian Federation], *Rossiyskaya gazeta,* May 6, p. 5 (in Russian).

Yeltsin, Boris. (1994). The basic provisions of the military doctrine of the Russian Federation. *Jane's Intelligence Review,* Special Report, January, 3–12.

Yeltsin, Boris. (1997). Kontseptsiya natsionalnoy bezopasnosti Rossiyskoi Federatsii [The National Security Concept of the Russian Federation], *Rossiyskaya Gazeta,* December 26, pp. 4–5 (in Russian).

Younge, Gary. (2002). No surrender. *The Guardian Weekend,* May 25.

Zadokhin, A. (2001). Globalizatsiya i natsionalnye interesy Rossii [Globalization and Russia's National Interests] *Nasledie,* http: //www.nasledie.ru/oboz/N01_02/1_08. htm (in Russian).

Zagorski, A. (1995). Geopolitik vetrsus geowirtschaft. *Wostok, 5*(6), 3–10 (in German).

Zagorski, A., Zlobin, A., Solodovnik, S. & Khrustalev, M. (1992). Russia in a new world. *International Affairs* (Moscow), *38,* 7, 3–11.

Zangl, B., & Zurn, M. (1999). The effects of denationalization on security in the OECD world. *Global Society, 13*(2), 139–163.

Zanini, Michele, & Edwards, Sean J. A. (2001). The networking of terror in the information age. In John Arquilla & David Ronfeldt (Eds.), *Networks and netwars* (pp. 29–60). Santa Monica, CA: Rand Corporation.

Zimin, P. (2002). Vyzov globalizatsii [The challenge of globalization] *Russkiy Zhurnal,* http: www.russ.ru/politics/20020212 (in Russian).

Zizek, Slavoj. (2000). *The fragile absolute—or, why is the Christian legacy worth fighting for?* London & New York: Verso.

Znachkov, B. (2001). Ekologicheskie argumenty v polzu i protiv globalizatsii [Ecological Arguments Pro et Contra Globalization] *Russkiy Zhurnal.* http: www.russ.ru/politics/20011015–zna-pr.html (in Russian).

# Contributors

**Ersel Aydinli** is an assistant professor of International Relations at Bilkent University, Ankara, Turkey and in 2004/2005 a post-doctoral research fellow at the International Security Program of Harvard University's Belfer Center. He is co-editor of *The Review of International Affairs* and *Ankara Papers*. His research interest areas include international relations theory, international security, globalization, and Turkish foreign and security policy. His articles have appeared in such journals as *International Studies Review, International Studies Perspectives, Current History, Middle Eastern Studies, Security Dialogue,* and *World Today*.

**Mohammed Ayoob** is University Distinguished Professor of International Relations, James Madison College, Michigan State University. A specialist on conflict and security in the Third World, he has written extensively on the subject both conceptually and as case studies relationg to South Asia, the Middle East, and Southeast Asia. He has also published on issues of IR theory, especially its neglect of the Third World. His books include *The Third World Security Predicament* (1995). His latest published articles deal with inequality and theorizing in International Relations, the war against Iraq, and humanitarian intervention and state sovereignty.

**Ken Booth** is E. H. Carr Professor and head of department, Department of International Politics, University of Wales, Aberystwyth, U.K. He is an academician of the Academy of Learned Societies for the Social Sciences, and a former Chair of the British International Studies Association. Previous posts include Scholar-in-residence at the U.S. Naval War College, Senior Research Fellow at Dalhousie University in Halifax, Canada, and Visiting Fellow at

Clare Hall, Cambridge. His latest book is *Security, Community and Emancipation in World Politics* (2003).

**Mark R. Brawley** has been on the faculty of McGill University's Political Science Department since 1990, except for one year he spent as a visitor teaching at Harvard. He is the author of several books including *The Politics of Globalization* (2003), *Afterglow or Adjustment?* (1999), and *Turning Points: Decisions Shaping the Evolution of the International Political Economy* (1997), as well as numerous articles. His work often examines the relationship between economics and security issues. His current research examines the economic roots of movements opposing globalization by exploring regulation of domestic markets for the factors of production.

**Barry Buzan** is a professor of International Relations at the London School of Economics, an academician of the Academy of Learned Societies for the Social Sciences, former chair of the British International Studies Association, and former project director at the Copenhagen Peace Research Institute. He has written or co-authored more than 80 articles and chapters, and written, co-authored, or edited 17 books, including *People, States and Fear: The National Security Problem in International Relations*, and, more recently, *Regions and Powers: The Structure of International Security* (with Ole Waever, 2003), and *From International to World Society? English School Theory and the Social Structure of Globalization* (2004).

**David Goldfischer** is an associate professor at the Graduate School of International Studies, University of Denver, where he directs the program in international security. He has had fellowships at the Brookings Institution, the University of Colorado, Boulder, and the Institute on Global Conflict and Cooperation at the University of California, San Diego. His publications include *Nuclear Deterrence and Global Security in Transition* (1992), *The Best Defense: Policy Alternatives for U.S. Nuclear Security from the 1950s to the 1990s* (1993), *War and the World Economy: A Historical Reader* (2003), and articles in such journals as *Political Science Quarterly*, *Review of International Studies*, and *Security Studies*.

**Bahgat Korany**, an elected Fellow of the Royal Soceity of Canada, is a professor of International Relations and Political Economy at the American University in Cairo. He is also a Research Professor at the University of Montreal. He has published 8 books, more than 20 chapters in other books, and 45 articles in international periodicals. Some of his writings have been translated into Arabic, Spanish, Italian, and Chinese. His first book, *Social Change, Charisma, and International Behavior*, was awarded the 1976 Swiss Hauchman Prize.

**T. V. Paul** is James McGill Professor of International Relations at McGill University and a former visiting scholar at Harvard University's Center for International Affairs and the Olin Institute for Strategic Studies. He specializes in international security, international conflict and conflict resolution, regional security and South Asia. He is the author of several books including *Power versus Prudence: Why Nations Forgo Nuclear Weapons* (2000) and *Asymmetric Conflicts: War Initiation by Weaker Powers* (1994), as well as co-editor of books such as *The Nation-State in Question* (with G. John Ikenberry and John Hall, 2003) and *International Order and the Future of World Politics* (with John Hall, 1999, 2000, and 2001).

**James N. Rosenau** is University Professor of International Affairs at George Washington University. A former president of the International Studies Association, his scholarship has resulted in more than 35 books including his most recent, *Distant Proximities: Dynamics Beyond Globalization* (2003). Earlier works include *Turbulence in World Politics: A Theory of Change and Continuity* (1990), and *Along the Domestic-Foreign Frontier: Exploring Governance in a Turbulent World* (1997).

**Alexander Sergounin** is professor and head of the department of International Relations and Political Science, Nizhny Novgorod Linguistic University, Russia. His fields of research are international relations history and theory, international security, Russian foreign policymaking, globalization, and regionalization. His most recent publications are *Russian Foreign Policy Thought: Problems of National and International Security* (2003), *Russia and the European Union's Northern Dimension* (with Pertti Joenniemi, 2003), *Are Borders Barriers?* (with Lyndelle Fairlie, 2001), *Political Science* (2000), and *Russian Arms Transfers to East Asia in the 1990s* (with Sergei Subbotin, 1999).

**Georg Sorensen** is professor of political science at the University of Aarhus, Denmark. His recent books include *The Transformation of the State* (2004), *Introduction to International Relations: Theories and Approaches* (with Robert Jackson, 2003), *Changes in Statehood: The Transformation of International Relations* (2001), *Democracy and Democratization: Processes and Prospects in a Changing World* (1998, 2nd ed.).

**Ole Wæver** is professor of International Relations at the University of Copenhagen. Among his publications are *Concepts of Security* (1997), *Security: A New Framework for Analysis* (with Barry Buzan and Jaap de Wilde, 1998), *European Integration and Natonal Identity: The Challenge of the Nordic States* (edited with Lene Hansen, 2001), and *Regions and Powers: The Structure of International*

*Security* (with Barry Buzan, 2003). Ole Waever has been involved in policy advising as a member of the board of the Danish Institute of International Affairs and of the Defense Commission of 1997. Since 1992 he has headed the national Danish school for Ph.D. education in political science.

# *SUNY series in Global Politics*
## James N. Rosenau, Editor

## LIST OF TITLES

*American Patriotism in a Global Society*—Betty Jean Craige

*The Political Discourse of Anarchy: A Disciplinary History of International Relations*—Brian C. Schmidt

*From Pirates to Drug Lords: The Post—Cold War Caribbean Security Environment*—Michael C. Desch; Jorge I. Dominguez, and Andres Serbin (eds.)

*Collective Conflict Management and Changing World Politics*—Joseph Lepgold and Thomas G. Weiss (eds.)

*Zones of Peace in the Third World: South America and West Africa in Comparative Perspective*—Arie M. Kacowicz

*Private Authority and International Affairs*—A. Claire Cutler, Virginia Haufler, and Tony Porter (eds.)

*Harmonizing Europe: Nation-States within the Common Market*—Francesco G. Duina

*Economic Interdependence in Ukrainian-Russian Relations*—Paul J. D'Anieri

*Leapfrogging Development? The Political Economy of Telecommunications Restructuring*—J. P. Singh

*States, Firms, and Power: Successful Sanctions in United States Foreign Policy*—George E. Shambaugh

*Approaches to Global Governance Theory*—Martin Hewson and Timothy J. Sinclair (eds.)

*After Authority: War, Peace, and Global Politics in the Twenty-First Century*—Ronnie D. Lipschutz

*Pondering Postinternationalism: A Paradigm for the Twenty-First Century?*—Heidi H. Hobbs (ed.)

*Beyond Boundaries? Disciplines, Paradigms, and Theoretical Integration in International Studies*—Rudra Sil and Eileen M. Doherty (eds.)

*Why Movements Matter: The West German Peace Movement and U. S. Arms Control Policy*—Steve Breyman

*International Relations—Still an American Social Science? Toward Diversity in International Thought*—Robert M. A. Crawford and Darryl S. L. Jarvis (eds.)

*Which Lessons Matter? American Foreign Policy Decision Making in the Middle East, 1979—1987*—Christopher Hemmer (ed.)

*Hierarchy Amidst Anarchy: Transaction Costs and Institutional Choice*—Katja Weber

*Counter-Hegemony and Foreign Policy: The Dialectics of Marginalized and Global Forces in Jamaica*—Randolph B. Persaud

*Global Limits: Immanuel Kant, International Relations, and Critique of World Politics*—Mark F. N. Franke

*Power and Ideas: North-South Politics of Intellectual Property and Antitrust*—Susan K. Sell

*Money and Power in Europe: The Political Economy of European Monetary Cooperation*—Matthias Kaelberer

*Agency and Ethics: The Politics of Military Intervention*—Anthony F. Lang, Jr.

*Life After the Soviet Union: The Newly Independent Republics of the Transcaucasus and Central Asia*—Nozar Alaolmolki

*Theories of International Cooperation and the Primacy of Anarchy: Explaining U. S. International Monetary Policy-Making After Bretton Woods*—Jennifer Sterling-Folker

*Information Technologies and Global Politics: The Changing Scope of Power and Governance*—James N. Rosenau and J. P. Singh (eds.)

*Technology, Democracy, and Development: International Conflict and Cooperation in the Information Age*—Juliann Emmons Allison (ed.)

*The Arab-Israeli Conflict Transformed: Fifty Years of Interstate and Ethnic Crises*—Hemda Ben-Yehuda and Shmuel Sandler

*Systems of Violence: The Political Economy of War and Peace in Colombia*—Nazih Richani

*Debating the Global Financial Architecture*—Leslie Elliot Armijo

*Political Space: Frontiers of Change and Governance in a Globalizing World*—Yale Ferguson and R. J. Barry Jones (eds.)

*Crisis Theory and World Order: Heideggerian Reflections*—Norman K. Swazo

*Political Identity and Social Change: The Remaking of the South African Social Order*—Jamie Frueh

*Social Construction and the Logic of Money: Financial Predominance and International Economic Leadership*—J. Samuel Barkin

*What Moves Man: The Realist Theory of International Relations and Its Judgment of Human Nature* — Annette Freyberg-Inan

*Democratizing Global Politics: Discourse Norms, International Regimes, and Political Community*—Rodger A. Payne and Nayef H. Samhat

*Collective Preventative Diplomacy: A Study of International Management*—Barry H. Steiner

*International Relations Under Risk: Framing State Choice*—Jeffrey D. Berejikian

*Landmines and Human Security: International Politics and War's Hidden Legacy*—Richard A. Matthew, Bryan McDonald, and Kenneth R. Rutherford (eds.)

*Globalization and the Environment: Greening Global Political Economy*—Gabriela Kutting

*Sovereignty, Democracy, and Global Civil Society*—Elisabeth Jay Friedman, Kathryn Hochstetler, and Ann Marie Clark

*Imperialism and Nationalism in the Discipline of International Relations*—David Long and Brian C. Schmidt (eds.)

*United We Stand? Divide and Conquer Politics and the Logic of International Hostility*—Aaron Belkin

*Mediating Globalization: Domestic Institutions and Industrial Policies in the United States and Britain*—Andrew P. Cortell

# Index

275